From Barbarism
to Chivalry

A Portrait of Europe 300–1300

From Barbarism
to Chivalry

Mary R. Price
and
Margaret Howell

Oxford University Press · 1972

Oxford University Press, Ely House, London W. 1

GLASGOW NEW YORK TORONTO MELBOURNE WELLINGTON
CAPE TOWN IBADAN NAIROBI DAR ES SALAAM LUSAKA ADDIS ABABA
DELHI BOMBAY CALCUTTA MADRAS KARACHI LAHORE DACCA
KUALA LUMPUR SINGAPORE HONG KONG TOKYO

Photoset by BAS Printers Limited, Wallop, Hampshire
and printed in Great Britain at the University Press, Oxford
by Vivian Ridler, Printer to the University

Editors' Preface

Recently there have been marked changes in the methods of teaching history and in our conception of what it is possible for young historians to experience and enjoy in school. The changes are designed to encourage them to make use of sources very early, to penetrate as deeply as they can into historical topics, to enjoy discovering for themselves what life was like in the past, and to develop their own individual interests. All this has had a very stimulating, in many cases a re-vitalizing, effect upon our presentation of the subject in school, and not least upon our attitude to the kind of books we need. There must now be few places where pupils are provided with only a single book for a year's work. Instead they are introduced to a multiplicity of publications dealing with separate topics, movements, and personalities, and the study of history is much enriched for them.

In view of this trend it may be asked if there is any place today for a series of background books such as these. Are they not quite outmoded and useless, if not positively harmful? We do not think so, for we are convinced that, if historical knowledge at any level is to be of lasting value and interest, such knowledge must not be piecemeal, but in the end set in a firm framework. Thus, in addition to books dealing with separate topics, young historians need books which will help to create this framework. It is not sufficient to relate topics solely to the history of our own country; historians will want books about the larger units with which their own country is particularly and obviously linked, about Europe in the first place, and ultimately about the world.

In these new Portrait books we have tried to avoid the superficiality of a brief chronological recital of events, and instead have chosen to highlight significant movements and people. Above all we have, wherever possible, introduced in the text and in the illustrations the sources of history, believing that this is one of the best ways to kindle the minds and imagination of the readers.

M.R.P.
D.D.L.

Contents

	Acknowledgements	8
	List of Maps	9
1.	The Roman Empire on the Eve of Collapse	11
2.	The West: Barbarian Attacks	21
3.	The East: The Emperor Justinian	35
4.	The Church: St. Benedict and Pope Gregory I	50
5.	The Rise of Islam	64
6.	The Age of Charlemagne	82
7.	The Break-up of Charlemagne's Empire	100
8.	The Manor	116
9.	The Empire of Otto	130
10.	Empire against Papacy	138
11.	Norman Conquests	147
12.	Cluniacs and Cistercians	164
13.	The Rise of the Towns	182
14.	Crusaders	196
15.	Feudal Monarchy in England and France	214
16.	Pope Innocent III and St. Francis	232
17.	Kings in a new style: Frederick II and St. Louis	247
18.	Men of Art and Men of Learning	263
19.	Epilogue	291
	Genealogical Tables	296
	Bibliography	298
	Index	302

Acknowledgements

Black and white photographs are reproduced by kind permission of the following:

Antikvarisk Topografiska Arkivet, Stockholm, page 108; Archives Photographique, 168, 177, 282, 287; Ashmolean Museum, 29, 33; M. Beresford, *New Towns of the Middle Ages* (Lutterworth Press, 1967), 190; Bibliotheque Nationale, Paris, 153; Bildarchiv Foto Marburg, 59, 113, 134, 248, 269, 284; Bodleian Library, Oxford, 94, 122, 123, 125, 128, 129 top left, bottom centre, bottom right; British Museum, 13 (right), 81 (right), 107, 203, 210–11, 254, 265 (bottom), 274, 275; J. Allen Cash, 77, 183 (top), 188, 240; Combier, Maçon, 165; Corpus Christi College, Cambridge, 253; Corpus Christi College, Oxford, 117, 129 (bottom left); Courtauld Institute of Art, 140, 286 (left); J. E. Dayton, 73, 75; Department of the Environment (crown copyright), 176; Editions Fallières, 279 (top); Fogg Art Museum, Harvard University, 246; G. Fossati, *Sante Sophia, Constantinople* (London, 1852), 47; Fotostampa Ficarelli, 256; French Government Tourist Office, 183 (bottom), 228; Giraudon, 221, 230, 259, 260; The Green Studio Ltd., 270; Gulbenkian Museum, Durham, 254; S. Kellig (University College, Dublin), 51; A. F. Kersting, 36, 44, 98, 131, 205, 277, 289; Kunsthistorisches Museum, Vienna, 137; Mansell Collection, 16, 19, 23, 32, 38, 40, 41, 53, 150, 148, 149, 150, 156, 233, 238, 243; Musées Nationaux, Louvre, 83, 86; Museen zu Berlin, 96; National Monuments Record (crown copyright), 114, 119, 155 (bottom), 157, 158, 159, 213; National Museet, Copenhagen, 286; Norwich City Museum, 155 (top); Public Record Office, 161, 225; M. Rayner, 191; Royal Scottish Museum (crown copyright), 81 (left); H. Trevor Roper, *The Rise of Christian Europe*, (Thames and Hudson, 1966), 88; M. Rostovtzeff, *Social and Economic History of the Roman Empire*, second edition (Clarendon Press, 1957), 13 (left); Edwin Smith, 268; Skjold fra. Gokstadskibet, Gokstadfumnet, 105 (middle left); Staatsbibliothek, Berlin, 63; Staatsbibliothek, Munchen, 136; Universitatsbibliothek, Jena, 143; Unversitetets Oldsaksamling, Oslo, 104, 105 top left, top right, bottom right, 107; University College, Dublin, 273; Victoria and Albert Museum, 133, 285; The Warburg Institute, 278.

Colour plates are reproduced by kind permission of: the Board of Trinity College, Dublin, facing page 265; Giraudon, facing page 188; Kimsthistorisches Museum, Vienna, bottom facing page 264; National Gallery of Art, Washington D.C.; Scala Instituto Fotografico Editioriale, facing page 189.

List of maps

The Roman Empire A.D. 300   10
The Barbarian Kingdoms c. A.D. 511   24
The Restored Empire of Justinian A.D. 565   42
The Muslim World today   65
The Muslim World A.D. 750   72
Charlemagne's Empire   91
Invasions of the Vikings, Hungarians and Saracens in the
    10th century   107
Charlemagne's Empire divided between his grandsons   109
The Empire of Otto I   135
Empire and Papacy in the 11th century   139
The Crusades   207
England and France in the 12th century   214
Europe in 1300   292

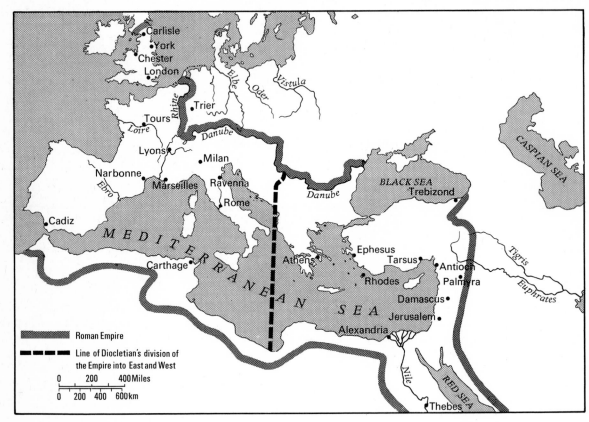

The Roman Empire in A.D. 300

Chapter 1
The Roman Empire on the Eve of Collapse

In the year A.D. 300 the Roman empire, vast and dominating, still straddled the known world, stretching from Northumberland to the Red Sea, as you can see from the map on the facing page. The number of people who inhabited the lands inside its long frontiers had never been very large as we now judge size, indeed only a fraction of the present population of those lands, and they had always been very unevenly spread. The desolate moors and uplands round Hadrian's Wall in the north of Britain were thinly populated compared with the Nile valley. The town of York, busy and thriving though it was with its seven or eight thousand soldiers and civilians, must have seemed very small to any of those soldiers who had seen service in such splendid crowded cities as Carthage or Alexandria or Antioch with their baths and temples and libraries, and perhaps 100,000 inhabitants. At the beginning of the fourth century the population of the empire was shrinking, and much of it was living in deep misery and constant danger. Once the citizens of the Roman empire had, in the main, known what it was to live for long periods in peace and security. Many of them had grown rich in the course of time, many more were comfortably prosperous, and even the poorest were not without hope and expectation of better days and fuller stomachs. The long roads, 90,000 miles of them, radiating to every part of the Roman world, along which the legions moved promptly and swiftly to deal with trouble spots, had also been alive with other traffic; farmers travelling to the local markets with their produce; merchants and traders with their packs bulging with goods—not only the commoner necessities like oil, fleeces, and cheap pottery, but also luxuries such as perfume, fine jewelry, costly glass, and furs which they had no difficulty in selling to customers by the way or at their journey's end. But at the time when this book begins things were very different. The 'Pax Romana' had largely disappeared, and with it had gone the well-being, even the hope, of countless Roman citizens of every sort and kind in Britain, Gaul, Italy, Africa, Asia Minor, and elsewhere, who now knew nothing but fear and hunger and looked out upon a black and threatening world.

Some of their troubles were due to natural disasters for which men knew no cure, such as outbreaks of plague and widespread famine which brought death and starvation to thousands, and left

great tracts of land, even in well-populated parts, empty and desolate. But the worst disasters came from incessant war, war which brought death and starvation just as surely as plague and famine and to even larger numbers, and which ruined those who were left alive and destroyed security everywhere.

Of course war had always been a danger to the empire. On the frontiers a ring of different peoples lay ever ready to invade and plunder if any sign of weakness in the defences appeared. Every section of the frontiers had been threatened, and there had been many times when these barbarian peoples had broken through them and ravaged towns, farms, and fields. But wholesale invasion had been prevented hitherto by the strength of the Roman army, its superior fighting qualities, and the speed with which it could move from place to place as danger threatened. Gradually, however, through the third century the awe which barbarians felt for that army had vanished, and by the end of the century barbarian attacks came more frequently, and when they came the Roman resistance was feebler, even at times non-existent. For the legions were far too often engaged in fighting, not on the frontiers to repel an outside enemy, but inside the empire and against each other. The chief cause of these civil wars was a dangerous practice which had become common: sections of the army would set up rival emperors or pretenders, and when soldiers were busy, in Britain or Gaul for instance, proclaiming new emperors of their choice and fighting to establish them—until they grew tired of them and began the process all over again—they had little time to spare for guarding the frontiers and repelling barbarians. So Romans fought against Romans as well as against barbarians on the soil of the empire, and everywhere the results were the same—death and ruin for the wretched civilians, ravaged towns, burnt homes, deserted fields, and neglected vineyards. About A.D. 265 a government official wrote a report on the district where he worked and the miserable state it was in. 'Very few vines are bearing grapes,' he wrote, 'they are in a terrible state of neglect and are overgrown with rushes, and the wine-presses and basins are in ruins'; and this neglect must have been true of many other crops besides vines, and in many parts of the empire. Countless farmers and traders disappeared, and those remaining were often too despairing to sow crops which might never be harvested, or to travel on roads which were now very unsafe. Food became scarce, and prices rose so high that the value of money dwindled almost to nothing. In the great cornfields of Egypt, for instance, the price of grain increased many hundreds of times, and three silver denarius would only buy a fraction of the bread it had once bought. It became quite common for poor people to sell their children because they could not afford to feed them.

To make matters worse, particularly for poorer citizens, there were incessant imperial demands for money and gifts in kind, and especially for the army. It had always cost a good deal to feed and equip the legions, but now the first thing that every new upstart emperor had to do was to satisfy and reward the troops who had proclaimed him, and so there were constant fresh and unexpected demands for oil, corn, leather, money, and even unpaid labour from the wretched civilians. And there was no help for them against the emperor, even if he only wore the purple for a few months, and no protection against the soldiers, who simply seized what they wanted if it was not immediately forthcoming. Near the end of the third century a writer described the outrageous behaviour of the army. He wrote: 'If you want to remain alive restrain the violence of the soldiers. Let none of them steal a chicken or take a sheep, let none carry off grapes nor thresh corn nor seize olive oil, salt, or wood . . . let them live on the spoils taken from the foe and not on the tears of the people.' From this it is clear that a man might easily lose everything, his whole livelihood and even his life, not to foreign raiders but to defenders of the empire. One petition to the emperor, after beginning very politely with 'Most blessed of all beings that have ever existed', went on to say 'we are most atrociously oppressed and squeezed by those officers and soldiers whose duty is to protect us.' Indeed, before the year A.D. 300 conditions in the Roman empire had become so chaotic and terrible that it seemed as if the whole great edifice was about to crumble into ruins. It was saved, though only for a time, chiefly by the magnificent efforts of two emperors, Diocletian and Constantine the Great.

Diocletian ruled the Roman world from A.D. 284 to 305. He was a soldier, the son of a freed slave, and he was born in Dalmatia, now Yugoslavia. He was a severe, tough-looking person with close-cropped hair and a short thick neck, deep grooves on his forehead and round his nose and mouth, and a melancholy expression. He

Portraits of Diocletian and Constantine on coins minted during their reigns. The Romans produced excellent coins. Compare these with those on pages 29 and 96 made by barbarians who had lost the art of good coin-making.

was proclaimed emperor by the Praetorian guard, the section of the army he commanded. There was nothing unusual about any of this. Men of many races and classes had worn the imperial purple, and emperor-making by the legions was, as we have seen, only too common. In the 50 years before Diocletian 20 emperors had been set up (and often knocked down) and you can easily work out how short the average reign was. What was unusual about Diocletian was that he remained securely in power for 21 years, challenged at times, as by the upstart Carausius in Britain, but never shaken; that in 305 he retired of his own free will from the most powerful— and perilous—position in the world; and that he tried to bring again some health and well-being to the empire. He was an astute and practical man, and saw clearly many of the problems which faced him, even if he did not always understand how best to solve them. He saw, for instance, that the crowning and uncrowning of emperors by the legions was fatal to any hope of general improvement in conditions, for no man who ruled only 'by the grace of soldiers' was likely to last long enough even to begin to restore the longed-for peace and security and prosperity. Much of the reverence that men had felt for the emperor had disappeared, and Diocletian's first move was to exalt the person of the emperor and so, he hoped, his power. He thought the throne would be made safer by deepening the mystery surrounding it. He intended that the emperor should be seen as a god in a human body, to be loved and worshipped and regarded again with deepest awe. Instead of the simple purple he appeared in gorgeous robes stiff with gold and jewels, jewelled scarlet shoes on his feet, a broad white band gleaming with precious stones round his head, and attended by a splendid but respectful retinue. This was a god-like figure, not to be approached with a simple military salute, but upon the knees, with oriental ceremony and many prostrations, and certainly not a human puppet to be tossed about at the whim of soldiers. Diocletian knew well that he could never weaken or diminish the army, for the safety of the frontiers depended on it. In fact he doubled its size, and oddly enough he recruited thousands of barbarians, even into the most famous legions, but he himself moved perpetually from place to place wherever danger threatened, danger that could come not only from barbarian invaders but from discontented soldiers and too-popular commanders turning covetous eyes on the imperial throne.

Diocletian decided that the empire was too big to be governed efficiently by one man. He therefore divided it into two parts by a line drawn roughly north and south through the Adriatic Sea, and subdivided each part into two sections called prefectures. He appointed a fellow-soldier to be his partner and rule the western half, while he took charge of the eastern. Both bore the supreme imperial title of Augustus. He then appointed two assistants with

the lower title of Caesar to be their adopted heirs and each to govern a prefecture. He probably hoped that these Caesars would slip into the shoes of the Augusti when they disappeared from the scene, so that there would be no awkward gaps in the succession to encourage more attempts at emperor-making.

He also began in other ways to reorganize the shaky empire. He fixed wages, he tried to keep prices steady, even the price of shoes and sausages, he called in worthless money and issued a new gold coin called an *aureus*. He ordered taxes to be simplified and made regular, so as to avoid the sudden unexpected demands that so 'atrociously oppressed' the people. But his reforms did not go to the real root of the troubles, and so had very little good effect. For instance, one of those roots was the vast imperial expenditure which could only be paid for by high taxation, but this became vaster still. There were now four rulers instead of one, and four courts to be supported, and more soldiers to be paid and fed, to say nothing of some splendid and expensive buildings in Rome, which Diocletian could not resist putting up, although he never had much interest in the city and never lived there. He also built an enormous palace in Dalmatia, where he went when he retired in 305, almost worn out by his labours. By then he had restored order and held the frontiers, but given very little relief to the ordinary citizen of the empire.

His arrangements for the division of imperial power between two Augusti and two Caesars did not work either; almost at once civil war broke out between rival claimants, and raged for 18 years, until one of the claimants, having destroyed his rivals, re-united the parts of Diocletian's divided empire and ruled alone. He was Constantine the Great.

Constantine, too, was born in Dalmatia, but his father was far from being a slave. In fact, he stood very near to the imperial throne, for he was one of the two Caesars adopted by Diocletian, and in 305 he moved up to become the Augustus of the west. That same year Constantine, then a young man of 32, fought with his father against the Picts in Scotland, and was with him when he died in York in 306. He was at once proclaimed Augustus by his father's legions, and so began the long conflict which ended in his becoming the sole master of the Roman world. Like Diocletian, he was a good soldier and had all the tireless energy and drive necessary to carry on the work of saving the empire from calamity; but he was a far more unusual person, subtle, far-seeing and capable of doing most unexpected things. During his reign the Roman army regained much of its old triumphant strength and spirit, and the frontiers were secured by new forts, like those, for instance, which were built round the coast of Britain from the Wash to the Isle of

Above *Relief from Trajan's Column in Rome, showing legionaries building a fort.*

The Porta Appia, one of the great gates in the walls of Rome. Built of brick by the citizens the walls were begun in A.D. 271 and were twelve miles long.

Wight—the 'Saxon Shore' as it was called—from which Roman and Briton together watched for the German invaders coming in across the North Sea. War galleys patrolled the waters of the Rhine, the walls of Rome were re-built and greatly strengthened, and many other cities, which had once had ample open spaces inside and around, were now for safety's sake encircled with close defensive walls, and so grew cramped and narrow-streeted, like those medieval towns that came after them. As the result of all these things the empire, though always on the defensive, was not dangerously threatened for 50 years after Constantine died, and some of its old peace and order returned. But of course there had been other emperors before Constantine who had achieved as much as this and more, and there are other reasons, two in particular, why he is called 'the Great' and why he is one of the most remarkable men in the history not only of Rome but of the world.

One of these reasons is that he completely transformed the position of Christianity from being a forbidden religion, which men followed in peril of their lives, into an honoured and protected faith. It was a strange and sudden transformation. Diocletian, a staunch believer in the old gods of Rome, had terribly harassed the Christians in the worst and longest persecution they had ever endured. No doubt he believed that he had every right to do this, for they were the only section of the community who would not give to the emperor the worship and adoration he demanded. They were quite ready to be good citizens in every other way, law-abiding and hard-working, but to 'worship the Augustus as a god in a human body' was something they utterly refused to do. Diocletian could not allow them to flout the imperial authority; their numbers were growing, and it must have seemed dangerous when Christian legionaries threw down their arms rather than worship the emperor, and civilians stubbornly refrained even from dropping a few grains of incense into the sacrificial fire before his altar and so admitting his divinity.

Yet not even the most savage cruelty allowed by Diocletian from 303 onwards could crush these invincible people or extinguish the light of their faith, and when in 305 he retired, ill and exhausted, there were really only two choices open to his successors: either to continue the persecution more and more harshly, and so add a long deadly war of religion to all the other hazards in the empire, or to find some way of winning the support of their Christian subjects.

Constantine, who was at the court of Diocletian at the time, must have been well aware of all this: the stubborn resistance of the Christians, the failure of death and torture to destroy their faith, and the urgent need to find some end to a conflict which

could only result in tearing the empire apart. Moreover, although officially a pagan especially devoted to Apollo, he had, in private, begun to doubt the power of the old gods to help those who sacrificed to them—for the help of the gods was something all Romans desired—and he had 'thought in his own mind what sort of god he ought to secure as an ally'. Then in 312, when he was in Italy challenging his most dangerous rival in the fight for the imperial throne, he and his army saw a vision. A shining cross appeared in the sky, with the words IN HOC VINCES written across it. Deeply impressed, Constantine ordered that all the standards of his army should be changed to the *labarum,* a cross with the initial of Christ's name upon it, so that his legions would march under the Christian symbol. Strangely enough, no written record of this vision appears till 25 years later, when Eusebius, Bishop of Caesarea, put it in his biography of the emperor, yet something must have happened to make Constantine act as he then did. Against all the advice of his generals, and all the omens of the oracles, with his whole future at stake, he advanced on Rome. It was a moment of great peril. His spies had kept him well informed and he knew that his enemy Maxentius, with a larger army than his own, was in Rome behind strong walls, his granaries stuffed with corn from Africa, and that he had consulted all possible oracles, made all possible sacrifices to the gods, and been promised victory. Yet with all these odds against him Constantine boldly marched against Rome under the Christian cross. He utterly defeated Maxentius, and by doing so became the undisputed master of the western half of the empire. He must have been convinced that the God of the Christians had indeed promised to fight for him and had kept His word.

From that moment Constantine having, he felt sure, secured the favour of God for the empire and himself, was committed to Christianity, although, rather oddly, he himself was not baptized until he lay dying 25 years later. He at once sent out a decree containing some famous words: 'Henceforth in perfect and absolute freedom, each and every person who chooses to belong to the Christian religion shall be at liberty to do so without let or hindrance.' With those words Constantine accepted Christianity, and henceforward he believed that he governed not with the blessing of Apollo, but under the eye of 'Almighty God who sitteth in the watch tower of Heaven' and whose gifts of 'heavenly benevolence', as Constantine later wrote, he could 'neither describe or number'. The old hostility between the pagan empire and the Christian Church, which had lasted since Pilate condemned Christ to death, was officially over. Although enmity between pagan and Christian did not by any means disappear and though at least one emperor tried to go back on Constantine's decree, nothing

The labarum *which took the place of the eagles and other standards in the Roman army after the vision of Constantine.*

could restore the past. Empire and Church were now linked, not divided.

Constantine's other moment of vision produced something more concrete. In A.D. 330 he founded a new capital of the empire, Constantinople, or New Rome, as he wished it to be called. (Constantinople is often called Byzantium, the name of the ancient Greek city which was there before the time of Constantine.) Many citizens of the empire must have been deeply shocked when they heard what he was doing, for many still thought of Rome as the sacred centre of the civilized world, that world, of course, being the Roman empire. But the truth was that Rome was no longer such a centre, and Constantine knew this. For years no emperors had lived there, it was much too far from the most threatened frontiers, the Rhine, the Danube, and the Euphrates. Most of the empire's trade was with the East; from the East came most of her wealth as well as the newest dangers from barbarians, Goths on the Danube and Persians on the Euphrates, and it was to the East that Constantine's new capital looked, across the Bosphorus and the Sea of Marmora. The city took $5\frac{1}{2}$ years to build, and it was meant to be in many ways a duplicate of old Rome, with a Senate House, a hippodrome, baths and aqueducts; a place where Roman law was obeyed and the Roman tongue spoken; but at the same time Constantine filled its libraries with Greek manuscripts, and adorned it with splendid works of art looted from Greece. It was a curious mixture of Roman and Greek, pagan and Christian, and probably the emperor's mind was a mixture too, since he set up a great statue to Apollo, the god of the unconquered sun, in the centre of the city, its face altered to be a portrait of himself; and yet he built a Christian church nearby—the church of Holy Wisdom, Sancta Sophia.

Chapter 2
The West: Barbarian Attacks

While Constantine lived and for some time after his death the conflict between Romans and barbarians on the frontiers, especially along the great barriers of the Rhine and the Danube, seemed to have turned in favour of Rome, and its fierceness seemed to have died down. But the danger was still there, lurking in the deep forests beyond the Rhine, on the foggy coasts which faced westward across the North sea, and in the vast lands beyond the Danube. It was a conflict which had harassed the empire, off and on, for more than two centuries, and it was bound to break out again sooner or later. Ahead lay many terrible years of tumult and disaster, during which the western part of the empire was to go down into darkness, and Rome itself, 'the city which had taken captive all the world', was to fall into the hands of barbarians—a terrible shock to those who still believed she was invincible. 'Her sword is broken, her walls have been scaled' wrote one tormented Roman after it happened, not realizing that 'her sword' had become an exceedingly blunt weapon. In A.D. 480 the last emperor of the west died, and after that there was only one capital of the empire, Constantinople, and only one emperor, in the east. How did all this come about?

The story is a very intricate one, and it is easy to become thoroughly confused in a maze of dates and events, and to get some quite wrong ideas, particularly about the barbarians themselves. For instance, it is easy to imagine that their invasions began suddenly and ended just as suddenly; that on a given day in a certain year a horde of uncivilized strangers, burning with hatred for Rome, erupted over the frontiers, overwhelmed the legions as they waited, neatly dressed in polished breastplates and helmets with horse-hair crests, and then proceeded to sweep away every sign of the Roman way of life. But, of course, the barbarian invasions were not like that, they were far more complicated, and it is important to understand certain facts about them.

For one thing, as you will have realized from reading Chapter 1, they were not suddenly begun and quickly over, but went on for a very long time, sometimes sharp and violent, sometimes dying away and almost forgotten. They did not always take the form of fierce fighting, with victory for one side and defeat for the other at

the end. Barbarians were not all uncivilized (the word simply means a 'stranger', not a savage). They did not all long to destroy the empire and everything in it they did not understand, but wanted to force their way into it and settle there to enjoy its wealth and trade.

The most dangerous kind of invasion was a subtle kind that no man could prevent and many Roman citizens were hardly aware of, or, if they were, preferred to forget. All through the third and fourth centuries thousands of barbarians, without bloodshed or battle-cries, had penetrated quietly, dangerously, into many parts of the empire and settled there. They had pressed in by countless little channels, just as the incoming sea trickles into the defences of a sand castle. They came as traders, concerned peacefully enough with daily buying and selling, but quite capable of acting as spies. They came as settlers, often invited deliberately by the Romans, and given empty tracts of country to farm and live on, in return for which they undertook to guard some piece of the frontier against other barbarians. They came uninvited, as refugees escaping from their own enemies, and it was not very difficult for whole tribes to slip unseen across frozen rivers in dark winter nights and disperse quietly into lonely parts. They came as servants to wealthy Roman households, and there were so many of these that at the end of the fourth century the Bishop of Cyrene said he hardly knew a single family without a Goth or a Scythian as butler, cook, or farm bailiff. And, perhaps strangest of all, there were thousands of barbarian soldiers actually serving in the imperial army; indeed, whole sections of it were barbarian like the Ist Cohort of Dacians, 'Hadrian's Own', as they were proudly called, which guarded part of the Wall in the north of Britain. Even in Constantine's reign the legionary did not often look much like the pictures of him that one usually sees in history books. The traditional armour, and helmet, the great rectangular shield, and the long *pilum* or throwing spear were not used, except perhaps by the magnificent Praetorian guard which surrounded the person of the emperor. Instead, most legionaries wore drab-looking padded leather tunics; they carried round wooden shields covered with leather, and weapons such as short-handled axes, daggers, and *spathas* (double-edged swords). Their standards were no longer the eagles of Rome but strange-looking dragon shapes, made of skins and then filled with air so that they floated from the tops of spears, and in the heat of battle wild barbarian war-cries were heard from both sides. But in spite of their rather uncouth looks and habits barbarians made excellent soldiers, and the Romans had always recruited them into the army as well as men of conquered races, for the empire was so vast that it could not be defended in any other way. This, of course, was a dangerous thing to do, for it meant that they could carry away much precious knowledge of the

Legionaries in traditional armour and their barbarian allies.

Right *Some of the standards replaced by the* labarum *and later by barbarian dragons.*

Far right *Barbarian soldiers with a dragon standard.*

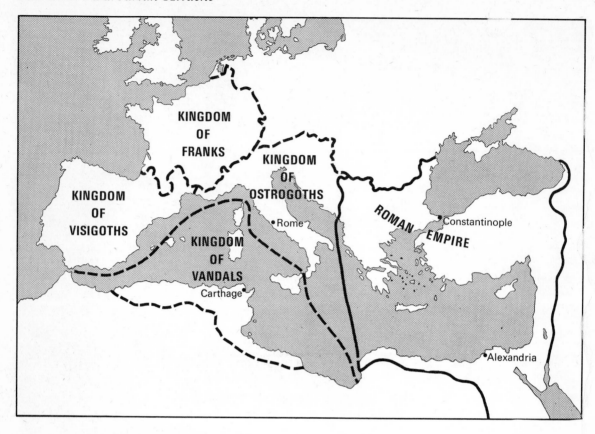

The Barbarian kingdoms, c. A.D. 511

Roman ways of fighting, and as a result become more deadly as enemies. But some among them were the best and ablest soldiers ever to be in the service of Rome, men who rose to the highest military rank of '*magister militum*', who spoke Latin better than their own tongue, had Roman friends, formed part of the imperial household, and occasionally married into the imperial family.

Clearly then all barbarians were not uncivilized savages. Many had lived and worked in the empire, many admired what they saw there, only a few sought to destroy it utterly. They were often greedy, envious, and violent, but they wanted land, homes, position, and power within the frontiers they attacked. Some who began by hating Rome ended by being fascinated by her laws, her buildings, and her skills, and longed to restore her glory. Ataulf the Visigoth was one of these. He was with his brother-in-law Alaric at the sacking of Rome in A.D. 410, and afterwards, when he married Galla Placidia, the sister of the emperor, who had been taken prisoner there, he insolently gave her as a wedding present 100 bowls of gold and jewels looted from the capital; yet at the end of his life his chief ambition was to be called '*restitutor orbis Romani*' —

24

restorer of the Roman world. But the time was near when it would be impossible for Ataulf or anyone to restore it, when the Roman world in the west fell apart, and its place was taken by the barbarian kingdoms you can see in the map on page 24.

The peoples who lived in these kingdoms nearly all belonged to the same race—the Germans—though the various sections of them are called by different names—Saxons, Franks, Vandals, Goths, and so on. Originally they were hunters and herdsmen, who scorned a settled kind of life and preferred to move about in their clans and family groups, searching for new pastures when their beasts had eaten the land bare, and new hunting grounds when they themselves had cleared the nearest forests of game. As time went on, however, some found it necessary to change their habits. The Franks, for instance, after moving south and west from the Baltic sea found themselves pressed against the frontier of the Roman empire and uncomfortably hemmed in by other barbarian people. They could no longer wander at will to find grazing and hunting, and had no choice but to settle down as farmers and follow the plough they had once scorned, varying this with a good deal of raiding and fighting to extend their lands.

Other Germans remained wanderers for longer, and among these were the Vandals and Goths, who moved south and east from the Baltic, whole tribes together with all their possessions, the Vandals into the lands beyond the Danube and the Goths into Russia and as far as the Black Sea.

By the end of the fourth century the Goths had separated into two great divisions, the Visigoths—or West Goths—and the Ostrogoths—or East Goths; and they were themselves living in considerable dread of another wandering people, the Huns, those squat, ugly, savage horsemen, whose mysterious speed of movement, slit eyes, and wiry black hair seemed so peculiar to Romans and barbarians alike, that they believed they were devils or evil magicians. Driven and crunched by the Huns, the Visigoths had crowded over the Danube and been allowed by the emperor in Constantinople, with some reluctance, to settle within the empire. In A.D. 393 they chose a warrior, Alaric, as their king. He had served for years in the Roman army, and the Visigoths were now pledged as '*foederati*'. *Foederati* were barbarian tribes who, in return for land and pay, were ready at one moment to fight for the empire, even against their own kin, but who might at the next moment change sides if they were not satisfied with their rewards. They were useful but untrustworthy, and Alaric was a typical example. He wished to see his people permanently settled in goodly homes and lands, and himself given a high commanding position in the Roman army. When none of these were forthcoming from the emperor in

Constantinople, 'he persuaded his people to seek kingdoms for themselves by their own efforts rather than live in subjection to others', and set off for the west to make a better bargain. The long slow trek to Italy of the whole Visigoth people took nearly 15 years, and the pattern of their passing was to be repeated over and over again in many other parts of the empire. Sometimes they moved through the country without delay, their warriors plundering, burning, and stealing; sometimes, when the Roman government seemed likely to give them what they wanted, they stopped and waited hopefully, to the dismay of the inhabitants in whose country they were who only longed to get rid of them. At one point, when Alaric was pacified by being made *magister militum* in Illyricum, they remained settled and respectable for four years. But he—and they—were never satisfied for long, and by 408 they had arrived in Italy. For the next 2 years Alaric fought, threatened and bargained fiercely, sometimes with officials in Rome, sometimes with the emperor, who had settled himself in Ravenna and did nothing to oppose the Visigoths. Twice he threatened to attack Rome if his demands were not met; the third time, furiously impatient at delay, he seized the city and sacked it. Its treasures, as always, were irresistible to the barbarians. Alaric's total share was 5,000 pounds of gold, 30,000 of silver, 3,000 pounds of pepper, 4,000 robes of silk, 3,000 skins dyed scarlet; but far more besides went to his looting troops. These were some of the things that made invasion worth while.

The sack of Rome in 410 sent a fearful shock through the empire. In Jerusalem the great Christian scholar Jerome, then an old man of 78, wrote mournfully 'When the brightest light on the whole earth was extinguished I was dumb ... and my sorrow was stirred'. Many others besides Jerome had a feeling of awe, even of love, for the city, and saw in its fall an omen of great evils to come. While men waited anxiously to see if the end of the world was upon them Alaric moved on to conquer the south of Italy, and began making plans to cross to Sicily and then Africa. But his plans came to nothing, and he never became one of the highest figures in the empire, as he had hoped to do, for in 412 he was suddenly taken ill and died in a few days. His warriors took extraordinary care over his burial. A gang of Roman prisoners was set to work to divert the river Busento, near which the Visigoths had camped, into a temporary channel, and the body of Alaric, with his armour and weapons, and some of the splendid spoils from Rome, was buried deep in the sand and stones of its dry bed. Then the water was turned again into the old course, hiding his grave for ever. The mourning Visigoths knew that no man of their race would dare to disturb the dead king, but, to make sure that others should not even know the exact position of his grave and be tempted to loot it,

they swiftly massacred the wretched prisoners, the only people who could have told the secret.

The new king was Alaric's brother-in-law Ataulf, the would-be *restitutor orbis Romani*, and he made peace with the Roman government, whose chief desire, since they could not crush the Visigoths, was to move them out of Italy as soon as possible and let loose their violent energy elsewhere. The best way of doing this was to employ them as Rome's shield against other dangerous marauders in the empire, and there were plenty of these, for while the Visigoths were rampaging in Italy, and the frontiers were thinly guarded, swarms of other barbarians had crossed the Rhine into Gaul. The Visigoths, therefore, were transformed into allies and were hurried off to deal with some of those who were plundering and destroying in the south of Gaul and in Spain. When the campaign was over, they were allowed by their treaty with Rome to settle at last on land forcibly taken from the Roman inhabitants, and to form their own kingdom, which, as you can see from the map, stretched through the south of France and over the Pyrenees into Spain.

Notwithstanding help of this kind the empire was everywhere desperately beset. Away on the outskirts across the North Sea the British found themselves almost helpless against the attacks of the Anglo-Saxons in spite of the forts of the Saxon Shore strung along the coast from the Wash to the Isle of Wight. They could get no answer from Rome to their appeals for the return of the legions, which had been withdrawn to fight nearer home. The gaps left gave wonderful opportunities to invaders, not only in Britain but also in Africa in the extreme south of the empire.

Among the tribes which crossed the Rhine at the beginning of the fifth century were the Vandals, and they, like the Visigoths, were not simply a raiding army but a whole hungry people on the move. They passed through the countryside like a scourge, and a far more terrible scourge even than the Visigoths, who were lambs compared with the Vandal wolves. By 428 they had travelled through Gaul, leaving a trail of broken towns and smoking farms wherever they passed 'If the waves over the ocean had overflowed the fields of Gaul they would have done less damage', and had reached the south of Spain; and in that year the most formidable man in their history was lifted on the shields of the warriors and proclaimed king.

His name was Gaiseric, and he was chosen first and foremost, of course, because he was a dauntless and successful fighter, which was absolutely essential in a Vandal leader. It was said that 'he was quicker in striking than any other man', and he was certainly as cruel and ruthless as any of them, but in certain other ways he was unusual. He did not stand out among the tall and physically splendid Vandals, for he was only of medium height and lame from a fall

off his horse. Instead of being noisy and boisterous and given to hard drinking, he was 'deep in mind and sparing of speech, a despiser of luxury'; and for years after his death he was still known as 'the cleverest of men'. His anger was terrifying, and he had an uncanny power of stirring up discord among enemies and friends, to their pain and his own profit. Like Alaric, he desired land for his people and a great position for himself; but, unlike him, he was intensely hostile to the empire and had no desire to become a Roman subject, however high and powerful. His intention was to rule an independent kingdom carved out at Rome's expense, and in 428 he made his first move towards this by what might seem the extraordinary action of shipping his whole people across from Spain to Africa. By then the Vandals had been on the move for 20 years, since they first crossed the Rhine, and had suffered many strange hazards; and now to cross the sea into the warm African sun must have seemed one of the strangest. But it was a calculated and far-seeing move by Gaiseric, for the long coastal strip of Roman Africa was one of the oldest and richest provinces of the empire. It was crowded with cities, some great and splendid like Carthage, the ancient rival of Rome, others smaller but beautiful and prosperous, and everywhere aquaducts and water channels made farming possible. Year by year a steady stream of tribute and trade, money, oil, and especially corn, went across the Mediterranean Sea to Rome and Constantinople. Thousands of soldiers were recruited there, and when Rome faced enemies in other parts of the empire she had always been able to rely on an obedient and busy Africa.

Gaiseric, of course, knew all this; he knew how greatly he would shake the empire if only he could make himself master of Africa and the Mediterranean, and so be able to cut off these supplies, and threaten Rome from the south. By the time the Vandals crossed from Spain the legions were already thin on the ground, for many had gone, just as they had gone from Britain, to face urgent dangers elsewhere. In two years the Vandals had sacked every city in the province, and the Roman rule was practically broken. By 442 Gaiseric was king in Africa, independent and dangerous, his ships free to scour the sea unchallenged by Roman galleys, his army able to plunder Sardinia, Sicily, and Italy itself; and while Rome struggled against foes in the north, the menace of this stubborn and relentless enemy was always present in the rear. It was a menace which, even though it did not last—for the Vandals gradually became fat and lazy in the warmth of Africa—, weakened the empire almost everywhere while it did.

There are still two more barbarian kingdoms on the map to be explained, the kingdoms of the Ostrogoths and of the Franks. When Alaric led his half of the Goths westward to Italy, the other half, the Ostrogoths, remained settled to the north of the Black Sea.

Coin portrait of Theodoric,
very crude compared with those
shown on page 13.

They were a strenuous powerful group, but even so they could not
stand against the quick fury of the Huns when it descended upon
them, and, like the Visigoths, they were at last driven, broken and
fugitive, from their homes. By a pact with the emperor at
Constantinople they were allowed to settle within the eastern
empire in return for an undertaking to guard the nearby frontier.
As they recovered from their mauling by the Huns, they became
too numerous and too hungry to live on the parcel of land they
occupied, and so there began the usual angry bickering with the
emperor, threatening demands for more land, more rations, and
more pay in return for their service as *foederati*. In 471 a young
prince of the royal family, the Amals, became their king. His name
was Theodoric. Like Alaric, he had been trained in the Roman
army, but he knew even more than Alaric about Roman ways and
government, for as a boy he had spent 10 years in the Court at
Constantinople as hostage for his father's good behaviour. There is
no doubt that Theodoric learned a great deal there, and admired
much that he learned, and he was—for a time—a high favourite of
the emperor, but this did not prevent him, when he became king
of the Ostrogoths, from being an intolerable nuisance. He cham-
pioned his people, quarrelled with the emperor, and though at
times he used his army in the service of the empire, he also led it
against Constantinople itself. With this menace on his doorstep,
the emperor decided that some way must be found of removing the
Ostrogoths as far away as possible, and he therefore played the old

game of setting one barbarian to dispose of another, this time in Italy.

In 476, after a procession of exceedingly ineffective emperors in the west, the last of them had been deposed, and now no remnant of the imperial line was left in either Rome or Ravenna. Italy was governed for the next ten years by a barbarian soldier named Odovacar, and the emperor at Constantinople, although now supposed to be emperor of the west as well as the east, had been obliged to leave him in power simply because he was not strong enough to do anything else. But in 488, with the turbulent Theodoric far too close to him to be comfortable, he invited the Ostrogoths' king to invade Italy in the imperial name and eject Odovacar. This would remove him from Constantinople, and if the two barbarians destroyed each other, so much the better. If Theodoric won, he was to be allowed to govern Italy as the emperor's agent, but he would be a long way off.

Theodoric accepted, called the Ostrogoths together, and told them to get ready at once for the journey. You can imagine the turmoil and confusion of their preparations, for 'with Theodoric went all the people of the Goths, putting their wives and children and as much of their goods as they could into their ox wagons.' The wagons, crammed with people, animals, corn, and even grindstones, were the only shelter the Ostrogoths had on a slow terrible journey, which, though it began in the warm October sun of Greece, took them over the high passes of the Alps in the depth of winter, when their shirts froze so hard that if they ever wanted to take them off, which cannot have been often, they had to break them in pieces first.

It took Theodoric three and a half years to dispose of Odovacar and take control of Italy himself, and afterwards he remained absolute lord of the country for thirty-six years, though he never wore the purple, never called himself anything but '*rex Gotorum*' or *magister militum*, and faithfully kept up the idea that he was the emperor's representative. He was more fortunate than Alaric, more civilized than Gaiseric, wiser, more patient, and certainly more splendidly successful than both. He never intended to obliterate the name of Rome, he had a vision of her greatness protected by Gothic spears, and although he settled the Ostrogoths throughout Italy, he managed to do this without reducing the inhabitants to abject misery or rousing them to revolt. His great object was to give the land peace and tranquillity. Fortunately for us, he had a most efficient secretary called Cassiodorus, who prepared countless letters for the king to stamp with a gold seal—he either could not write or was too busy to sign his name—, and from these letters we know a good deal about Theodoric and his work. For instance, we

know that he carefully put the defences of Rome in order, for there is a letter about the supply of 25,000 square flat bricks each year for patching the walls, and another saying 'We are earnestly anxious to keep the walls of Rome in good repair. . . . If anyone has in his fields stones suitable for the building of the walls let him cheerfully and promptly produce them.' And evidently they were produced, for some have been found with the words 'Our Lord Theodoric, benefactor of Rome' cut in them.

Aquaducts were repaired, and marshes drained, and even the hot springs at a village called Aponum were cleaned out and made to flow properly, so that by bathing in them people might have their pains soothed and sickness removed. Theodoric had a very keen eye, and never keener than when he was watching food supplies, especially of corn, for the Vandals still prevented shipments of the precious stuff from Africa. There is an angry letter to a certain official which says 'We are exceedingly annoyed at finding that the crops which are generally sent by your district . . . have not yet arrived though it is near autumn. What are you waiting for? Put this to rights promptly.' No doubt the official hastily did what he was told, for though, as Cassiodorus was constantly saying, Theodoric had great patience, it could become exhausted and then the results were unpleasant.

But of course the peace and tranquillity depended on more than the walls of Rome and the supply of corn. It could be utterly destroyed by war, and Theodoric therefore did everything in his power not only to secure his own frontiers but to keep peace with his neighbours. Without tying himself too closely to any single other barbarian leader, which would immediately have caused the rest to join forces and attack him, he tried to be on friendly terms with them all. He arranged convenient, if not very comfortable, marriages for one of his sisters to the king of the Vandals, and one of his daughters to the king of the Visigoths, and he himself married a Frankish princess, sister of Clovis, king of the Franks.

Cassiodorus wrote a good many letters for Theodoric to Clovis. He arranged for a particularly skilful doctor from Constantinople to attend him, a man who had very strong ideas about diet and disapproved of hard-boiled eggs and old dry cheese, and he wrote about a harper that Clovis had asked for. There are letters congratulating Clovis on his victories, but also urging him 'with frankness but all affection' to be moderate and not attack his neighbour, and not to persecute refugees. But 'frankness and all affection' did not make much impression on Clovis when he had made up his mind to do something, and though Theodoric was successful in keeping peace in Italy, he could not restrain his tempestuous brother-in-law, the king of the Franks. The Franks were a group of German tribes

Above *Frankish gold ornaments.*

Left *Theodoric's tomb at Ravenna.*

who little by little had moved south from the coast of the North Sea until they found the way barred by the frontiers of the empire. After many clashes with the Romans they made the usual bargain with them, so that by the time that Alaric invaded Italy many of them were living in the north of Gaul, holding their land in return for helping in the defence of the empire. They were far more faithful than most barbarian *foederati*, and for generations were the trusted allies of the emperor, and exceedingly useful ones too, for they were good soldiers, clever at making weapons and using them—especially their favourite *francisca*, a throwing axe of deadly sharpness—and they had invincible courage. 'Death may overtake them but not fear' wrote Sidonius Apollinaris, a man of Roman family who lived in Gaul under the Franks and certainly knew them well. They were pagans but not savages, they had a taste for Roman ways, and seem to have been generally cleaner than most barbarians, for they did not smear their hair with rancid butter as some did, nor go about wearing the skins of fox, wolf, and badger, which, when not properly cured, smelt abominably. The Franks dressed in close-fitting tunics fastened with brooches and decorated belts, for they loved fine gold and precious stones and wore all the brooches, rings, bracelets, and collars they could afford. Goths and Vandals usually peered out through a fuzz of beard and long matted hair, but the Franks preferred to shave their chins and cheeks and cut their hair short. Only their kings were exceptions, for the mark of royalty was to wear the hair uncut and falling thick and long to the shoulders.

Clovis became one among a number of Frankish kings in A.D. 481, when he was 15 years old; when he died, aged 65, he was the only one. For the first 5 years of his reign he watched what was going on round him and waited, but, being a mixture of high intelligence, cunning, and ruthless daring, he was not likely to remain quiet for long, especially as he was ready to destroy any man who stood in his way. He saw that the remains of Roman power were no longer of the slightest account, and that soon the whole of Gaul would be possessed by barbarians. Clovis meant to have his full share. He first demolished the last representative of Rome, and then, one after another, attacked and ruined the rival barbarian kings, until at the end of his reign, either through open war or by plain murder, he had made himself master of practically the whole of Gaul. Not surprisingly, he became a much dreaded man, treacherous, crafty, with a habit that he never lost of suddenly raising his axe and burying it in the head of any man who crossed his will or seemed a possible danger to him.

But he did not rely simply on brute force. He married the Princess Clotilde of Burgundy, like himself a person of unusual intelligence, but quite unlike him in being kind and gracious far

beyond the cruel fashions of the time. She was a steadfast Christian and an exceedingly determined woman, who set to work at once to convert her husband: 'Without ceasing she urged the king to confess the true God and to forsake his idols for, as she said, these cannot aid themselves or others seeing they are but images carved in wood and stone.' A hundred years later her great grand-daughter was to bring the same persistent pressure to bear on her husband Ethelbert, King of Kent. Clovis, like Ethelbert after him, took a long time to decide to accept a God 'not even proven to belong to the race of gods', as he told his wife, but while he hesitated he calculated carefully what the result on his fortunes would be if he was baptized. By now there were many Christians in Gaul and their influence was great, and Clovis knew that baptism would turn every bishop, priest, and Christian man and woman into his friend rather than his foe. Partly for this reason, and partly because he respected, even if he did not really understand, his wife's religion, Clovis at last abandoned the gods of his ancestors: he was baptized with much ceremony in a church splendidly adorned with white hangings, mysterious with the scent of incense and perfumed candles. From that day forward he could count on the support of the Church, even though he remained distinctly superstitious—he briskly axed one of his soldiers who stole some hay from the lands of the cathedral of Tours, saying as he did so 'Where shall our hope of victory be if we offend the blessed Martin?'—and he did not drop his bloodthirsty habits. Even Gregory, Bishop of Tours, who wrote a history of the Franks and on the whole approved of Clovis, had to admit that the king constantly searched 'to bring to light some new relative (and possible rival) to kill'.

But he governed his lands wisely, he listened to the advice of those remaining men of Gaul who had received a Roman education, and often took it, he came to see that sometimes the settlement of dispute by agreement rather than by blows had something to be said for it, and he caused the law of the Franks—called the Salic Law—to be collected and written down.

Clovis, the last of the barbarian leaders in this chapter, died in A.D. 511 and was buried in a church of his own building in Paris. He is the only one of the four whose territories are still to be found on maps of western Europe. Visigoths, Ostrogoths, and Vandals have disappeared; the name of the Frankish kingdom alone survives—as 'France'.

Chapter 3
The East: the Emperor Justinian

While the western part of the empire was enduring the torment and confusion of being overrun and parcelled out among barbarian kings, the eastern part remained unconquered, though not undisturbed. There were alarms and attacks from various quarters, from Huns, Goths, and Persians, and Constantinople was threatened many times, but always the enemy was somehow vanquished, or pacified, or persuaded to move on elsewhere. A great stone column still stands in Istanbul (the modern name for Constantinople) which commemorates a victory over the Goths, for on it are cut the words '*Fortunae reduci ob devictos Gothos*', that is 'Thanks for the return of fortune on account of the defeated Goths', and, of course, when Theodoric departed for Italy he no longer menaced the eastern capital.

So the Roman empire, though much diminished, still lived on, and Constantine's city, jutting boldly out into the Bosphorus toward Asia, presented its greatness to the east, and was not sacked as Rome was in 410. Though often in peril it remained invincible, full of tempestuous life and extraordinary contrasts between squalor and wealth. There were—and of course still are—some drawbacks to its position, for it lies in an earthquake zone and has suffered terrible disasters because of that, and the climate can be very unpleasant, scorching sometimes in summer, when hot winds blow from Asia Minor and Arabia, and bitter in winter, when they come from the bleak steppes of Russia, and in a few hours can lay an icy wall of fog, so cold that it almost takes your breath away, round the city. But in other ways the position is superb, with the sea on all sides but one, protecting the city and also continually feeding it with rich trade from Europe, Africa, and Asia. Constantine had secured it on the landward side by a massive wall, but the population grew so fast that in 413, only 83 years after its founding, another one had to be built, enclosing nearly twice as much land. This great wall still stands, a good deal patched, but towering magnificently above the houses and the market gardens which now lie at the foot of it. What with sea and walls, Constantinople was, for those days, a reasonably safe place to live in, and certainly it was a splendid one, with buildings as fine as any in Rome, and adorned with wonderful works of art taken from other great cities of the empire, Athens, Antioch, and Rome itself. It was

The walls of Constantinople (Byzantium) built in A.D. 413.

splendid in spite of its narrow filthy streets, the widest only 15 feet wide, lined with dark little shops and overhanging balconies. Rich men lived luxuriously in magnificent houses of stone or brick, built round cool open courtyards shaded with trees, and musical with fountains and miniature waterfalls, the rooms glowing with walls of coloured marble and golden ceilings, and almost every piece of furniture inlaid with silver and gold. In the hot summers they moved into equally splendid houses on the shores of the Bosphorus.

The poor enjoyed life too, though they lived in squalid, dirty, ramshackle houses of wood, crowded together and often swept by fire and outbreaks of plague. Constantine had given all citizens a free daily supply of bread, treating them just like the citizens of Rome, and when Justinian became emperor in 527 this bread was baked in twenty State bakeries, and distributed each day from 117 'steps' or stalls throughout the city. Most of the corn for it came from Egypt and North Africa, so that the Vandal conquest of those places had threatened the food supply of thousands far away in Constantinople, as Gaiseric had known it would. The poorest families were given special wooden tallies to show at the steps, and then they received some oil, wine, and a little meat, as well as bread. But meat was much less eaten than fish, for however disagreeable the north winds might be they brought huge shoals of fish from the Black Sea into the waters round the city, and men had only to cast their lines or nets into the sea to catch plenty. You can see their descendants still doing just the same today, even though the Golden Horn and the Bosphorus are now crammed with shipping and the sparkle of the water is dimmed by oil and scum.

At the heart of the city stood the forum, the senate-house, the imperial palace, the church of the Holy Wisdom (Sancta Sophia), and the vast hippodrome, an open-air theatre which seated 40,000 people, and where all the entertainments—the chariot races, wild animal shows, gladiator fights, and displays of captured barbarians—, like the bread, were free. The palace looked out over the sea to the distant hills of Asia. It was not a single building, but a vast enclosure dotted with banqueting halls, summer houses, baths, churches, and private apartments, their marble walls and gilded domes showing above trees and fountains; and it contained an enormous number of people, besides the imperial family—officials, secretaries, soldiers, priests, and servants of every sort, many of them barbarian slaves. It was a very spectacular crowd, for their clothes were elaborate and often brilliantly coloured. The nobles who attended the person of the emperor wore white robes, with broad red girdles and black shoes. His body-guard had green or red tunics faced with gold, and heavy gold chains round their necks. They had golden helmets and carried gleaming spears, and their shields were decorated in red and blue. Officers wore yellow

Portrait of Justinian in mosaic from Ravenna. The artist has captured his odd smile.

and purple tunics and gold chains, and their shields were a wonderful sea-green colour bearing the Chi-Ro mark—the monogram for the name of Christ—inlaid in gold upon them.

The most important place in the palace was the throne room. Here the Sole Augustus, the Basileus, the Lord and Master—all these names were used for the emperor—, seated on an ivory and gold throne, raised on a dais of purple marble and under a canopy of pure silver topped by silver eagles, gave audiences to his subjects and to important foreign visitors. In the days of Diocletian and Constantine, though both men had deliberately emphasized the magnificence and god-like nature of the emperor, to approach him was still quite simple. A subject or a visitor simply dropped on one knee and then stood to receive a ceremonial kiss on the head, a somewhat awkward place unless the emperor happened to be tall. But in 527 the man on the ivory throne expected very different behaviour. Although Justinian was outwardly a courteous and affable person—he had a violent temper, but it was very well controlled in public—, no one could approach him, or the empress Theodora, without showing humility and adoration. Three times he must prostrate himself, flat on his face with arms stretched out

in front, and then kiss the imperial feet. Only after this might a man stand up and speak or be spoken to. Seated gorgeously on his throne, which, to be even more impressive, was sometimes raised in the air by a hidden mechanism, Justinian must have looked rather more like an idol than a human being, for he would be swathed in a purple robe stiff with gold embroidery and jewels, caught up on the right shoulder with a jewelled brooch, bright scarlet shoes showing under it, on his head an elaborate and heavy crown studded with precious stones, and enormous pearls dripping round his neck. However much he loved ceremony, he must often have been thankful to shed these trappings, and move freely in the white silk tunic he wore underneath. Without his ceremonial robes and crown Justinian was not a particularly impressive person to look at. He was of middle height and distinctly plump, though he was not at all greedy. In Lent he often fasted for two whole days together, and at other times drank only water and ate green herbs sprinkled with a little oil and vinegar. He had a smooth chubby face, and curly brown hair, which turned grey as he grew old and tired; and nearly all his portraits, even those on small coins, show an odd little smirk on his face, as if he was always just about to smile. He was one of the most conscientious and hard-working men who ever lived, and was known as 'the emperor who never sleeps'. He got up at 7 a.m. and laboured all day at the business of the empire, going into every detail himself, but even after such toil he would 'sit without guards till late hours in the night in the company of old priests deep in the study of the holy books of the Christians', for next after imperial ceremonies, plans, and duties, his great interest was in religion.

Justinian was determined to be a worthy emperor, and had very clear ideas about his responsibilities. First and foremost, being shamed by the diminished size of the Roman empire, he felt bound to recover the lost fragments that had been torn out of it—in his own words, 'We have good hopes that God will grant us to restore our authority over the remaining countries which ancient Rome possessed . . . and lost by neglect.' This was Justinian's dream, but he had to wait for five years after he became emperor before beginning to make it come true. First he was held up by a war with Persia. Rome and Persia were old enemies, they banged away at each other for 400 years, neither being completely victorious, and Justinian ended this war as quickly as he could by agreement. Then came terrible danger in Constantinople itself, danger which very nearly destroyed him. In spite of all the free bread and amusement, the people of the city were never very docile; they were excitable, often violent riots broke out in the streets, either between the two parties, the Blues and the Greens, into which the citizens were divided, who hated each other, or

The Emperor and his courtiers

because some frenzy of general discontent exploded into violence.

One day in January 532 one of these explosions came, caused chiefly by the very heavy taxes and the cruel ways used to get the money out of people. For once the two parties were united, and in the hippodrome the crowds hissed the emperor—an act of blasphemy—, and then began to rage through the city yelling 'Nika, Nika' ('Victory, Victory'), killing, destroying, and burning. Soon the whole city was in flames and chaos. After a few useless attempts at pacifying the rioters Justinian lost his head completely, shut himself up in the palace, and prepared to escape. His servants were told to load as much treasure as possible into ships which were lying just under the palace walls, and he and his ministers sat wavering and twittering with panic. Suddenly the empress Theodora rose to her feet among them. This extraordinary woman, small, slender, and pale, with huge dark eyes, had been born in the poorest slums of Constantinople, and in many ways seems to have been a most unpleasant person. She could be absolutely merciless to people she disliked—she tortured them with relish; if they escaped her secret police, she hunted them down and dropped them into dungeons under her palace. She was quite unscrupulous and seldom, if ever, spoke the truth. But she was very intelligent, and had enormous courage, which she now showed to her shrinking husband and his council. 'When safety lies only in flight,' she said, 'I still will not flee.

The Empress Theodora and her attendants.

These stately processions done in mosaic are in the church of St. Vitale in Ravenna. They reveal the splendid ceremonial of Justinian's court.

I will never live to see the day when I am no longer saluted as empress. Flee if you wish, Caesar; you have money, the ships await you, the sea is unguarded. As for me, I stay. I hold by the old proverb which says that purple' (she meant the imperial purple worn by the emperor) 'is a fair winding-sheet.' This scornful courage was irresistible. Justinian pulled himself together and gave orders to his generals to sally forth and set upon the crowds in the streets and the hippodrome. All through the rest of that day and the next night the soldiers restored order, simply by slaughtering thousands upon thousands of people, until the streets of Constantinople, red with blood, lay quiet and empty. This act of violence, which would never have been necessary if Justinian had not lost his nerve when the riots first began, crushed all opposition, and bit deep into the memory of the citizens. No wonder that Justinian's power over his capital was never challenged again, and no wonder that Theodora's power over him, after those moments of naked cowardice, was absolute, and that as long as she lived he never did anything important without consulting her.

In 533 Justinian was able to begin the recovery of the lost provinces. The signs were hopeful. Everywhere Roman people, governed by barbarian kings (who, curiously enough, thought of themselves as Romans too, and did not think they were really destroying the empire), longed for the emperor in Constantinople

41

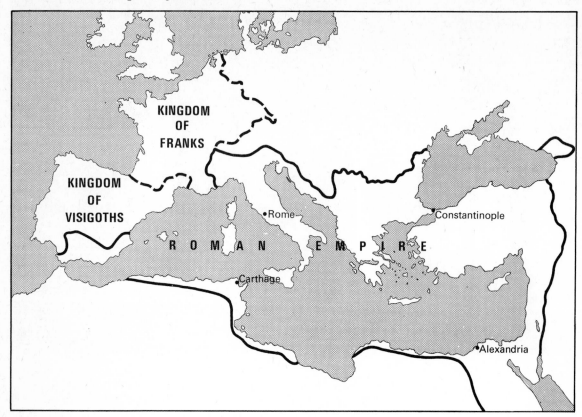

to deliver them. In Africa, in the 100 years since Gaiseric crossed from Spain, the Vandals had lost their fire and ruthless strength, and had become soft and indolent. In Italy the great Theodoric was dead, and only his daughter remained to govern for her ten-year-old son. In Gaul and Spain the barbarian kings, endlessly jealous of each other, bickered and plotted. Besides all this, Justinian had a powerful army, well armed and led by excellent generals. Most of the soldiers were hired barbarians and most of them were mounted. One usually thinks of imperial legionaries as foot-soldiers, slogging to war along the roads at the Roman military pace of 20 miles in five hours, which ate up distances in a way that had often astounded and alarmed their foes; but now the greater part of Justinian's army was heavily armed cavalry. They were called '*cataphracti*', and in battle they broke the ranks of the enemy by the tremendous violence of their charge, using lances or bows and arrows with marvellous skill. These hired soldiers were not in the army because of any particular loyalty to the emperor, but for what they could get out of it; they were difficult to keep in order and appallingly greedy, ready to loot at the slightest opportunity. Only remarkable generals could lead them, and fortunately at this point in history Justinian had three, his nephew Germanus,

The restored empire of Justinian A.D. 565

Narses, and Belisarius, the hero of the reign, all three of them almost worshipped by their soldiers, who would follow them anywhere. So it was that in twenty-one years, 533–54, the imperial armies recovered much of what ancient Rome had lost—Africa, Egypt, Italy, part of Spain, and all the islands in the Mediterranean Sea. Justinian added to his title, 'Imperator Caesar Flavius Justinianus', the new ones of 'Gothicus', 'Vandalicus', 'Africanus'. He also added others to which he had not the slightest claim; 'Francicus', for instance, was one of these, for the Franks were unconquerable and he never recovered Gaul from them. Nor did he rescue Britain, which remained in the dark under Saxon masters. Even so, the empire was almost doubled in size, a dazzling triumph for Justinian, if you did not look too closely. If you did, you would see darkness behind the dazzle. Justinian's determination to restore the empire to its old size was, of course, quite natural for a man who was passionately interested in imperial power and glory, but he did not stop to think if it would benefit his subjects, and in the end it certainly did not. The cost in money and lives, and in the ruin of people whose homes were fought over and trampled by the armies, was enormous, far more than the empire could afford. And the cost did not end when fighting stopped for of course the reconquered provinces, as well as all the rest of the empire, had to be defended, and this needed a multitude of soldiers and strongholds spread out along remote frontiers. Justinian had to pour out money for defences, and he built walls, watch towers, castles, and fortified towns. Yet in spite of this he did not really make the empire secure, for some of these defences were never finished, some were not kept in repair, and some were useless because there were not enough soldiers to man them. At the end of his reign he was also spending large sums in buying the fickle friendships of barbarians, especially on his eastern frontier, and bribing them not to attack. As you can guess, that money was often wasted.

This was not all. Like many other emperors, Justinian had a passion for building, and the results of this expensive passion, aqueducts, baths, bridges, cisterns, churches, granaries, harbours, and palaces, could be seen going up everywhere during his reign. Some of these were wisely planned and much needed. For instance, he built a granary on the island of Tenedos, near Constantinople, to store corn for the city, because when the grain ships were prevented by contrary winds from reaching harbour—which often happened in winter—they sometimes lay so long at anchor that the corn rotted in the holds. He brought relief to many places where water was scarce by building great storage cisterns; two of these you can still see in the middle of Constantinople, one of them even now filled with water and so large that a guide rows you across it in a boat. Then there were churches like those at Ravenna, built of

thin rose-coloured brick and adorned inside with mosaic pictures
in clear vivid colours which have not faded at all, even after 1,400
years. But there were other buildings that were not necessary and
were simply put up to remind the world of the glory and greatness
of Justinian, '*Pius, Felix, Gloriosus*', as he liked to be called, and you
can be sure that the people who had to pay for them by taxes that
steadily grew heavier were not particularly interested in his glory.

*The water cistern of Yerebatan,
Constantinople, one of
Justinian's useful buildings.*

Justinian died in A.D. 565, aged 83. For the last 17 years he had
been a lonely, decaying figure, for Theodora had died in 548 and
this was a mortal blow to him. To someone who saw him then he
seemed 'an old man who no longer cared for anything'. Almost at
once dangerous facts began to come to light. The very day after he
died his nephew, the new emperor, was given a report by court
officials which said 'We found the treasury crushed by debts and
reduced to the last degree of poverty, and the army so short of
necessities that the empire was exposed to increasing invasions and
insults of barbarians.' More dangerous still for the future was the
poverty and despair in many parts of the empire, and especially in
the reconquered parts which had never settled down into the

'peaceful order' that Justinian hoped for. In fact, the first joy at being rescued had quickly changed, first into disappointment and then into sullen hatred for all the imperial officials who ceaselessly squeezed money out of people, until in desperation they fled from their homes; so that, as one official wrote, 'the tax gatherers could find no more money to take to the emperor because there were no people left to pay the taxes.' Those that were left were ready to welcome other invaders when they came.

A Greek scholar of the sixth century wrote a grim epitaph for Justinian: 'Thus died this prince having filled the whole world with noise and trouble', and if in the end that was all that could be said about him he certainly would not rank as one of the great Roman emperors. Yet he is the only one after Constantine whose name is known to many people who have never read a word of history. This is because, besides the conquests which did not last and the burdens which crushed his people, he left behind also certain notable achievements that have not perished or done harm. One of these you can see today if you visit Istanbul: the great church of Sancta Sophia, which Justinian raised over the place where Constantine's first church stood, and which far surpasses anything else that he built. In 532, when the terrible Nika riots ended, the whole centre of Constantinople lay in smoking ruins, but on this occasion Justinian certainly did not falter. He was determined to make his capital the wonder of the world, and within a month he had the charred remains cleared, the ground levelled, and plans drawn up. From the ashes there rose a set of buildings even more splendid than before, crowned by a marvellous church, which is now, after more than 1,400 years, after earthquakes, fires, and wars, the only one of them still standing whole. For its building Justinian gathered together 10,000 workmen and 100 master craftsmen, and they finished it in the month of December 537, that is in less than 6 years. When you go inside you are immediately struck by its size, which even by modern standards is immense (it is not surprising that in 1453, when at long last Constantinople fell into the hands of the Turks, the pagan conquerors found it amusing

> For to let theyr hawkys fly
> In the church of Saint Sophy

—for there was plenty of room for their sport), and by the daring height of the dome. This was a very bold thing to attempt in the sixth century. Domes are never easy to build with safety, and when Michelangelo built the one at St. Peter's in Rome nearly 1,000 years later, it was considered a masterpiece of architecture, and so was Wren's dome at St. Paul's Cathedral, built in 1695. But though we can still marvel at the boldness and the size of Sancta Sophia, we can never realize to the full its first glorious colour and decoration,

45

which in the sixth century was so splendid that the sight reduced men to speechless wonder. Today the interior seems rather faded and shadowy, but then it must have been ablaze with colour, for the floor, the huge pillars, and the towering walls were of gleaming marble, freshly dug from quarries all over the empire, green and gold and white, rose-red and purple, glittering black and 'the deep blue of the summer sea', and when you entered by one of the 9 great doors 'you might imagine that you had come upon a meadow with all its flowers in full bloom.' Then the ceiling was gold, the altar was pure gold; by day the sun streamed in at the windows and filled the whole place with light; at night hundreds of silver lamps, burning perfumed oil, lit up every part, and shone through the openings in the dome and far out to sea, so that sailors were guided into the harbour below 'by the divine light of the church itself'.

Of course, in this, as in so many other matters, Justinian ignored the whole question of expense, and to pay for men, marble, silver, and gold he dipped deeply into the imperial treasury, which his suffering subjects had to fill. Naturally, as the great church grew he saw to it that his own name and glory were not forgotten. His monogram appears on 56 of the carved capitals, and when he stepped over the threshhold for the opening ceremony he cried aloud, so that all men could hear, 'I, Justinian, have surpassed even thee, O Solomon.' But in spite of his pride and extravagance this plump affable man was not simply a rich royal patron with no knowledge or understanding of what he was doing or of the skill and effort that went into the building of such a church. He knew enough for the architects to go to him for advice if they were in difficulty—as, for instance, when some of the marble columns began to shed little flakes of stone from their surfaces, as if they were crumbling under the weight they carried. Justinian inspected the columns, decided that the cause was the dampness in the stone, and briskly ordered the upper part of the work to be taken down, and the columns left until all the moisture had thoroughly dried out of the marble. This was done, and after a time the structure was rebuilt and stood safely. And not only was his knowledge and commonsense valuable. Without his imagination and driving force we should never have had the splendid church of Sancta Sophia, once called 'the most interesting building on the world's surface'.

His other great and lasting achievement is not a splendid sight, in fact is not easily seen at all, for it lies hidden away in books of law that only enthusiastic lawyers can really enjoy, or in a few ancient yellow manuscripts, covered with stiff black handwriting, which do not look inviting. Yet the work of Justinian in law has affected the lives of far more people than all the beauty of Sancta Sophia.

Sancta Sophia, the church of the Holy Wisdom, built by Justinian in Constantinople. Try to imagine it without the minarets, the low dome on the right, and the building with fourteen windows. These are all later additions.

The Romans had a very strong sense of law and order. They believed—as of course we do too—that laws were necessary, and were 'made for the safety of citizens . . . and the tranquillity and happiness of human life'. They wanted every Roman citizen in every part of the empire to live under the same laws, and one of the greatest of Romans, Cicero, wrote 'There shall not be different laws at Rome and at Athens but one law for all nations and at the same time.' They also thought that all men accused of wrong-doing—all free men that is, slaves were not included—ought to be allowed a fair trial. 'It is not the custom of the Roman', said Festus, governor of Palestine, proudly, to the Jews who wanted him to hand over St. Paul to them without a trial, 'to give up anyone before he has met his accusers face to face and had a chance to make his defence'; and even the most violent of Paul's enemies, who had sworn not to eat or drink until they had killed him, dared not flout the Roman laws.

By the time of Justinian an enormous mass of laws had accumulated, and they were in the deepest confusion. For the past 1,000

47

years they had been added to, altered, copied and recopied, sometimes with mistakes. They were so complicated, wordy, and contradictory that even the most excellent lawyers could not always make them out, and added to the confusion by their explanations and opinions; different judges often gave different punishments for the same crime. The idea of clearing up any kind of confusion appealed to Justinian's orderly mind, and as soon as he became emperor he appointed ten men, all high officials and expert lawyers, and set them to sort out and arrange the unwieldy mass of the Roman laws. After years of work they produced two great books, by which Justinian has been remembered ever since. First came the *Codex*, an up-to-date collection of 4,652 laws, written down as simply and clearly as possible. After that the oldest of all the laws and decrees, many of them made before the birth of Christ, were pruned and arranged clearly in what has been called 'the most remarkable and important law book the world has ever seen'. It is called the *Digest*, and is certainly not a book for light reading, for it has 50 parts, and to compress the laws even into these 50 Justinian's committee had to cut down 3,000,000 words to 150,000.

When the *Codex* and the *Digest* were finished Justinian ordered a third book to be produced—the *Institutes*—an official textbook for the training of lawyers, and he then closed all the law schools in the empire except three, in order to make sure that budding lawyers were all taught in the same way, and all by first-class teachers. At first the *Codex*, the *Digest*, and the *Institutes* were only used in the empire, but gradually they became known all over Europe, and through them the laws of Rome have had an influence in every country in the world. Anyone who trains as a lawyer has to study them, and if you were to rummage about in legal books and documents in half a dozen languages you would find that Justinian's laws are frequently mentioned and some, indeed, are still in force. They, at least, have made an indelible mark on the world, and it is for them more than anything else that he is known. In fact, a good many people have no idea that Justinian was an emperor; they think he was a very clever lawyer.

So you can think of Justinian as a conqueror, a builder, or a law-giver, a man who could make plans on a grand scale and carry through great enterprises. But you can also think of him as a person who would give the same dogged and detailed attention to much smaller matters than the war in Africa or the building of Sancta Sophia, if he thought they might bring prosperity to the empire, and thereby, of course, to the emperor. One of these minor matters was the silk trade, for silk was in great demand all over the empire, and particularly in Constantinople. There was never enough of it and it was exceedingly expensive, for the raw silk for weaving came only from China, and it was brought by sea only by

Persian merchants, who sold it in the markets on the eastern fringe of the empire at almost any price they chose to demand. Whenever the old hostility between Romans and Persians flared up, the supply of silk was cut off abruptly or the price shot up far above what the imperial weavers could afford. Justinian was always trying to find some way of by-passing the Persian merchants, breaking their monopoly, and getting more silk at a reasonable price. He tried to bring raw silk from China by another route, the long overland trail to the north of India and Afghanistan, but it was too uncertain and too costly. He tried to smuggle silkworms into the empire, but the tiresome creatures died long before they arrived. Then one day, probably in A.D. 550, two monks arrived in Constantinople and went to the imperial palace. They had come from China and an audience with the emperor was arranged for them with surprising speed. After the usual elaborate ceremonies they began to speak to 'Justinianus, Pius, Felix, Gloriosus', on the subject of silk, and it was clear that they knew a great deal about it. Silkworms, they said, were fragile things which would die at a touch, or even from a shake, and it would never be possible to carry them far by land or sea, but their eggs were tougher and took weeks to hatch. You can imagine Justinian, who, a few moments before, had been deep in discussion perhaps with his generals over some great military plan for Italy, or with his architects over the building of a massive aqueduct, seizing upon this small matter of silkworms' eggs, giving all his attention to the monks and plunging into the details of a secret plan. The monks left the palace and shortly afterwards set off once more for China. But they did not stay there long. Soon they were back in Constantinople, and again they went to the palace and were taken to the audience chamber. This time they produced from the folds of their habits a few short hollow canes, in which Justinian, no doubt to the surprise of his noble attendants, showed an extraordinary interest. The canes were stuffed with minute pearly-grey eggs, each smaller than the head of a modern pin, and from these precious dots there duly hatched thousands of silkworms which took kindly to the mulberry trees of the empire, and so multiplied that in time the Persian stranglehold over the silk trade was broken. Silkworms have flourished in Europe ever since, and Justinian started them off.

Chapter 4
The Church: St. Benedict and Pope Gregory I

If you had lived in the sixth century you would surely have thought that the only hope for the future lay in the eastern part of the old Roman empire. There, in the rich ceremonial of Justinian's court, among the fine buildings of the capital city of Constantinople, thronged with lawyers, scholars, statesmen, and nobles, was an elaborate and colourful civilization which had been preserved while the barbarian hordes were parcelling out the West. In fact you would have been wrong. It is true that the eastern part of the empire was to survive for almost another 1,000 years, but the story was one of decline. The splendour of Constantinople was to grow tarnished and corrupt; invaders were to come from the west to loot its wealth and tear apart its lands, and finally Turkish invaders were to come from the east to crush and annex it. The future, strangely, lay with the West, and if we want to find the roots of our own modern world, and to study the very beginnings of that enterprise and vigour which have brought us to the space age, we must turn our backs on Justinian and look carefully at what was happening in those western parts of the old Roman empire, bordered by the Rhine and the Danube.

First we must look at Italy, the heart of the old empire. Here, about A.D. 500, in a little place called Subiaco, in the quiet seclusion of the hills not far from Rome, a man called Benedict was living as a hermit. He ate the plainest food, he wore old rough clothes, and his home was a little cave which gave him some shelter from the heat and the rain. He spent his time in prayer. We must find out more about him, because his life was to have as great a power over the future as that of the glorious Emperor Justinian in his resplendent court on the Bosphorus. Justinian was the younger man, but he and Benedict were contemporaries. Benedict was a Roman, not a barbarian; he was of good birth and well educated, but as a young man he had turned away from the prospect of a promising career in Rome to become a solitary monk, cutting himself off from the world and devoting his life to God.

Benedict was by no means the first person to do this. There were many monks in Ireland and Gaul and other western countries at this time, some of them living completely alone and others living in loose-knit communities called 'monasteries'. In Ireland these

Beehive cells on the Irish coast. Each monk had his own cell where he spent much of his time alone in prayer.

monasteries were usually groups of draughty little stone huts, each hut built in a shape rather like a beehive, often situated on some wind-swept island, or bleak headland jutting out into the Atlantic, as you can see from the picture on this page. The monks lived a very hard life, training themselves to do without all comforts. They could never marry, they went for long periods without food, they would spend many hours in private prayer in their cold stone cells. All this was for a purpose. An astronaut only goes through a period of intensive training and discipline because he is absolutely caught up in his aim to venture into space and to try out the unknown. The monk had the same kind of completely absorbing and demanding aim; in his case it was to reach God. The monks were absolutely sure that the only way to do this was to deny themselves all other pleasures. Only by crushing their desires for comfort and good food, ease and pleasure, could they train themselves to put God first in their lives instead of thinking about themselves and their own wants.

These men looked back for inspiration to the very early Christian monks who had gone out into the desert in Egypt, and had lived an exceedingly harsh life, full of rigour and suffering, and full of scorn for the worldly pleasures that most people were eagerly seeking, in the days when the Roman empire was in decay.

Clearly Benedict had chosen a very hard way of life. People respond to disaster in very different fashions. Many Romans of Benedict's generation, realizing that the great Empire was falling about them in ruins, and that they were at the mercy of upstart barbarian kings like Theodoric, had simply decided to make the best of it. They tried to go on living as comfortably as they could in their town houses or country villas, clinging to their own property, trying to avoid the unpleasant things and the havoc of war for themselves and their families, and trying not to think too much about all that was happening. That was one way. But there was another. There were those who turned away from the violence and cruelty and suffering, not to look after themselves but to look to God. Benedict was one of these.

At first Benedict lived entirely alone, a life of prayer and utter solitude. But he was a man who cared very much about other people, and before long a little community of monks gathered round him and he did not turn them away. From this point he found himself having to organize the lives of other men, and finally he became the head or 'abbot' of a large community of monks at Monte Cassino. It was here, soon after the death of Theodoric, when Italy was once more plunging into confusion and war, and while Justinian in Constantinople was planning his schemes of building and reconquest, that Benedict set himself to writing one of the greatest documents in the history of the world. He did not think of it this way; he simply saw himself as drawing on his long, hard, and often disappointing experience to write down a simple practical set of rules for his own community of monks, and any other that might find it helpful: a 'little rule for beginners' he called it. He could not foresee the future. This Rule was to be for centuries the accepted way of life in thousands of monasteries all over western Europe; it was to be copied and recopied; it was to become a weapon of peace which was to tame and civilize those barbarian tribes who had swarmed into the empire, and many who were yet to invade. Nor could he have known that in the twentieth century his Rule was to be reprinted and read by many people who were not monks at all. But even if he could have known these things it would have made no difference to him; for St. Benedict believed that a true monk should be entirely humble. He had used the works of other monastic writers in drawing up the Rule, and he would have thought his own contribution small.

An early monastic cloister in Milan. The courtyard of this monastery of S. Ambrogio is very like that of a Roman villa.

To see why the Rule was great we must study it. We must turn, too, to our own experience of working together with other people in a community, like a school for instance, with all the problems of any such community, rules, quarrels, friendships, boredom, excitement: 'the times when things go well with me, the times when things go ill', as a later follower of St. Benedict put it.

We may imagine the monastery of Monte Cassino as a large Italian villa, built round a courtyard, with a few big rooms, like the *triclinium* or dining room, which the monks could use as communal rooms for eating and sleeping, and some smaller rooms. Benedictine monasteries continued to be built round a courtyard (or 'cloister', as it came to be called) throughout the Middle Ages— as you can soon see if you visit any ruined abbey of their order in England today. The picture on this page shows an early Benedictine cloister in Italy. A Roman country villa would be surrounded with

53

farming land, and St. Benedict advised that a monastery should have close by all the things that were really necessary for the simple daily life of the monks. There should be a stream for water supplies and fishing, a mill for grinding corn, a garden for growing vegetables, and workshops for craftsmen like carpenters or tailors. These practical points meant that a Benedictine house was self-contained, able to feed itself and rule itself quite independently of the outside world, a tremendous advantage in the troubled times of war and violence that lay ahead. The Benedictine monastery was built for survival in a rough world. It could survive almost anything, except the direct plundering and sacking of the monastery itself. And that sometimes happened, too. Monte Cassino, built high in the rocky Appenines, was sacked by the Lombards in 577. It was rebuilt.

If you had visited Monte Cassino in St. Benedict's time, as a traveller wanting a night's rest and safety, we can tell from the Rule that you would have been kindly received. Benedict had much common sense. The porter's room was to be at the gate of the monastery, 'so that those who come may always find someone to answer them'. Better still, he knows that stupid people who never know the answers to your questions can be thoroughly tiresome, and so he adds thoughtfully that the porter should be 'a wise old man who understands how to give and receive a message'. How sensible. Benedict says that he thinks it is better to have an old man, because he is less likely to want to rush off after another job just when he has learned how to do this one properly.

The visitor would then be taken by one of the monks to buildings set apart for guests and given a meal. The monk looking after him would be allowed to share this meal, to put the visitor at his ease, and at night there would be a bed neatly made up. Benedict stressed that special kindness should be shown to poor guests, and remarks crisply that the wealthy visitors inspire enough awe to be sure of being well looked after.

When the visitor had eaten and rested, he might perhaps have had some glimpses of the life of the monks themselves. He would not see everything and many parts of the monastery he would not visit at all, but he would certainly take away an impression of the atmosphere of the place. Later, one royal visitor to Monte Cassino wrote a poem about what he remembered. He remembered the food, as one usually does, the fish, fine herbs, and plentiful bread, but also 'the holy peace, the serenity and harmony of the monks in their life together, and the love and worship of Christ'.

It was a fine impression for a visitor to have, but this peace and harmony was reached only because Benedict knew the worst side

of human nature, and guarded against it at every turn. Benedict had known many ordinary people who wanted to lead a holy life in a community, but who so quickly gave way to all the temptations that most of us give way to any day. They grumbled, they liked getting their own way; they were jealous and upset if someone else was treated better than they were; they made good resolutions about being punctual and about being good-tempered, and then slipped back into their old ways, because they tired of the effort. It was to help men like this, beset by all the usual dismal and tiresome human failings, mixed up with their longing to lead a good life, that St. Benedict wrote his Rule. Many would have become disheartened in one of the Irish or Egyptian monasteries where the fasting and discipline were extremely severe, but St. Benedict says clearly that he hopes he will order 'nothing too harsh or too burdensome'.

Daily life in most communities is based on two essential ideas— routine and variety. Think of the way in which the day is divided up in a school or an office. There is always a familiar pattern to the day, and it is always divided into manageable stretches of time by such devices as tea breaks. Benedict, like any modern business man or headmaster, knew that if you keep people working at any one task for very long they will flag. So he planned for the monks a very regular, ordered life, in which there was plenty of change of occupation. The most important work was the *Opus Dei*—the work of God. This meant the services in the church, where seven times a day the monks filed silently into their places, to offer praise and worship to God. Whatever the monks were doing when the signal was given for one of the services, they had to lay down their other work and make their way straight to the church. The services were short and simple, but they had to be performed with the greatest reverence and care. Here the monks were to aim at the very highest standards, so that their service of God might be as near perfection as possible. Not everyone kept up the standards; some got slack. Benedict has some firm and sensible things to say about those who carelessly arrive late for services; for he knows that there will always be some people like this. These monks are to go inside the church and stand in a special place apart, where they will be in full view of the rest of the monks, and may be shamed into being more punctual in future. Benedict explains that if you let such a monk stay outside the church until the service is over, maybe he will slip back to have a few more minutes in bed! or at least he may see his friend at the other side of the cloister and go over to have a chat with him. As you read the Rule you have an odd feeling that you have met all St. Benedict's monks somewhere before.

The church was at the very centre of the life of a monastery, but the services did not go on all the time. Yet the church was always

left open, so that a monk could slip in quietly to pray when he had a little time to himself.

For about four hours a day the monks worked with their hands, labouring in the fields, looking after the garden, doing craftwork like weaving or pottery, or simply doing the ordinary household jobs in the monastery kitchen, like preparing the vegetables or cleaning the dishes. For about two hours a day they were to read books which would encourage them and inspire them in their own lives. Some monks delighted in reading and developed a deep love of learning. Through the reading and copying of books Benedictine monasteries eventually handed on much of the literature and learning of the Roman past to future generations. But some monks hated it. In Lent, when they all received a book from the library, to be read from cover to cover without skipping, two of the senior monks were to go round the cloister, when the monks had had time to settle down, to make sure that no lazy monk was settling himself to a good gossip, 'so that he not only does himself harm but disturbs others'. Nearly every school class has someone like this in it: such people were to be found other jobs to do.

Unlike the monks of the Egyptian desert, Benedict's monks had enough to eat and a regular eight hours' sleep. The whole programme was reasonable, though not easy, and not meant to be.

We must now face a key question. Was a monk's life in fact selfish? You might argue that these monks were simply running away from the turmoil of the real world instead of facing up to it. Italy was suffering devastation and invasion while the monks of Monte Cassino lived their ordered lives apart. St. Benedict did not think in this way. He believed that in a rough and violent world, where men were struggling for land or power or just for loot, it was pleasing to God to establish 'a school for the Lord's service', as he called his monastery. In a Benedictine monastery men prayed for each other and for the world, and all prayer and praise were directed to God. The life of a monk was a God-centred life, and in St. Benedict's view this was what mattered.

You may think that life was pretty easy for the monk, and it is true that usually the monastery offered some shelter from the violence of the outside world. But living in a community is never easy, especially when you have solemnly promised that you will never leave it. A Benedictine monk could not go off to another monastery if he found that he did not get on with some of the other monks. He had to take a fresh look at himself instead. He gave up a great deal in becoming a monk—all his own property, however wealthy he might be, the right to marry and have a family and a home of his own, and, above all, the feeling that he might choose to do what he wanted. Most people would feel that these were tremendous

sacrifices. St. Benedict required absolute obedience. This obedience was really obedience to the will of God, but Benedict knew that obedience is partly a habit of mind, and so he ordered that the monk must be entirely obedient to the abbot and, below him, to the senior monks in the monastery. The monk must learn to 'hate his own will'; he must thrust down the feeling of what *he* wanted to do, and instead must bend his will to obey his superiors, for the love of Christ.

In the end the Rule is founded on love. Benedict's ideas about obedience strike many of us as severe, even to harshness, but nothing could be more tender or considerate than his insistence on care for the sick and those in trouble. Elderly monks and children should be spared the full rigours of monastic life and be allowed to take their meals early. If a monk is being punished for a serious fault, one or two wise and trusted monks should talk to him and comfort him, so that he is brought round to repenting his fault and is not left to brood on things and despair completely.

The abbot himself had great power, and therefore great temptations. Benedict urges him not to become a tyrant; he must give careful attention to the advice of the wiser monks before taking important decisions. Some of the monks would be hard, proud, and disobedient, others would be gentle and sensitive; it was the abbot's business to know them all and use quite different methods with each. One he must rebuke, another he must persuade, and he must love them all, even when he is appalled by their wrongdoing. It was surely a very wearing and difficult task that the abbot undertook, but Benedict goes on to say that if he worries too much that will be bad too, because he will never be at rest, and it is important for the monks that the man at the head of the community should be calm and serene.

Perhaps we begin to see that the monk's life was not an easy one. We may still feel that they should have been helping other people outside the monastery. This was not their first purpose, but in fact they did help enormously. It was not only that they received guests with kindness, nor even that they preserved much of the learning of the ancient world that might otherwise have been lost. More than all this, they had great influence on the life of the people around them. Lay folk admired the life of the monks, and often gave their young children to monasteries to be brought up to become monks; they gave presents and land to monasteries and founded new houses; rulers often relied for advice in government on abbots and bishops (who had themselves often been brought up in Benedictine houses). As the Rule of St. Benedict came to be a guide for monks throughout Europe, so there grew up innumerable little centres of Benedictine influence radiating out into the lives of

the communities around them. Wherever a Benedictine house was founded the teaching of the Rule went too. The qualities that St. Benedict himself thought so important, kindness, self-discipline, love, obedience, goodness, were set before a world which certainly valued courage and loyalty, but which also accepted terror, cruelty, revenge, and greed in their most ruthless forms. In the crude and violent world of the barbarian invaders the message of the Rule of St. Benedict commanded wonder, and eventually respect.

★   ★   ★

When Justinian's armies were shattering the Ostrogothic kingdom in Italy and trying to regain control of the western part of the old Roman empire, another Roman was born who was to become as great a leader as Benedict. This young boy, Gregory, must have been a delight to his wealthy well-born parents; he was highly intelligent and sensitive, but also very practical and firm. He received a good education and entered the lower ranks of the imperial civil service. His career prospects seemed good since he was so clever, but Italy was in such a wretched state that some men began to wonder, as Benedict had done, whether any career was really worth the effort. Rome had been besieged and captured three times during Justinian's wars; its fine buildings, the Colosseum, the basilicas, aqueducts, and lovely spacious houses were falling into ruins after the battering by the troops. No one appeared to have the will or the wealth to rebuild them, and the representative of the emperor of Constantinople, an official called the exarch, lived in a palace far off on the north-east coast, in the marsh city of Ravenna. Gregory felt keenly and bitterly the long-drawn-out decline of the city of Rome and of all that Rome stood for. 'She that once appeared mistress of the world,' he wrote, 'we have seen what has become of her. . . . Rome is deserted and in flames, and as for her buildings we see them fall down of their own accord.' 'The present world is bitter for those who love it, and its decay teaches us that we ought not to love it.' Yet Gregory, like every true Roman, had loved it, and he felt the utter desolation of living in a period of decay and destruction.

Worse was to come. A new race of barbarians had appeared, 'fierce with more than the usual fierceness of the Germans'. In 568 the Lombards swept down on the plains of North Italy. They cared nothing at all for Roman culture. They slaughtered and sacked and destroyed, with a ruthless vigour that even Italy had not known before. Where they settled, the Roman landowners were wiped out or reduced to serfs. By 571 the invaders had conquered the northern plain; the next year they seized Benevento and Spoleto further south, which later became smaller Lombard states; and in 573 they

Pope Gregory the Great, from a manuscript of the 10th century, copied from an earlier one.

threatened Rome itself. Gregory was in Rome. Still a young man, he was now holding the highest post in the Roman civil service, that of prefect of the city. Everyone admired his competence and efficiency in this time of crisis. The next year he resigned his high position and gave up his career.

Many people must have thought Gregory crazy to have done such a thing, except that it was difficult to think this of so level-headed a young man. To Gregory it now seemed clear that the cause of Rome was a lost cause and that the only cause worth fighting for was the cause of God. He sold the rich family lands that he had inherited from his father in Sicily, gave the money to the poor, and retreated to his father's large house on the Caelian Hill outside Rome, with a few companions, to live the life of a monk.

One is bound to be struck by the likeness of this story to that of St. Benedict's early life, and Gregory, indeed, knew of St. Benedict's work and had meditated on Benedict's Rule. And for five years, inspired by the writings of Benedict and other great Christian thinkers, he lived a quiet life in his monastic home, while the 'unspeakable Lombards' waged fierce war; the exarch abandoned all thought of protecting Rome, to concentrate on trying to hold on to Ravenna itself, and save his own skin.

Gregory's life of peaceful seclusion was soon doomed. In 579 the pope, that is the head of the Church in Rome, commanded Gregory to go on a mission to Constantinople, to urge the Emperor to send help to the West against 'that impious nation, the Lombards'. Gregory went, and stayed there for six years. In 590 the pope died, and Gregory, by the wholehearted wish of the Roman people, was elected as the new pope. Gregory had withdrawn from the world to dedicate his life to God, but now as a servant of God he was thrust back into it, right at the centre of the turmoil.

Gregory as pope was the most respected man in Rome. As the bishop of the city where both St. Peter and St. Paul were believed to have preached and died, the city which had also been the capital of the Roman empire in its days of greatness, Gregory had great authority over the Church in the whole of western Europe. He was to increase that authority still further by his own actions.

The first task was to take care of the people of Italy. And once more, as in 573, his clear duty was the defence of Rome. The exarch in Ravenna was useless as a protector, and Gregory found himself taking on many of the jobs which should have been done by the imperial civil servants. He took them on because no one else was doing anything about it. He appointed military commanders and paid the imperial troops; he collected the taxes and distributed corn. In the end, he made a peace with the Lombard king, Aigulf.

The exarch was furious; he wanted the Lombard king to weaken his strength in fighting against the upstart Lombard dukes of Benevento and Spoleto. But Gregory saw the miseries and suffering of the victims of war, and he could not look at things as the politicians did. He had at last found work that was worth doing, work to which he was prepared to give every ounce of will-power and energy that he had.

Help for those who were homeless, hungry, and ill was the first call on his resources. At seven fixed places in Rome food was given to the starving; buildings called '*xenodochia*' were built to shelter people who were sick or old or without a home. The dues of wine, cheese, vegetables, bacon, fish and oil which were regularly carted into Rome from the lands belonging to the pope were distributed to the poor every month. Food was cooked in the papal palace and taken to people who were sick. When a very poor man was found dead, from lack of food, in a miserable room in an old boarding house, Gregory would not say mass for several days, because he blamed himself for not having got to know about the old man before it was too late.

This was certainly practical Christianity. Gregory was by instinct and by training a first-rate organizer. The estates belonging to the pope were now well farmed and efficiently administered as never before. It was a big task. There were 13,000 to 18,000 square miles of land to be dealt with, in Italy and in southern Gaul. He kept in personal touch with his bailiffs, who had to be churchmen themselves, and he wrote as much as once a month to consult them and give instructions.

It might seem that Gregory's task in Italy was so wearing and demanding that he could not possibly have dealt with more, but he did. As pope, Gregory felt a special responsibility for the whole of the Church in the West, and things were as bad in other lands as in Italy. To the north of the Alps, in the kingdom of the Franks the warlike queen Brunhild treated the Church as though it was her personal property, giving bishoprics to young boys and to greedy lords who were not priests at all. Men openly bought bishoprics from the queen, and the Church was in chaos through lack of discipline. Gregory could not do very much as yet about this huge problem, but he made a start. He wrote forthright though tactful letters to Brunhild, urging reform, and he began to strengthen his own hold over bishops in Gaul, and also in Spain and North Africa as well as Italy, realizing that in the end it was only by firm control from Rome that the Church would be likely to regain its spiritual tone, and clergy once more command respect.

To the far north, beyond Gaul itself, was an old province which had been on the fringes of the Roman empire, but which was now

almost completely overrun by pagan Germanic tribes: Britain. There is no reason to doubt the famous story that Gregory had seen Anglo-Saxon boys being sold as slaves in the market in Rome, and had from that moment longed to go to England to convert their people to Christianity. He was a man of strong and generous impulses, and he had a deepening personal belief in the Christian faith as the one thing that really mattered for the torn and battered world in which he lived. His many cares as pope never gave him time to go to England himself, but he chose instead Augustine, a monk of his own monastery in Rome, and forty other monks, men who were disciplined and accustomed to hardship and obedience. The little party set off on the dangerous and tiring journey across Gaul, to go to the court of the Anglo-Saxon king of Kent, Ethelbert, who was married to a Gallic Christian princess. As they made their way across the north of Gaul, brave men though they were, their courage failed, and they sent Augustine hurrying back to Rome to beg Gregory to call the whole thing off. 'They were appalled', wrote the English historian Bede a century later, 'at the idea of going to a barbarous, fierce and pagan nation, of whose very language they were ignorant.' Was Gregory's eager dream of bringing Christianity to the English to be abandoned, after all? Gregory stood absolutely firm. He did not show contempt and tell them they were cowards; he did not turn on them for letting him down; but he did not let them turn away either. He simply sent Augustine back to his companions with a letter from himself. As we read that letter now, we suddenly find ourselves face to face with Gregory. We feel his quiet confidence, and the courage and resolve that he could inspire in others. He knew that the monks would obey him: 'My very dear sons, it is better never to undertake any high enterprise than to abandon it once it is begun. So with the help of God you must carry out this holy task that you have begun.' It was this same quiet determination to see a very great enterprise through to the end that in our own lifetime took Aldrin and Armstrong to achieve a landing on the moon. Augustine and his companions went on.

One cannot read Bede's account of Augustine's mission to England, the successful conversion of the kingdom of Kent, and the spread of the faith beyond this into neighbouring kingdoms, without realizing that Gregory was behind the mission at every step. Augustine tended to worry, and to write to Gregory a great deal for advice on practical matters. He wanted to know whether the pagan temples of the Anglo-Saxons should be destroyed. Gregory said not; rather, destroy the pagan idols in them, and then change them into Christian churches. Again he advised Augustine to keep some of the festivals that the people were used to, but to give them a Christian meaning, 'for it is certainly impossible',

wrote Gregory sensibly, 'to root out all mistaken ideas from ignorant minds at one stroke.' The pagan winter festival of Yuletide became linked with the Christian festival of Christmas, and the name of the pagan goddess of springtime, Eostre, was given to another great festival of the Church.

The organization of the Church in England presented Gregory with problems too, but his keen administrator's mind was well able to deal with these, and the pattern of organization in the Church of England today bears the marks of the decision that Gregory made. The English Church was to be divided into two provinces, one centred on London and one on York, each with an archbishop. In fact the pull of Ethelbert's capital at Canterbury, where Augustine had first preached, prevented London becoming the head of the southern province. The archbishop was to receive his authority direct from the pope by receiving from Rome a white wool vestment known as a *pallium*. The deep reverence for the pope which was so natural a part of Augustine's work among the English became an essential part of Church life in this country, and in the eighth century missionaries from England were to take the faith (and also this special veneration for Rome) into the lands of the Franks, with momentous consequences, as we shall see in a later chapter.

It may seem strange that so humble a man as Gregory, who called himself 'the servant of the servants of God', should so stress the importance and authority of his position. He did so, not because of any personal pride, but because he believed that great authority and power had been given to the Roman Church by Christ. The chief challenge to this belief came, as one might expect, from Constantinople. When the bishop (or 'patriarch', as he was called) of Constantinople claimed the title of 'universal bishop', Gregory sharply rebuked his pride. The Empress Constantia then asked Gregory to send her some relics of St. Paul from Rome, because she wanted to put them in a great church that she was building in honour of St. Paul in Constantinople, near her own palace. Gregory said forthrightly that this would be most wicked sacrilege, and told her what terrible punishments she would endure if she attempted any such thing. He went into such blood-curdling details that Constantia pressed the matter no more.

At the centre of Gregory's life, amid danger, war, violence, and distress, there was a calm. As a young man he had known bitter disappointment at the prolonged wrecking of Roman civilization; he had seen more than most men of human weakness and cruelty and selfishness, but he had come through all this to a patient and vigorous resolve to do the will of God as he saw it, and this gave him peace of mind. The papacy has been one of the great historic

VICARIVS VRBIS ROMAE

PROBIANTE...

...OREN...

An early impression of the 'vicar of the city of Rome'. This was made about the year 400, when the head of the Church in Rome was less important than he came to be when Gregory the Great held this position. The figure here is dignified but very simply dressed and has none of the splendour of later popes.

institutions of our own civilization. In many ways it is so still. If we had to select one man who in its early years did more, perhaps, than any other to shape it to good ends, that man was Gregory the Great.

Chapter 5
The Rise of Islam

In the whole history of the world there have been only three great religions which set forward the belief that there is only one God. The Romans and Greeks, advanced as they were in other ways, worshipped a whole sky-full of gods and goddesses; so did the Anglo-Saxons, and some of the other barbarian tribes, before they became Christians. Of the three monotheistic ('one-God') religions, the first in time was that of the Jews, and the second, which partly sprang from the first, was Christianity. The third was Islam. You may have heard it called Muhammadanism (there are various spellings), after its great prophet, Muhammad (Mahomet), but the followers of Muhammad themselves prefer to call it Islam, which means 'submission to God', and the believers in Islam are known as Muslims.

How many Muslims are there in the world today? If you look at the map opposite you will see in which countries most of them live. They are spread over three continents and there are 475 millions of them. The startling thing is this. When Gregory the Great became pope in 590 there were no Muslims. When Charlemagne became king of the Franks some two centuries later, the horsemen of the Arabian desert had carried their new faith of Islam as far as the Atlantic coast of Africa in the west, and to the borders of northern India in the east, and had utterly changed the course of world history; all these countries are still Muslim today, and you cannot properly understand their problems in the twentieth century without knowing how it all began.

If we search back into the very beginnings of this tremendous movement, we shall come to the land of Arabia in the sixth century. Much of the country has not changed very much even today, nor have the ways of its people. If you look at Arabia on the map you will see that it is a peninsula, and, apart from a few fertile strips near the coast, where the prosperous cities of Mecca and Medina are to be found, the interior was, and still is, dry dusty desert, intensely hot, with stretches of only slightly less barren steppe country, rough scrub fit only for grazing sheep, goats, camels, and horses. Dotted over the desert are pleasant oases, where almonds grow and fruit trees, especially date palms and water-melons. For man to survive in this part of Arabia he must be tough and determined, and the Bedouin Arab is both. He lives a nomadic life,

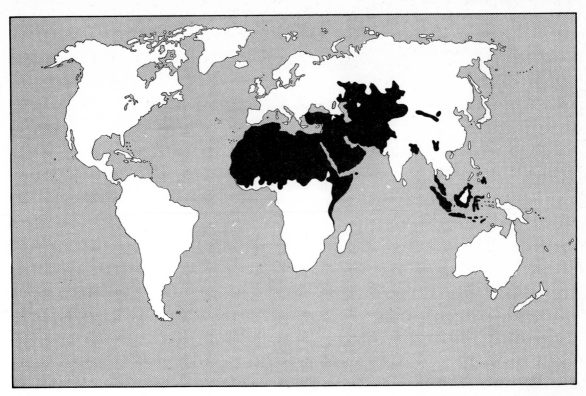

The Muslim World today

feeding on dates, camel-flesh and milk. His home is a tent made of camel's hair; he uses camel skins as coverlets and camel dung as fuel. He loads all his household possessions on to the backs of his camels as he moves across the desert, and it is in terms of camels that he measures his whole wealth, whether in reckoning a dowry for his daughter, or in throwing dice with his friends. The Bedouins refer to themselves as 'the people of the camel'. Since one cannot grow crops in such country, the Bedouin makes his wealth by breeding camels and the famous Arabian horses, beautiful strong intelligent creatures that are highly valued by horse-racing men throughout Europe. As a sideline, there are sharp sudden raids on neighbouring tribes, which may bring in rich loot in spices and silks that have come originally from the East. To his own tribe the Bedouin is intensely loyal. It was from these men of the desert that the brave and daring warriors of Islam were to be drawn, and without them the new faith might never have spread.

The religion of Arabia before the birth of Muhammad was primitive and superstitious. The Arabs worshipped gods of streams and hills and sacred stones; and they imagined the desert to be haunted by evil spirits called *jinn*. In the city of Mecca was the shrine called the *Kaaba*, where it is said that 360 gods were worshipped, and

where there was a particular black stone which was specially holy. Here many Arabs would come on pilgrimage from all over Arabia, and the shrine was carefully guarded by an Arab tribe known as the Quraish. It is here that the story of Islam really begins.

In or about A.D. 571 a boy was born into the Quraish tribe who was to be called Muhammad. At the start life was hard enough for this little boy, for his father died before he was born and his mother by the time he was six years old. He was an orphan, left to face a very harsh world without the comfort of his parents' care and affection. We do not know much more than that about Muhammad's early life, but as a young man he came to be employed by a merchant's widow, Khadijah, who was a woman of strong character. When her husband died she had roused herself to carry on his business, and by her courage and her ability she had become quite wealthy. When he was 25 Muhammad married Khadijah, and although it was a custom among the Arabs for a man to have more than one wife, Muhammad himself would have no other wife until after Khadijah's death, for he was deeply devoted to her. Khadijah, for her part, was to give him all her support, and to show men that she at least believed in her husband when most people were laughing him to scorn; but this lay in the future.

It was some years later that Muhammad became fully aware of God's call to him. Sometimes during the hot summer day he would climb the rising ground outside Mecca, and seek out a quiet little cave in the hillside where he might meditate and try to understand what God wanted him to do; and it was here that he received the kind of call that the Old Testament prophets like Amos and Isaiah had once heard so clearly. Muhammad felt an overwhelming urge to proclaim to his people a great message: that there is only one God, that he is all-powerful and the creator of the universe, and that he will judge all men. Jews and Christians believed these truths too, of course, and Muhammad knew about their teaching, but to the Arabs this was a call to a great new religion and a new way of life.

A very few of his relations listened to Muhammad, and believed his prophetic sayings—Khadijah his wife, his cousin Ali, and his kinsman Abu Bakr; but the wealthy and influential members of the Quraish just laughed at him and made sarcastic jokes. At first they did only this, but then they got angry. Muhammad had a following among the slaves and the poorer people of Mecca, and the Quraish began to think that if this nonsense about 'one God' went too far it might become more than a joke, and perhaps pilgrims would no longer flock to the *Kaaba* sanctuary. This was like threatening a modern seaside resort with the end of its tourist trade. They began to treat Muhammad as a trouble-maker, and to persecute his

followers until some were forced to flee to Abyssinia. Muhammad himself remained and continued to preach fearlessly the worship of the one true God, whom he called 'Allah'. '*La ilaha illa-'llah*' ('There is no God but Allah') was his resounding cry, and it is echoed daily by millions of his twentieth-century followers.

It was at this point that Muhammad, trained from an early age to fend for himself, showed that he was more than a prophet; he was a man who could plan and who could act decisively. With daring and secrecy, he planned that two hundred of his followers should leave the dangers of Mecca and go to his mother's native city of Medina, where he had friends. He followed them himself on 24 September 622, and this is the event from which Muslims now reckon the date of the year, in the same way that Christians reckon from the birth of Christ. Muhammad's journey to Medina is known to Muslims as the '*hejira*' or 'flight', but it was a carefully planned move, not a flight in the ordinary sense.

In Medina Muhammad rose swiftly to success. He first rallied his followers to attack their enemies. Trading and raiding were the Arab's favourite pursuits. Each year several caravans, great convoys of camels, carrying goods from Syria down to Mecca, passed close by Medina. Muhammad decided to lead his companions in an attack on the Meccan caravan. When the caravan leader heard of the plot he sent for reinforcements from Mecca, but Muhammad's 300 followers won a complete victory over 1,000 Meccans. This was the first sign that the Muslim religion was to be a fighting faith; Muhammad had declared a 'holy war', and it was a dark hint of what was to come. Muhammad soon ran all the affairs of Medina, and won more and more recruits, until in 630 he was able to lead a triumphal following of Muslims back into his native city of Mecca, which now submitted to him completely. He smashed the idols in the *Kaaba* sanctuary, and declared it to be in future the sanctuary of the true God, Allah. 'Truth has come; falsehood has been overthrown' was his glad cry.

Muhammad had now broken finally with the Jews and Christians and his religion had become an essentially Arab faith. It was a far nobler and finer religion than the Arabs had ever known before, but it was chiefly because they recognized him to be a great man and an outstanding leader that the tribes of the Arabian desert came pressing into Medina to pay tribute and make submission to Muhammad. He had broken with Christian tradition because, while he believed him to have been a great prophet, he did not regard Christ as the Son of God. He regarded himself, too, simply as a prophet, and so Muslims have done ever since. They do not worship Muhammad; they worship Allah, and they revere Muhammad as the prophet of Allah.

Two years after Muhammad's triumphal re-entry into Mecca he died, in the tenth year of the Muslim era, the year 632 by Christian reckoning. Before we investigate the exciting events that swiftly followed on the prophet's death, and the alarm that was soon to spread through the whole civilized world, we must take a closer look at the teaching of Muhammad. This can be studied in the Koran, which holds much the same place in the religion of a Muslim as the New Testament does in that of a Christian. It is in the Koran that we come closest to Muhammad's deepest thought, for the book consists of statements made by him when he felt himself to be directly inspired by God. These were written down in the Arabic language, which before had only been used for everyday speech and for poetry. The Koran became the great book on which the whole education of a Muslim was based. Today in Arab countries many Muslim children still learn to read by using the Koran as a textbook.

The first statement that Muhammad made in the Koran is the foundation of his whole religion; that clear haunting phrase '*la ilaha illa-'llah*'. No god but Allah: this was the mighty truth that he wanted above all to proclaim, and which gripped his followers by its fine inspired simplicity. Five times a day from the tall shapely minarets, or towers, which are to be found scattered throughout Muslim countries, there still comes today the call to all faithful Muslims to turn to Mecca and repeat this declaration in a prayer.

Although Muhammad allowed men to have more than one wife, as the custom of Arabia had always been, he was not a man who lived in luxury. Both he and his early successors, Abu Bakr and Omar, lived very austerely and simply, and this was in keeping with Muhammad's own disciplined teaching. He forbade men to gamble, would not allow them to drink alcohol, and insisted on their fasting from dawn to dusk throughout the Muslim month of Ramadan. We can see that he was very strict. Above all Muhammad never forgot what it had been like to be an orphan, needing kindness and help. He made it a binding duty on all Muslims to care for the weak, for children, and for old people, for all those in any community who find it difficult to cope with life at all, and who tend to be forgotten and ignored by those of us who are happy and comfortable ourselves. He urged men to free their slaves, to protect and care for orphans, to show kindness and hospitality to strangers. Just having kind thoughts and good intentions was not enough; Muslims were to give generously from their own money to provide places where the sick and homeless might be looked after, and this tradition is still a strong one among the followers of Islam.

Every Friday at noon all the men in a Muslim community came together for the weekly service in the mosque (they still do). Here

they followed the *imam*, or prayer leader, with great devotion and concentration. There were no priests in the Muslim religion, and any man, however humble, might act as *imam*. The Friday service brought Muslims together regularly and helped to make them feel that they belonged to a real brotherhood of believers. So, too, on a vast scale, did the final duty of the Muslim, to make a pilgrimage to Mecca once in his lifetime. This pilgrimage has been the great event in the lives of countless Muslims of all ranks throughout the centuries. They would put a little money aside each year, and gradually, as the small savings mounted, they would look forward eagerly to the day when they would actually set out on the long journey to Mecca. Trekking across the African desert from the west, journeying by sea from Malaya, setting out from Pakistan or from Persia, Muslims in their thousands might be met every year as the pilgrimage season came round. They made their way in groups, some on foot, some on camel-back, some by ship, all pressing on towards the holy city of the prophet. Mecca was ready to receive them and make them welcome. A pilgrim in Mecca must surely have an exhilarating sense of being a member of a world-wide movement, which is his birthright. Here the pilgrims meet men of many other races, strangers in speech and dress, but all are fellow Muslims; all follow one prophet; all worship one God: *'la ilaha illa-'llah'*. The mosque at Mecca, with its fine courtyard and impressive buildings, is enormous, but only Muslims may enter it. Fewer than twenty European-born Christians during the 1,300 years since Muhammad's death have contrived to penetrate this inner heart of Islam, and return to tell the tale.

We may now go back to 632, and the death of Muhammad. What would happen? The tribes of the desert had hurried in to submit to Muhammad and claim the new faith, simply because Muhammad himself was a very remarkable man. No one could be sure that they would accept his successor, and, in any case, who was to be his successor? At this point Islam might simply have petered out. That this did not happen is one of the most important facts of history.

Faced with this crisis, the group of Muhammad's closest companions acted speedily and chose the wise and respected Abu Bakr, the prophet's kinsman, as his *caliph*, that is his successor. In one sense, of course, Muhammad could have no successor, because he himself was the final 'seal of the prophets'. But Muhammad had been more than a religious leader; he had actually ruled his Muslim followers, and in this sense he could and must have a successor. Abu Bakr was strongly supported by the man who was to become the second caliph, Omar. Together they renewed the 'holy war' against any of the tribes who would not submit, and Abu Bakr quickly succeeded in regaining control in Arabia.

Yet it is not Abu Bakr's leadership alone that explains what comes next. The truth is that the Arabians were hungry, hungry for land which could produce wealth. There were far too many mouths to feed in Arabia. Much of the land was so poor and barren that for years some of the tribes had been edging up towards the north, in the direction of the territory bordering on Syria and Persia which is sometimes called the Fertile Crescent. There it would seem they could go no further. Look at the map. Two mighty empires blocked their way, Persia to the north-east and the Byzantine Empire, once ruled by Justinian, to the north-west. There seemed no chance for the Arabs.

Here we need to think back to the chapter on Justinian. You will remember that he had ruled over the eastern part of the old Roman empire, which included all the lands which bordered the eastern end of the Mediterranean. This is usually known as the Byzantine empire, because it was ruled from Constantinople and Byzantium is another name for Constantinople. Justinian's reign had seen great triumphs, and so had the reign of the Emperor Heraclius, the latest of his successors in Constantinople, but the cost had been staggering. All was not well with the seemingly rich, populous, busy provinces of Syria and Egypt. Taxation bore down relentlessly on the poor, and the native population had always hated the rule of the Roman empire; to them it stood for cruel foreign oppression. Christians and Jews alike in Syria and Egypt would have been glad of an excuse to throw off the yoke of Constantinople.

This was the picture of the lands to the north-west of Arabia. Let us now look to the north-east. Here stood the ancient empire of Persia, which had lasted for more than 1,000 years. Yet here too we find decay and discontent and bad government. Worse still, these two empires had greatly added to their troubles by constant bitter warfare between themselves. There they now stood, prosperous and civilized if you did not look beneath the surface, but in fact dangerously exhausted. Dangerously, because of the Arabs.

Probably neither Abu Bakr nor even Omar would ever have been so bold as to sit down and plan deliberately that the Arabs should found a mighty new empire. It happened quite differently. Among the Arabs at this time there were some very able eager young men, with powers of leadership that they themselves as yet hardly suspected. They longed to prove themselves in the holy war, and to lead raids on neighbouring territory. Among them were Khalid ibn al-Walid and Amr ibn al-As. (We will call them simply Khalid and Amr.) Khalid had joined Islam in Muhammad's lifetime, and he was a strong and adventurous fighter, inspired by the new faith. He led some of the early raids on the Fertile Crescent with startling success. Khalid's hopes rose high. In 634, while he was raiding in

southern Iraq, he was suddenly ordered to go to the help of some Arab troops who were in danger of being overwhelmed by the forces of the Emperor Heraclius, on the borders of Syria. The north Arabian desert lay in between Khalid and Syria, but what was this to a Bedouin Arab? The camels could move with incredible speed; the morale of Khalid's troops was high, and his organization was perfect. Water for the men was carried in bags slung over the camels' backs, and for the horses there was water in the paunches of old camels that were slaughtered for food on the way. Khalid struck straight across the trackless desert, and appeared dramatically before the walls of Damascus, the Syrian capital, long before anyone had dreamed of expecting him. Damascus surrendered to the Arabs after a six months' siege, and other Syrian towns fell quickly. The Emperor Heraclius was now deeply alarmed and sent an army of 50,000 men to meet the Muslims in open battle. Khalid had only half that number, but his courage was high. The climate and the battle ground favoured him. The two armies came to grips on a day of intense heat and swirling dust storms on 20 August 636, in the valley of the Yarmuk. Khalid's men, all sons of the desert, undaunted by the wind-blown sand, charged the enemy with tremendous vigour and won a devastating victory. The power of Heraclius was crippled, and the Roman province of Syria then fell to Islam.

It seemed almost impossible that this striking victory could be repeated, but within the year, in 637, in yet another day of dust storms, the Arab force swept down on a large Persian army at Kadesiya, and dealt a death blow to the might of a second empire. The Persian emperor fled from his capital at Ctesiphon, and met a miserable death at the hands of one of his subjects, who killed him to get hold of the crown jewels. As the Arab horsemen entered Ctesiphon they saw for the first time the luxuries and splendour of an oriental capital. This was a very different way of life from that of the tents in the desert or even the mud homes of Mecca or Medina. They had much to learn. One Arab had a nobleman's daughter as his share of the booty; he promptly sold her for 1,000 silver coins. One of his friends told him he was a fool for making such a poor bargain, to which he solemnly replied that he never knew that there were any numbers above a thousand. By 643 the push to the east had reached to the borders of India. Meanwhile our main concern is with the west, where Khalid, 'the sword of Allah', had won Syria for Islam. Beyond Syria lay Egypt, and this was to be the prize of Khalid's young rival, Amr. In 639, with 4,000 horsemen, he took the road from Syria to Egypt. His army was joined as it went by recruits from Arabia, and finally, with 20,000 men, Amr stood before the massive walls and towers of Egypt's wealthy capital, Alexandria. It was a city of magnificent buildings, beautiful

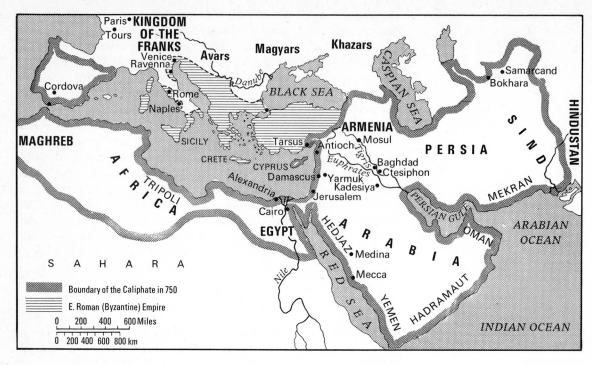

The Muslim World in A.D. 750

churches, a famous library, and outside the walls, dominating everything else, stood the mighty Pharos lighthouse, one of the seven wonders of the world, flashing its light by night to guide the shipping into this great Byzantine naval base and port. Amr must have gazed on all of this, and perhaps his eye was caught by two tall pointed granite shafts, so high that they would show above the walls of the town, one of which, over 1,000 years later, was to be brought to England. You can see it for yourself on the Thames embankment just below Waterloo Bridge. It is called—mistakenly—Cleopatra's Needle. Amr pitched his camp outside the city. He had no siege machines, no ships, and yet he was determined to force the surrender of this city, garrisoned as it was by 50,000 men and with the whole strength of the Byzantine navy behind it. A year later Amr wrote to the Caliph Omar, 'I have captured a city, from the description of which I shall refrain———.' The fair town of Alexandria had fallen to Islam.

Beyond Syria there had been Egypt. Beyond Egypt the North African coastal provinces stretched in a narrow strip the whole length of the Mediterranean Sea, far away into the west towards the outermost Atlantic edge of the African continent. Behind that fertile coastal strip was the desert, and here lived the warrior-like Berber horsemen, whose way of life was rather like that of the Arabs themselves in their own homeland. For many years the

Berber chieftains held the Arabs back, but eventually they were won over to Islam, and then nothing could stop the whole African coastline from falling to the Arabs. If you look at the map on the opposite page, you can work out how far the Arabs had now got. Once the Berbers joined the Arabs, their joint forces were so restless and so powerful that they almost *had* to go further still. As you can see from the map, 'further' could only mean into Europe.

It was in 711 that a Berber freedman, Tariq, landed on the huge rock that lies off the southernmost point of Spain. 'The hill of Tariq' we still call it, *Jabal Tariq*, or Gibraltar. Tariq had only a small force, but the Visigothic kingdom in Spain was rotten at the core. The wealthy landowners lived in idleness, and the poor were terrorized by robber bands who raided the countryside simply to get food. Recruits flocked to join Tariq's army, and what had started as a coastal raid became a campaign for the conquest of the whole country. By the end of the summer Tariq was master of half of Spain. Musa, the governor of North Africa, who had sent Tariq to Spain, now came over to share the spoils and the glory.

By this time the capital of Islam had been moved from Medina to Damascus, where the Omayyad family, the aristocracy of the Quraish tribe, ruled the Arab empire as caliphs. When news of the

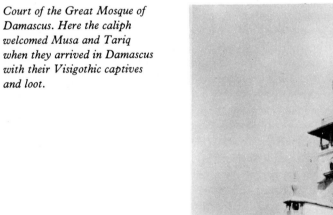

Court of the Great Mosque of Damascus. Here the caliph welcomed Musa and Tariq when they arrived in Damascus with their Visigothic captives and loot.

conquest of Spain reached Damascus, Musa and Tariq were summoned to the capital, and they made a slow and splendid triumphal journey the whole length of the North African coast from west to east, with an enormous retinue of 400 captive Visigothic nobles, decked out with gold belts and other finery, hundreds of newly-made slaves, and load upon load of Visigothic treasure captured in booty. It must have been a strange and impressive sight, though rather sordid too. The whole vast procession was welcomed by the caliph in Damascus with an elaborate official reception in the court-yard of the Omayyad mosque, against the background of its lofty arches and glowing golden mosaics.

The conquest of Spain was not yet finished, but the Arabs and Berbers, cheered by their early successes, now overran the north of the country. On they went again, over the Pyrenees, across Aquitaine, and deep into the heart of France, to the Frankish town of Tours. Only here did they stop. Charles Martel, ruler of the Franks and grandfather of Charlemagne, had gathered an army to meet them. Some of the Frankish army were foot soldiers, but some were mounted knights, because Charles knew that the Arabs won their victories because of their fine horsemanship. Charles Martel matched the Arabs in toughness and courage. A great battle was fought between the two armies somewhere between Tours and Poitiers, and the Arabs never went further into France after that.

Western Europe was in a poor state at this time, and much of it must have seemed very primitive and backward to the Arabs, as compared with other lands where they had been. Everywhere men were seeking lords to give them protection; in the monasteries the monks knew little Latin, and the only kind of history that most monasteries managed to produce was a list of short, bald statements, set side by side with a list of dates. In the 'annals' written at this time in the German abbey of St. Gall, all that they could manage to put against the date 710 was 'Hard year and shortage of crops'. For 712 the entry is shorter still: 'Great flood'. For 722, more cheerfully, the scribe has written 'Great crops', but then by 732 he roused himself to write a whole sentence, for he knew that something very important had happened in this year. The scribe wrote proudly, '732. Charles fought against the Saracens at Poitiers on Saturday.' In his excitement he did not actually mention the important fact that Charles won!

To turn from Europe as the monks of St. Gall knew it, a scene of landowning knights and counts, of peasants eking a hard living from the soil in their little village communities, and kings who had to travel round from one estate to another eating up the food rents, to life as it was lived in Muslim lands at this time is to enter a charmed and wonderful world. One big difference was that the Muslim empire was a world of wealthy cities. When the Arabs had

The Dome of the Rock, Jerusalem. The plan and style of the mosque show how much the Arab architects had in mind the fine Byzantine churches of Constantinople, such as Sancta Sophia.

seized the provinces of Syria and Egypt, which had belonged to the Emperor of Constantinople, and the great kingdom of Persia, they did not destroy what they found; they were simply delighted by it, and they wanted all the trade, the elaborate system of government, the beautiful building, and the study of law and literature, philosophy and medicine, to go on. In fact they joined in. They learned quickly, eagerly, and intelligently from the people they had conquered; they too wanted to trade, to build, to study books. We have already seen that the caliphs in Damascus had built a fine mosque in that city, for which they used craftsmen and engineers and artists who were trained in the traditions of Constantinople. In Jerusalem rose the Dome of the Rock, a large octagonal mosque, built in rich marbles, its splendid dome reminding us of the church of the Holy Wisdom in Constantinople. It was built by one of the Omayyad caliphs, eager to impress his subjects with a temple worthy of the greatness of Allah.

Far in the west of the Islamic empire in Spain was another capital city, Cordova. A German nun, living in a bleak and draughty

Saxon monastery, had heard such wonderful fairy-tale descriptions of the exquisite palaces and mosques of Cordova that she called it 'the Jewel of the World'. The Arab rulers had certainly lavished their wealth and skill here. By the tenth century there were half a million inhabitants in Cordova, 700 mosques, and 300 public baths. An aquaduct brought a supply of pure water to the city and the streets were properly paved and lighted. In any western European town north of the Pyrenees you would have been up to your ankles in mud if you had stepped out into the street on a rainy day, and even kings were thought very soft and effeminate if they bathed more than about once in three months! The bookshops and fine libraries in Cordova made it a centre of learning, and here men translated the works of the great Greek scholars, such as Aristotle, and the physician Galen, which were later to find their way across the Pyrenees and into Christian Europe. The beautiful mosque at Cordova is still standing, and there is a photograph of it opposite. Its graceful slender columns, carrying their delicate scalloped arches, give a wonderful sense of lightness and elegance to the whole building. One of the rulers of Cordova had a luxurious palace built for his mistress, al Zahra ('she with the bright face'). Marble was shipped from North Africa, and the basins for the fountains and the golden statues were specially imported from distant Constantinople. 10,000 workmen were said to have laboured for 20 years to build al Zahra's palace.

Scalloped arches in the mosque at Cordova, Spain.

Spain, which had been backward and oppressed under its Christian Visigothic rulers, now became prosperous and civilized under its Muslim governors at Cordova. In Spain, and indeed everywhere in Muslim lands, the Christians were allowed by the Arab conquerors to speak their own language and keep their own religion, but it is hardly surprising that many young Spaniards felt the strong attraction of the Muslim culture and way of life. One Christian writer living in Cordova in the ninth century grumbles bitterly about the younger generation: 'All the young Christians, noted for their abilities, know only the language and literature of the Arabs, read Arab books and study them with zeal, building up great libraries of them at enormous cost and loudly proclaiming everywhere that this literature is worthy of admiration.'

Spain was not quite the only European country to be occupied by the Arabs, though it was the most important. The island of Sicily fell to the Arabs too. There were 300 mosques in Palermo alone, and even when the Normans eventually conquered Sicily in the eleventh century, the Norman rulers went on minting coins which bore Arabic inscriptions and were dated from the *hejira*, although they were issued in the name of a Christian king!

Spain and Sicily have a special fascination, because they were

absolutely on the frontiers between Christendom and Islam, between the Cross and the Crescent, but to get to the very heart of the Muslim world we must leave the west and go far into Persia, to Baghdad. The Omayyad rulers in Damascus were challenged in 747 by their cousins, the Abbasids. Eighty Omayyads were invited to dinner by an Abbasid general, and in the course of the feast their host had them all murdered. He then seized power for his own family. He abandoned Damascus and at his death his son and successor Mansur chose Baghdad as the site for his capital city. Those of you who have read the *Arabian Nights* will know that this is the city of 'Sinbad the Sailor' and 'The King of the Ebony Isles' and many other stories, but Mansur spotted it for a very practical reason. 'This island between the Tigris in the East and the Euphrates in the West', he said, 'is a market place for the world. . . . Praise be to God who preserved it for me and caused all those who came before me to overlook it. By God I shall build it. Then I shall dwell in it as long as I live and my descendants shall dwell in it after me. It will surely be the most flourishing city in the world.' If you look at the map on p. 72 you will see what a clever choice it was. It was a meeting-point for very many trade routes.

Let us look for a moment at these trading tentacles that wind away from Baghdad to the furthest parts of the Muslim world and beyond. Up the Persian Gulf and the River Tigris came the merchants from India and the Far East; by caravan route from Syria and then up the Euphrates came all the produce of the West, which had first been brought to the Syrian ports by ships from Spain and Sicily, and also from Constantinople. Camel caravans took the produce of Egypt first to Syria and then to Baghdad. Goods from Armenia and from the heart of Russia came from the north, and there were overland routes to such romantic places as Bukhara and Samarkhand in the far north-east of the empire.

It is not often that a mere list of imports is very exciting, but just listen to this. From China came silks, paper and peacocks, swift horses and saddles and cinnamon; from Africa there was gold dust, ivory, and slaves. India sent tigers, panthers, elephants, rubies, ebony, and white sandalwood. Down the Volga and in through the northern route came goods which have a whiff of Scandinavia about them: fox and beaver skins, wax, arrows, birch bark, honey, amber, falcons—and fur caps. But perhaps the most curious assortment of all came from the Byzantine empire. This list of imports included not only gold, drugs, locks, and slave girls but also marble-workers and hydraulic engineers! Few empires have ever been better placed to attract and control trade from such a rich variety of areas.

At the very heart of this trading network Mansur had built his city of Baghdad, defended by mighty triple walls and a deep moat.

There were four main gates in the walls, through which a busy throng of people were usually to be found hurrying and jostling: messengers, merchants, clerks, sailors, royal ambassadors, and scholars, some of them about to set off for the furthest corners of the Islamic empire. In the very centre of Baghdad, the 'abode of peace', as Sinbad the Sailor always called it, there stood a great mosque and the caliph's Palace of the Golden Gate, the huge dome of its audience-chamber rising to a height of 130 feet. Inside, the chamber was luxuriously decked out with richly woven rugs, curtains, and cushions, for Arab craftsmen specialized in producing beautiful fabrics of intricate designs. History often leaves us with everyday words which bring us echoes of remote empires of the past. Every time we speak of a 'tabby' cat we are using the Arabic word for a gay striped material first produced in Baghdad, and perhaps it was some English merchant doing business with the Baghdad traders who first called his stripy kitten '*Tabi*'. Again, European ladies of the Middle Ages bought at the great fairs the stiff silky cloth from Persia called *taftah*—and 'taffeta' we still call it.

The caliphs lived in sumptuous luxury inside the Palace of the Golden Gate. At one royal wedding the groom and his bride were showered with a thousand pearls as they stood on a golden mat studded with pearls and sapphires. It sounds a little painful. It was a very far cry from the simplicity of the lives of Abu Bakr and Omar to the oriental splendour of the caliphs of Baghdad, who enjoyed using the title 'the Shadow of God'. Surrounded by palace chamberlains, singing-girls, slaves, and guards, the Abbasid caliphs led a very artificial life; some of them gave themselves up to it to the full, and left most of the tiresome business of state affairs to the 'grand vizier', the chief minister.

A caliph who is well known in the West, because poems and stories have been written about him, is Harun al Raschid. His court was always full of poets, musicians, and dancers; he had gay river parties on the Tigris, for which special barges were made, shaped like animals, one in the form of a dolphin, another a lion, and another an eagle. Sometimes the court was entertained by performances of ballet that went on all night. Charlemagne, king of the Franks, was a contemporary of Harun and sent ambassadors to the caliph's court. They were well received, and came back to the palace at Aachen with a bewildering assortment of presents from the generous Harun. There were fabrics and spicy perfumes, but also a very intricate clock, and, most exciting of all, an elephant. Men of western Europe were fascinated by elephants. The trouble was that when an elephant was on show there were so many people wanting to see it that it was very difficult in the crowd to see more than the top half. This must surely be why the manuscript writers who enjoyed drawing them in their books, and the craftsmen who

sometimes carved them in wood on the tip-up seats of cathedral choir-stalls, always made a splendid job of the upper half of the elephant: its head and tusks and trunk and back came out beautifully, but the artists were full of uncertainties when they got down to the feet.

Not all the caliphs were out for mere pleasure. One of the most famous, al Mamun, founded in his capital in 830 'a house of wisdom'. This was to be important not only for the whole Muslim world but eventually for the Christian world too. Mamun endowed his house of wisdom with a fine library, and employed many scholars in translating works of the ancient Greek writers into Arabic. These were works which in western Europe had been completely lost since the time of the barbarian invasions. Men of great learning, especially from Syria and Egypt, were attracted to Mamun's court, and a tradition of study and scholarship was begun which was to save for the world some of the finest works of the Greek genius. In certain directions Arab scholars were able to go further still, beyond the discoveries made by the Greeks, especially in mathematics and in medicine. From India the Arabs, with their special flair for picking up useful knowledge, learned the use of what we call 'arabic' numerals. We learned them from the Arabs, but the Arabs more correctly call them Indian numerals. They also took over the decimal system from the Indians.

The caliphate of the Abbasids lasted until 1258, when Baghdad fell to the Mongols, but although successive tribes have overrun the eastern parts of the Islamic empire since then, they have always in the end become Muslims themselves. There is no doubt that to the end of the period covered by this book the world of Islam was far more cultured, learned, and civilized than the Christian world of western Europe. Men of the West were afraid of Islam; many of them wished to attack it; a few wished to learn more about it. There was a great deal, in fact, that the two cultures of the Cross and the Crescent had in common. They both believed in a single God, and the religion of both was firmly based on a single tradition, the Jewish faith of the Old Testament. For Jews, Christians, and Muslims Jerusalem is still a sacred city, and in this fact lies one of the problems of the government of Jerusalem today. Muslims and Christians also inherited together the civilization of the Roman empire, with its mingling of Greek and Roman traditions of art and learning, law and politics.

Wild rumours were to be heard in western Europe about what the Muslims believed. Some westerners maintained that the Muslims worshipped as many as 30 gods! It is interesting to find that it was an abbot of the great Benedictine abbey of Cluny, Peter the Venerable, whom we shall meet again in Chapter 12, who

Left *Bowl from the Muslim city of Nishapur. The design is boldly painted in black on a smooth white ground and it was made in the eighth or ninth century.*

Right *Glass mosque lamp. This was probably made in Syria in the fourteenth century. It shows how Arabic writing was used for decoration.*

showed a far more intelligent approach, when he employed an English scholar, Robert of Ketton, to translate the Koran from Arabic into Latin, so that he would at least know exactly what the Muslims did believe. He wanted to go on from there to show the Muslims where their religion went wrong.

Peter was exceptional. The much more common attitude for many years to come was the crusader's simple belief that Islam stood for all that was evil, and must be destroyed by ruthless warfare. We shall hear much more of this in Chapter 14. It only very gradually dawned on the West that there was absolutely no hope of destroying Islam. Meanwhile, some European scholars had found out, through contacts in Sicily and Spain, what treasures of learning the Muslims enjoyed. More and more of the works of Aristotle, long since lost to the West, but available in Spain in Arabic translation, were now translated one after the other from Arabic into Latin, to be eagerly snapped up and read and re-read by scholars at the universities of Paris and Oxford. This did not happen until some 600 years after Muhammad's death, and several hundred years after most of the events described in this chapter, but western Europe could never have reached the position in science and other branches of learning that she holds today without first absorbing the learning of the Greeks, much of which was carefully preserved, studied, and handed on by Islam to the western world.

Chapter 6
The Age of Charlemagne

In the summer of the year A.D. 793 a letter arrived at the monastery of Jarrow in Northumbria and was probably read aloud by the abbot to the monks in the chapter-house before being passed round to individuals. Evidently the writer was in a very troubled state of mind, for he wrote 'Who is not afraid of the terror which has struck the church of the holy Cuthbert? Now in our time is fulfilled what was foretold by the prophet, "Out of the north evil shall break forth", for behold the flying robber has overrun the northern parts of our land.' The letter must have been a considerable time on the way, for it had travelled by land and sea from the palace of the king of the Franks at Aachen (now called Aix-la-chapelle), but the monks knew at once that it was referring to the Viking raid on the holy island of Lindisfarne in the spring of that year, and they also knew the writer. He was the scholar Alcuin, who had been born in Northumbria and brought up in the monastery of York, just as the great Bede had been at Jarrow, but who now had lived abroad for eleven years. Alcuin often wrote to his friends at Canterbury, Jarrow, and York, for he had a passionate love for England, and, though a busy and important man, was still homesick at times. 'O my brethren,' one letter says, 'beloved beyond all others, do not forget me; I shall be yours, as in life so in death'; and indeed he often said he wanted to end his days in Northumbria, so it seems odd that he had ever gone so far away from home and there must have been a compelling reason for it. What was he doing in the palace of the Frankish king? What was it like there? And what sort of a man was this king, 'so eager in making search for wise men' that he had drawn a reluctant English scholar into his court?

Alcuin's employer was Charles, king of the Franks and Lombards (768–814), also known as Charles the Great, Charlemagne, Karl der Grosse, or Carlo Magno, depending on the language you use, a man who in the 1,100 years since he died has puzzled or fascinated scholars, historians, and poets, and caused them to argue hotly, to write learned articles, books, songs, and poems; a man who, according to one point of view, was only 'a barbarian warrior of great energy, limited intelligence, good humour and no education', according to his secretary, was 'a great and glorious king', and, according to the poets and song writers, a hero of matchless courage and virtue. The arguments about him are still going on.

A Carolingian warrior on horse-back. This is probably a portrait of Charlemagne.

Charlemagne became king of the Franks about 250 years after the energetic and ruthless Clovis, but was not descended from him. Clovis, as you know from Chapter 2, steadily increased his lands and his power until he dominated Gaul, ruling the Franks by right of birth, and the native population (the Gallo-Romans, as they are called—you can easily understand that name) by right of conquest. He treated his kingdom, as the custom then was, exactly as if it was his own private estate, held and managed for family profit, and when he died he left it divided as equally as possible between his four sons. When the last of these died, having collected together the shares of his three brothers who happened to die before him, the whole process was repeated and all was re-divided. This happened time after time and, as you can imagine, it was not an arrangement which led to peace. In fact it caused much trouble and bloodshed,

for there was nearly always envy and bad feeling between the heirs of the kingdoms, who coveted each other's lands and stopped at nothing to seize them. In a barbaric world of passion and violence men used violent ways to get what they wanted, and much of the history of the Frankish kings is a long tale of treachery and sudden death. They ruled their kingdom by force and fear, but this was not then thought at all peculiar. No one was surprised when royal decrees ended bluntly with the words 'Whosoever sets at nought this our order shall have his eyes put out', and what may seem to us rather odd advice, given by one writer to young warriors, was really sensible and necessary: 'When making your way up the hall,' he said, 'you should observe and note *all the doorways*, for you can never be certain when you will find enemies present.' Violence bred violence and one murder led to another, for this seemed the best way of holding your own and dealing with rivals. One Frankish noble, knowing well that the king had just disposed of his two brothers, said harshly to him 'We know where the axe is that cut off the heads of your brothers, and its edge is still keen', but the words and the threat they carried were no great shock to the king. They simply told him what he already knew, that one black deed was certain to be followed by another, and that his own life was far from safe.

There were of course, strange contrasts in this long story. One king at least, according to Gregory of Tours, 'ruled with justice, relieved the poor, and distributed many benefits with piety and friendliness', and one of the most ruthless of Frankish queens was a highly educated woman who spoke and wrote excellent Latin. Even Chilperic, grandson of Clovis, who sounds as if he was more a monster than a man, for he murdered two wives and an indefinite number of enemies, robbed the poor, and was 'ever on the watch for new ways of torturing people', was fascinated by the remains of Roman civilization, added four letters to the alphabet, and wrote poems and hymns.

For more than 100 years after Clovis this strong family, the Merovingians, so crude and uncivilized, yet at times so touched by the crumbled greatness of Rome, and at times moved to better deeds by the gospel of Christ, kept their toughness, added to their lands, and held them against all enemies. But at last their vitality began to fail. Weakling followed weakling on the throne, some pathetic, some nasty, and nearly all delicate and short-lived, dying in their twenties, or even earlier. As the kings weakened there were plenty of bold men around them who grew stronger, the leaders of war-bands, for instance, and the officials of the court. Chief among these were the royal stewards, the mayors of the palace, whose duty of managing the royal domains gave them a finger in every pie and much knowledge of the king's business. Gradually the mayors drew

all royal power into their own hands, and looked after the kingdom and all that had to be done at home and abroad, while the kings — the 'do-nothing kings' as they are called —, still bearing the signs of royalty in their uncut hair and flowing beards, lived in seclusion and idleness on a single farm, attended by a few servants who made some show of respect and reverence for them. The mayors became so powerful that they were able to pass on their great office from father to son, and yet, strong and dreaded though they were, none dared actually to take the name of king of the Franks or wear the crown. This was partly because of the hostility of other great families, but also because of the strange awe which the Franks felt for their royal family, descended, as they believed, from the ancient gods of their race and therefore still sacred to them, even though the last feeble remnant only appeared on certain state occasions, or when some important foreign envoy had to be received with unusual ceremony. Then, like a kind of puppet, the king would be brought from his estate, would mumble a few suitable words which were put into his mouth by the mayor, and disappear again into seclusion.

Charlemagne's father Pepin the Short, his uncle, his grandfather, and his great-grandfather were all mayors of the palace, but only his father, after being in power for 10 years, at last took the final step. In 751 his desire for the crown and title of king became urgent. There had been a deep peace in the kingdom for 2 years — a most unusual thing for those days — and he felt strong enough to act. But he knew that he must somehow break completely the spell of the Merovingians, and that he would only do that if he was supported by something more than sheer force of arms, by the help of some power greater than the sword, which would seem to the Franks more potent than the dim gods of the past. One power alone could do this, the Christian Church. By this time most Franks were baptized Christians, even if some of them, to be on the safe side, quietly made offerings to the old spirits and gods, and breathed a charm or two; Pepin certainly was. He had been educated by the monks of Saint Denis near Paris, he listened with attention to the advice of bishops and abbots, he fostered monasteries, he protected and encouraged missionaries, like Boniface, in their work, he was on good terms with the Pope. Some reward for all this was due, and besides, he was a very powerful person, the sort of man much needed as friend and ally by the Pope, who was continually beset by enemies.

So in 751 Pepin sent two envoys to Rome to ask his Holiness the Pope a plain question requiring a plain answer. Was it right — or not — that one man should have the name of king while another ruled? The answer came back promptly and clearly, that it was *not* right, and armed with this statement from the highest personage in

the Church of God, who surely must be able to tell right from wrong, Pepin summoned an assembly of the leaders of the Franks. We do not know exactly how he told them that he meant to take the crown, but they must have been expecting it to happen; the Pope's approval finally broke down any lingering doubts and superstitious fears, and Pepin was elected king according to the Frankish custom. Afterwards he was blessed and anointed with holy oil by the saintly Boniface, and this was a new ceremony—a Christian one—which gave a special halo to the new royal line of the Franks. The last of the Merovingian do-nothings was shorn of his hair and beard and hurried into a monastery.

Thereafter Pepin wore his crown for 17 years, and his two sons, Carloman and Charles, peacefully succeeded to his kingdom, still by custom divided between them. Carloman lived for only two years, and then Charles was made sole king 'by the consent of all the Franks'. A few years later he began to build the palace of Aachen, where Alcuin wrote his letter.

It was always his favourite palace and the one he returned to most often, though, like all the kings and great men of the time, he had many domains and houses on them, and travelled about continually from one to another, living on the produce of the royal lands which were stored against his coming. This may sound a laborious business, but it was safer and easier than collecting all the produce in one place. Most of the houses were simply large farms, countrified places, with a stone or wooden 'hall' of two or three rooms, some stables and barns and cow-sheds, and some huts for serfs to live and work in, all surrounded by a wall or a stout fence. One of these royal estates at the time of Charles had 200 lambs, 150 ewes, 165 pigs, 30 geese, 80 chickens, 22 peacocks—not only for ornament but because they were a great delicacy to eat—, and 17 beehives. Honey was the only sweetener, and beeswax made the candles the king required, though of course most people went to bed at dark. There was also a good store of rye, wheat, oats, and barley.

Aachen was bigger than most royal houses, and though much of it was was built of wood and so has disappeared, parts were of stone, and for the chapel, which still exists, Charles fetched marble columns and pavements from Theodoric's palace at Ravenna. According to our standards it must have been crowded, draughty, and possibly smelly, for people had dirty habits and there were few drains; but there were a few baths, and some of the rooms were warmed by large fires, though the Roman skill in laying on running water and underfloor heating had been lost. Charlemagne lived in considerable state and magnificence, though not in the mysterious scented magnificence and elaborate ceremonial of Constantinople.

Charlemagne's sword and scabbard.

He was a naturally friendly man, who enjoyed mixing freely with all sorts of people and was always ready to talk. Like all wealthy Franks, who loved silver and gold and jewels, he had plenty of treasure. In his will he left three tables made entirely of silver, and one of gold 'of remarkable size and weight', and he had chests full of precious things, gold cups, platters, basins, jugs, swords, brooches, belts, armlets, and so on, thick, chunky, and rather clumsy-looking, but marvellously wrought by the cunning smiths who were always attached to the royal court. The bloodthirsty Chilperic once showed Gregory of Tours a huge gold platter made by his favourite smith, which weighed 50 pounds and was crusted with jewels, and Charlemagne had a sword which he called Joyeuse and preferred to any other, with a hilt and scabbard of pure gold.

On state occasions he appeared in barbaric splendour, wearing richly-coloured robes and a heavy crown of gold, towering above everyone, for he was very tall; but he was much happier in the simple clothes of an ordinary Frank, and usually wore them, a linen shirt and breeches, loose stockings bound to his legs with long garters, a short tunic, and a cloak of fine blue wool. Only his belt, richly ornamented with gold, and of course the gleaming gold of Joyeuse by his side, marked him out as a great man. The scabbard alone would do this for this item was very costly and not everyone could afford it. A plain sword-blade without a scabbard was worth 3 good cows, and 3 cows could secure a good wife. In winter, even though he was a man of great physical endurance, the bitter cold forced him to protect his chest and shoulders with the soft thick pelt of an otter or a pine-marten, but he was just as happy with a sheepskin, and usually wore one for hunting, especially as he knew it would wash. He often jeered at nobles who wore their best furs when tearing through the woods, and spoiled them. Such simplicity in dress was unusual but Charlemagne was an unusual person. For instance, at a time when it was quite normal for men to drink so much that they rolled off their benches and under the table at the end of every meal, he hated drunkenness and never himself took more than two or three cups of wine. But he ate heartily and often, and could not go for long without food; he could never resist large helpings of roast meat brought straight to the table, hot and juicy, on spits from the kitchen. After the midday meal he took off his shoes and outer garments and went to sleep for two or three hours. The result of this Churchillian habit was that he slept only slightly and briefly at night, and often got up and wandered about, or read a book, or, like Theodoric the Goth, tried to learn to write: like Theodoric, he never managed more than his signature.

One of his secretaries, Einhard, a busy little man who ran 'back and forth with ceaseless pace like some tiny ant', wrote a biography

This bust of Charlemagne was made long after he died and is largely imaginary but the artist was inspired by the legends of his greatness passed down in stories and songs.

of his master, which described him clearly, and this is very useful to us, for no true portraits of Charlemagne survive. The one on the coin on page 96 is not very helpful, and the other on the page opposite was made 500 years after he died. Einhard said that the king was tall and powerful, with fair hair—the Franks were famous for their fair hair—and large bright eyes, but he also said honestly that his nose was 'rather larger than is usual . . . his neck rather thick and short and he was somewhat corpulent'. His voice must have been a shock when you heard it for the first time, for instead of being a deep bass, coming out of the mouth of this big powerful man, it was high and rather squeaky, though perfectly clear. He was very healthy, and only towards the end of his life began to suffer from rheumatism, so that in the end he was lame. Being a true Frank he was never happy unless he took violent exercise by riding and hunting. The great forests round Aachen were excellent for this, and there king and court chased to their hearts' content wolves, bears, boars, deer, and possibly the wild black cattle called 'aurochs', which have now quite died out. One of the courtiers described a hunt in which a wild boar escaped from the hounds, dashed across a valley, and bounded away up the steepest of places. 'At last grunting fiercely but exhausted by its efforts it sits panting on its haunches. At that supreme moment the king arrives. Fleeter than a bird in its flight he breaks through the crowd, strikes the beast with his sword and drives the cold blade home.' The whole of the royal family, women included, watched from a safe distance.

Charlemagne also enjoyed swimming. Aachen was known to the Romans because of its healing springs and now the barbarian king 'delighted in the hot vapour of the water' that his forerunners had enjoyed. He built a swimming pool, with fine marble steps going down to the water, where he swam as often as possible, together with as many other people as he could persuade to come in, often 100 at a time. For he lived continually surrounded by crowds of people; he did not like being alone, and his friends were expected to appear early in the morning, while he was still dressing, and begin to talk, to talk at meal times unless a book was read aloud, to talk in the swimming bath. They discussed serious matters, but they also made absurd jokes and asked each other riddles. The palace was crowded with his family, friends, war leaders, fighting men, clerks, huntsmen and servants, priests and monks. As he married four times, and also had a number of mistresses, all of whom had children except two, his family was large and he loved them dearly. His sons he could not keep at home, for they soon had estates and titles and duties of their own; but his daughters were always with him, because he was so possessive of them that none ever married and left the court for their husband's homes.

There was also a steady stream of visitors: perhaps a poor man

who came with a plea for justice, and 'no man cried out to him (Charlemagne) but straightway he could have good justice'; or a foreign envoy with greetings and requests for friendship, bringing with him suitable gifts. Harun al Raschid of Persia, for instance, sent monkeys, spices, scents, and an elephant called Abulabaz which lived at Aachen for ten years. The King of Africa sent a lion, a bear, some iron, and some fine Tyrian purple, and Charlemagne, who knew that, in spite of these gifts, the king and his subjects were very poor, sent back a good supply of oil, wine, and corn by the envoys. But this was an unusual gift; generally he sent Frankish robes of white, grey, blue, and red, fine swords, and dogs of remarkable swiftness and ferocity.

But, of course, the king's time was not entirely taken up with hunting and swimming, with his family and his official guests. All through his long reign he was incessantly active in the business of governing his vast and growing territories. He gave a great deal of time to his royal estates, of which he had a marvellously complete knowledge. It was important that they produced as much as possible, and he ordered his stewards to keep the buildings and fences in good repair, to see that on each estate the chambers were provided with 'counterpanes, cushions, pillows, bed clothes, and coverings for tables and benches', so that these did not have to be brought along when he came to stay. There were to be plenty of cooking utensils and tools, and these were listed, even down to frying-pans, axes, knives, and spades. All the food produced on the estate, sausages, salted meat, lard, butter, beer, honey, wax, and so on were to be prepared 'with the greatest cleanliness'. The separate buildings where the women worked at their spinning and weaving were to be properly heated in winter. Charlemagne must have had an extraordinary knowledge of farming and gardening, of seeds, animals, and implements. Horses were bred with special care, for they were very valuable for military service, and he ordered their food: fresh grass, hay, straw, oats, peas and beans. He also sent his stewards a list of 74 plants he wanted grown on his estates, including many of the vegetables we still eat today, and of the trees to be set in the orchards, apples, plums, peaches, cherries, figs, and several kinds of nuts. There were to be flowers too, and the stewards were to keep a number of specially beautiful birds, swans, pheasants, peacocks, and turtle doves 'for the sake of ornament' and not only for food.

But Charlemagne had far grimmer occupations than closely watching over his estates. In the 46 years of his reign he made war almost continually, he ordered and often led no fewer than 60 military expeditions. Einhard busily gives a list of the victims. 'This great king', he says, 'waged war with the utmost skill and success' against Aquitanians, Lombards, Saxons, Gascons, Bretons,

Empire of Charlemagne.

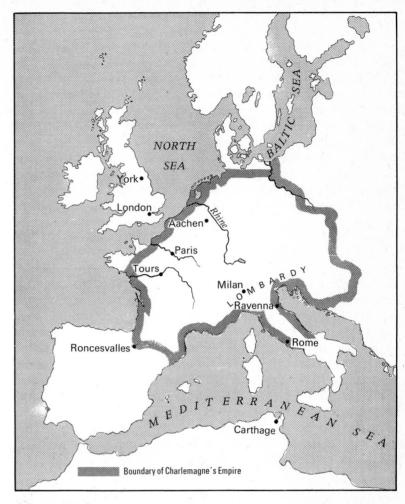

Boundary of Charlemagne's Empire

Slavs, Bavarians, Huns, Avars, and Northmen. Nearly every year, after he had met the important warriors and leaders of his kingdom in May, he or his war-leaders set out in the summer months on a merciless march into enemy country. 'The king is gone to lay waste the land of the Saxons' says Alcuin in one of his letters. Many of these expeditions were in defence of the frontiers, but in others Charles pushed those frontiers so far forward and in so many directions that by the end of his reign he had almost doubled his kingdom, and, as you can see from the map on this page, he ruled over almost all western Europe, except Spain and the south of Italy. The most merciless of all his wars were the ones he fought against the Saxons, whose kith and kin had crossed to Britain in the fifth century, and, being more ignorant than other barbarians, had there blotted out almost every trace of Roman civilization and nearly extinguished the British people themselves.

These 'detestable and oath-breaking pagans' lived to the north and east of the mighty Rhine and were a perpetual menace to the Franks. Their small villages were scattered about in deep forests and boggy plains, and here they hunted, drove their herds of pigs, goats, and scrawny cattle, and grew wretched crops of rye, barley, and oats, for they were most ignorant and unskilful farmers. It was a dark and uncertain existence, squatting there in poverty and squalor, and sheer hunger often drove them to unite in their favourite exploit of raiding peaceful or unsuspecting neighbours. For years Charlemagne tried to quell them by ferocious counter-raids. He laid waste the land, he destroyed the great mystic tree which the Saxons worshipped, for they believed it held up the sky above the world, but nothing had any permanent effect. At last he decided to wage war on them till they were conquered or totally annihilated, and after three more years of furious fighting he had them at his mercy. Perhaps to rule the Saxons with a rod of iron was the only way of ruling them at all, but it seems very strange to us that he also felt it right to convert them forcibly to Christianity. Baptism was made compulsory on pain of death. Death, too, was the penalty for attacking a church, a priest, or a monk, or for being found worshipping a pagan god. Charlemagne must have felt that to drag or drive a pagan into the Christian faith not only would save his immortal soul, but was the best way of making him behave himself, and there were some priests and monks who had the same crude idea. But some did not, and among these was Alcuin the Englishman, who had the courage to disagree with the king: 'Our Lord commanded us', he said, 'to teach the Christian faith and then, *after it had been accepted*, to baptize. How can the wretched Saxons be forced to believe what they do not believe?'

Obviously there were times when Charlemagne was as cruel and barbaric in his deeds as any of his forerunners, even though by nature he was a kindly lenient man. His third wife Fastrada was well-known for her cruelty, and, according to Einhard, as long as she was alive she often seems to have persuaded him to turn aside from his usual easy-going generosity. For he was really very far from being a complete barbarian. He believed it was part of his duty as a king to enlighten the minds of his subjects—impatiently forcing the Saxons to become Christians was a rough and ready way of doing this. He did all he could to foster the Christian faith. He himself was hungry for learning and knowledge of every sort, and this is why Einhard could write that he was 'beyond all kings most eager in making search for wise men, in giving them such entertainment that they might pursue philosophy in all comfort, whereby he made his kingdom radiant with fresh knowledge, hitherto unknown in our barbarism'.

As you know, one of these wise men, and the most dearly loved

of all by Charlemagne, was Alcuin. The two men, who were to be close friends for more than 20 years, first met in Italy, where Charlemagne had just spent months in subduing the Lombards, the most constant and bitter enemies of the Pope, and Alcuin was on his way home to Northumbria after a visit to Rome. The king took an instant liking to him, and pressed him to come to Aachen and take over the palace school there; and though Alcuin refused at first, for he was very reluctant to leave home permanently, at last he consented, gave up his work in York, and went to Aachen. His quiet and unspectacular arrival—all his life he was simple in his tastes and did not go in for grandeur—was one of the most important things that ever happened, because from that day on, until he died in 804, he had more influence than any other person over the most powerful man in Europe.

Alcuin did not start the school in the palace. Every great household of the time contained a number of boys of noble birth who went there to learn the behaviour and the habits of their class, to hunt, to fight, to dress properly, and generally to find their feet in society, and the greater the household the greater the advantage of being trained in it. They learned chiefly by attending the king's person, waiting at his table, mixing with his family and retainers, and having some instruction dinned into them by elderly and experienced warriors. It was not unknown for some of them to learn to read, but this was far from necessary, and at Aachen the young sprigs of nobility must have been surprised—and not very pleasantly surprised—to find that with Alcuin as their tutor their education was to go far beyond a hazy knowledge of their ABC, and was to include reading, writing, arithmetic, astronomy, and the art of arguing in a reasonable way. These were matters that seldom troubled the heads of Frankish warriors, and which many of them probably felt were beneath them and best left to monks; and to teach them to rumbustious boys and fierce young men could have been an impossible job for Alcuin, but for three things. He was a born teacher, able to intoxicate his pupils with what he liked to call 'the old wine of ancient studies and the apples of grammar', which simply meant that he had the gift of making everything interesting; he had a great gift, too, for making friends; he had also the king and his family as his pupils, and their example must have subdued the resistance of the most unruly young noble. In fact the school was an extraordinary mixture. There was Charlemagne himself eager to study anything that Alcuin put before him, specially interested in astronomy and 'the marshalling of the stars', scratching his ear, we are told by Einhard, and snorting through his nose when he was thinking deeply; there was his fourth wife, the fair lady Luitprand, and all the flaxen-headed royal children; there were courtiers of every age and kind. Some were themselves to

Cover of a Gospel book beautifully carved in ivory and made in Charlemagne's court.

carry their learning far beyond Aachen and its palace, and to have a deep influence on men and women in many parts of the kingdom. Others, who usually led lives of violent exercise and vast meals, whose pleasure lay in deep drinking and hunting rather than reading

books, could cudgel very little into their thick heads, but came to school because it was the will of the king. Among them all was Alcuin, who rose with the sun to prepare his lessons, was always busy, always ready to answer questions, exceedingly respected for his learning, but also loved and teased, when, for instance, even at the most splendid feasts he insisted on eating only porridge and cheese. He was helped at first by three young monks, Witzo, Fridugis, and Sigulf, who went with him from York, and later by others, who came and went between Frankland and Northumbria, bringing back to Charlemagne's court what Alcuin called 'the flowers of Britain', those choice books for which he hungered. No doubt they also helped him to write his own textbooks for his pupils, among them one specially produced for Charlemagne's second son 'The Royal and most Noble Youth Pepin', and one called 'Problems for sharpening the wits of youth'. The book contained 53 problems, some of which seem very familiar to us, like this one, which goes:

A ladder has a hundred rungs. On the first rung sits one pigeon, on the second two, on the third three, and so on up to the hundredth. How many pigeons in all?

The king's enthusiasm for learning and the teaching of Alcuin had an influence in Europe which grew steadily as the years passed, for they never ceased to kindle enthusiasm in others. Both men grew old, but still they laboured on. 'In the morning with the zeal of youth I sowed the seed in Britain' wrote Alcuin, 'Now as evening draws on and my blood grows cold I still sow in Frankland.' Many who lived and worked with him in the palace school were made bishops and abbots by Charlemagne, and in their households and monasteries other schools were started and libraries grew. Monasteries, which in any case impressed the toughest Frank or Saxon with their holy peace and 'marvellous freedom from the tumult of the world', were, by the king's desire, to be places where at the very least there were to be copies of the Psalms, and of arithmetic and grammar books, where 'the faithful might send their children for the learning of their letters'. Many were, of course, far more than that—great centres of learning, where not only were books read and studied, but also produced: they were workshops where manuscripts were copied slowly by hand and bound with care, sometimes, with the most amazing skill, in glorious materials, like the one shown on page 94. Charlemagne even kept his eye on that, and had directions sent round to say that books must never be copied carelessly or by boys, but only 'by men of full age with all diligence'.

By the year 800 Charlemagne was without a doubt the most famous man in Europe and even beyond, known not only as a great warrior, victorious and rich in treasure, but as a ruler 'surpassing all others in power and outshining them in wisdom' and in the vastness

of his dominions. In December of that year he was staying in Rome, having gone there to extricate the Pope yet again from difficulties, this time the malice of his personal enemies. For years now, ever since the conquests of Justinian crumbled and the Lombards over-ran Italy, the popes had relied on the Franks for help, and Charlemagne, who had conquered the Lombards, now bore the title 'king of the Lombards'. On Christmas Day 800 he went to Mass in the church of St. Peter, and just as the service ended Pope Leo III lifted a golden crown from the altar and, turning to where Charles still knelt in prayer, placed it on his head. Immediately the congregation rose and shouted aloud the words 'Carolo Augusto, a Deo coronato, magno et pacifico, imperatori Romanorum, vita et victoria' ('Life and victory to Charles Augustus, crowned by God, the great and peaceful emperor of the Romans'). It must have been a startling moment, yet probably very few people in the church were taken by surprise. Charles must have known what the Pope intended to do—in any case he could hardly have missed seeing a large gold crown on the altar—and the acclamation was too long and too carefully thought out for the congregation to say it all together, unless they had rehearsed beforehand. Charles was, in fact, being publicly recognized as the greatest ruler in Europe, a man for whom the title of king no longer seemed enough, for whom the ancient titles by which the rulers of imperial Rome were known, Augustus and Imperator, seemed more fitting. But he was not the new ruler of a resurrected Roman empire. In the West that had been destroyed for ever: in the East, in Constantinople, there was still an emperor.

Charlemagne dressed up as a Roman emperor. The coin is still crude though slightly less so than the one on page 29.

The ceremony in St. Peter's made little difference to Charlemagne in day-to-day affairs. Although he used his new titles on official documents, which went out in the name of 'the most glorious Charles, Imperator et Augustus', and on coins like the silver penny shown on this page, he never went to Rome again, nor did he suddenly begin to appear in a toga and a laurel wreath, even though he is shown wearing these on the coin. According to Einhard, 'he turned his attention to the laws of his people', and spent the remaining 14 years of his life labouring at the business of governing those vast dominions, which, though they were never the size of the Roman empire at its greatest, were far too big for one man, even a man like Charlemagne, to rule over with complete success.

He had enormous problems. Rome had built up, bit by bit, elaborate machinery for the government of the empire, with cohorts of judges, tax-collectors, civil servants, and governors of cities and provinces, all quite apart from the imperial army. The machine had worked efficiently because communications were good, because there was, as you know from Chapter 3, the same law for every free Roman citizen, whether he lived in Gaul, Italy, North

Africa, or Britain, and because written records were carefully kept of taxes due and paid, and other official business. But by the ninth century practically all of this had either disappeared or long ceased to work. The roads along which not only legions but imperial messengers and officials had moved with impressive speed were now full of ruts and holes and empty of legions, and travel was slow and dangerous. For instance, it took the best part of a year to go from Aachen to Constantinople and back by the quickest route. Many of the cities where governors had lived and judges had held their courts were gloomy ruins. The Franks did not keep records, and there was no thought of one law for men of all races, for the Frankish way was for a man to be judged according to the laws of his tribe or group, however crude and savage this might be. Because the Franks did not understand the Roman system of law and order they had no idea how to keep it going, so it simply fell to pieces. In its place was only the king, who governed by his own personal efforts and the work of the chief men of his household. Charlemagne used such men for all kinds of royal business. Some were made counts and sent to live in every part of the kingdom, to represent him, and guard the royal rights, and keep the peace. Counts had great power over the people in their districts, and because of this they could ill-treat them very badly. They had to be carefully watched, and four times a year each one was visited and inspected by two royal envoys called *missi dominici*—*missus* means messenger—who linked them with the king's person, and if necessary gave them a sharp reminder of his will.

The *missi* had a tough job. Obviously a good many counts, much enjoying their power, and a comfortably long way from their royal master, resented these visitations and did not like to be reminded of their duties. They were obliged to listen to the latest decrees from Charlemagne, which would be read aloud—one of the *missi* was always a bishop or an abbot, so there was always one who could read—, but you can guess that, though they kept quiet while the visitation took place, some of them made little attempt to carry out the orders when the *missi* had departed. They did not try to see, for instance, that churches were well built and kept in repair; they did not reprove priests who got drunk, failed to teach the Creed and the Lord's Prayer to their people, and used the church for storing hay; they did not punish men for the crimes that specially dishonoured 'the peace of the lord king'.

Besides bringing royal decrees the *missi dominici* inspected churches and monasteries, reprimanded lazy priests and monks, listened to complaints, and judged those accused of oppressing widows, orphans, and poor folk who could not defend themselves, or of burning down a man's house and stable, or breaking down his fence.

One of Alcuin's friends, Theodulf, Bishop of Orleans, a scholar and poet who had lived in the royal household at Aachen, was used by Charlemagne as one of a pair of *missi dominici*, and he wrote a long witty poem warning others of what they would have to face. People are so dishonest, he says, that everyone will try to buy your favour, and they will offer you bribes of every sort and kind, ranging from jewels, armour, and horses from rich men, to hats, shoes, gloves, and face-towels from the poorer ones. These should all be refused by an honest judge, but there is no harm in accepting small friendly gifts like eggs and cheese and garden produce, and an occasional fat pullet. Theodulf himself enjoyed good food—he was one of those who teased Alcuin about his cheese and porridge—, but he urges judges not to eat and drink gluttonously, for this will make them flabby and inactive and unfit to concentrate on difficult matters that need close attention and quick thinking. A judge must be punctual at the court, and he must keep order and be able to quell insolent men, but he should be able to control himself when people are exceptionally tiresome and not be tempted to seize a stick and beat them. Theodulf, though himself a man of barbarian descent— he was a Visigoth—, found the many different kinds of law by which men were judged clumsy and he disliked the noisy habit of oath-taking in court. He longed, as barbarians often did, for the old dignity and order of the vanished Roman ways.

Backed by the power and glorious name of Charlemagne, the *missi dominici* strove to keep a check on the counts, but you can imagine how quickly, when they had gone, the worst and greediest would throw off their good behaviour, would oppress the weak, and build up their own power till they were dangerously strong, strong enough, in fact, to flout the will of a weaker king than Charlemagne. And Charlemagne could not live for ever. In January 814, now lame and very lonely, for he had lost his wife, the gentle Luitgard, two of his sons, and nearly all his old friends including Alcuin, he died in his palace of Aachen. He was buried in the church he had built there, under the great marble columns he had brought from Rome and Ravenna, and at a moment when the skies were darkening over his empire.

Chapter 7
The Break-up of Charlemagne's Empire

The empire over which Charlemagne had reigned for 47 years—called after him the Carolingian empire—passed to his son Louis whole and undivided. For a time men must have rejoiced that Louis seemed so like his splendid father. Like Charlemagne he was impressive to look at, handsome, tall, strong; like him, he revelled in hunting and in all sorts of violent but fashionable exercise; like him, he had been one of Alcuin's most eager pupils, had learnt to speak Latin, and was a diligent reader, which was unusual for a man of high birth who was not a monk or a priest. He was 'of all emperors the most zealous on behalf of the Church of God'. But there the likeness ended, for Louis had none of his father's greatness. He was given the nicknames of Louis the Pious, Louis the Good, and Louis the Monk; indeed, he would have made a useful and learned monk, even a successful abbot, but as an emperor in those tumultuous times he was a failure. When he died the empire was rapidly falling apart, and there lay ahead another long confused period of darkness and insecurity as dreadful as any so far described in this book, and perhaps even harder for men to bear, because they had seen glimpses of peace and order under Charlemagne.

Of course, this was not all the fault of Louis the Pious, though his weakness made matters worse. In any case, the empire was too big for anyone but a tremendous person like Charlemagne to quell, defend, and hold together, and even he did not manage it completely. For one thing, it had no unity of its own. It contained a great mixture of races, Franks, Saxons, Lombards, and Gallo-Romans, to mention only some; races which spoke in different tongues, so that even the men who were about the person of the king could not always understand each other. Latin had once been used all through the Roman empire, but now only churchmen and a few unusually well educated nobles spoke it—often rather badly, too—, and nothing had taken its place as a common language. For instance, an oath sworn in 842 by two of Louis's sons had to be written down first as 'Pro Deo armour et pro Christian poblo', and then as 'In Goddes minna und in thes Christianes folches'—both meaning 'For the love of God and for Christian People'. Otherwise their two armies would not have known what was going on.

Another difficulty came from the different laws and customs by which the different races lived. Theodulf of Orleans was not the only person to lament the confusion caused by this. Another bishop equally irritated by it wrote: 'It constantly happens that out of five men walking together or sitting side by side, no two have the same earthly law.' Such differences divided the people of the empire.

Then, again, the Franks still stuck to their custom of dividing the lands of a dead man as equally as possible between his sons, and Charlemagne had not tried to alter this, perhaps because he was a Frank to the core, perhaps because he did not realize its dangers. Louis the Pious had become sole ruler of the empire only because his other brothers were dead and he got their shares. He himself had four sons, and he at once set about arranging for each to have a part of his dominions to govern under him, three as kings and the eldest with the title of emperor. The results were disastrous. His sons, and later his grandsons, hardly stopped quarrelling and fighting among themselves, and the empire was torn in pieces by their struggles for bigger shares and more power. Such a state of things would have been bad enough in peaceful times, but now it was fatal, for all through the ninth and tenth centuries the empire was threatened on every side by new dangers.

So far each chapter in this book has had something in it, even if only a few sentences, about barbarian invasions, and you might expect that after 500 years and more, these really ought to be over. But they were not, and the storm which broke over the Carolingian empire came from the last barbarian invasions. You may have heard of the prayer used by the unhappy people of England in the time of Alfred the Great: 'A furore Normanorum libera nos Domine' ('From the fury of the Northmen, deliver us, O Lord'), but the Anglo-Saxons were not the only people at that time to plead for deliverance from a dreadful enemy. All over Europe men must have prayed much the same prayer; 'Deliver us, O Lord', they cried, 'from the arrows of the Hungarians' or 'from the pagans' or 'from the savage Northmen', and while the descendants of Charlemagne were distracted by their family quarrels and jealousy, their lands and their wretched subjects were being attacked by Hungarians, by Saracens (always known as pagans), and by Northmen, and sometimes by all three.

The Hungarians, 'a people greedy, reckless, ignorant of God, and only eager for murder and robbery', as an Italian monk wrote at the time, came in the ninth century from the east, from beyond the River Danube. They chiefly harried the eastern part of the empire, though they got through to France, and crossed the Alps to raid Italy and plunder Rome.

The Saracens, who won control of the Mediterranean sea, and

101

mastered Sicily, also plundered Rome. They struck chiefly in the south. Besides being sea pirates they had an unpleasant habit of making a nest in some inaccessible spot on land, and darting out from it like furious wasps to attack everything within reach. One of these nests was hidden deep in the desolate marshes round the mouth of the river Rhone, and another was on a mountain, also in the south of France, which is still called 'Mont de Maures'. Thick thorn scrub covered three sides of the mountain, on the fourth was the sea, and only one secret track led to the top, which no one was very keen to look for. Year after year the Saracens swooped out of the thorns, through the forests, and down to their hidden boats to raid the seas, or inland to fall on distant villages and monasteries, so that men lived in constant dread, for nowhere seemed safe from them, and when they climbed back to their eyrie with spoils, and prisoners to be sold as slaves, they left the land behind them like a desert.

Hungarians and Saracens were bad enough, but more terrible still were the Northmen, the Vikings, who plagued the whole of Europe for more than 250 years—as you can easily calculate, if you remember that their first raid on Lindisfarne, which made Alcuin so unhappy, was in 793, and their last two expeditions to England were in 1066. One of these was defeated by Harold the king; the other, which was not, we call the Norman Conquest.

The Northmen came from Scandinavia, from Norway, Sweden, and Denmark, and can also be called Norwegians, Swedes, and Danes. Their other name, Viking, means 'seafarer in search of adventure', and to go viking was an old pastime of theirs. It meant making occasional short sharp plundering raids, quick-in and quick-out, on any desirable places within reach by sea. For they were most skilful and daring sailors, who began to handle boats almost as soon as they could walk, since in their homelands it was often much quicker and easier to travel from place to place by sea than overland. The Lindisfarne raid was one of their lightning attacks, but soon afterwards they changed their ways, and instead of making quick raids in small numbers, perhaps only a single ship-load, they began to descend in great swarms all through the summer months on undefended places, and to travel much farther to do so. In the autumn they sailed home, and if the expedition had been profitable they spent the winter in plenty, living on their spoils. Then it was that in the long dark evenings they enthralled their kinsmen with the tales of their adventures as they sat by the fire and planned for the next spring sailing. They told of villages and towns lying open and unprotected, of monasteries and churches full of rich hangings and gold and silver crosses and vessels, and of warm farm-houses and deep pastures, all to be won by the bold and

cunning. Their minstrels made songs out of their talk, and one of these tells how

> They bent their backs to the oars
> They hewed with their axes
> They put their fingers to the bowstrings and shot deftly
> And reddened their swords far and wide.

It is easy to imagine how such stories stirred men's hearts, and how the desire to sail with the next host drew them like magic, but this was not the only reason why the menace from the Northmen grew so formidable. Another was that they became desperately hungry for land, land to grow crops of barley, oats, and rye for themselves and hay for their cattle. And they were very short of land. In Norway, for instance, they had to cultivate every small patch of soil that could be reached by clambering high up among the rocks, even if it was not much bigger than the sail of one of their ships, and this meant hard bitter work. In winter, when hay ran short, as it often did, the cows were fed on a mixture of birch twigs, moss, and pine needles, and this might keep them alive till the spring, but did not produce much milk or butter for hungry families. If the summer was a bad one and the crops failed, the winter seemed long and cruel almost beyond endurance, and when the weather was too stormy to go fishing, hunger drove people to eat seaweed, bark, and the grey lichen from the rocks. As families grew, it became more and more difficult to make the food go round; the little fields crept up the mountain sides till they reached the snow line, where nothing would grow however hard a man worked; and you can understand why the Northmen were greedy for the rich pastures of Ireland or England or France, where, according to the story-tellers, every green blade dripped butter.

Another reason why the Northmen were driven to go viking was that, unlike the Franks, they had the custom of leaving the whole of their property at death to the eldest born; and as they usually had big families this meant that there were always many younger sons who got nothing when the father died, and were forced to find some way of winning land and fame for themselves. These were young hot-blooded men, fearless, hard, and boisterous, 'who loved the clang of iron and the clash of shields', and eagerly filled the ships that might carry them to adventure and wealth. It was far better to seek the unknown than to idle in a brother's house and have to look to him for everything. 'Time it is to fare', two of them sang as they left home, 'over the misty ways. We shall both return unless all-powerful death shall seize us.'

And the last reason for the great upsurge of voyaging in the ninth and tenth centuries was that the Northmen had by that time so

Viking weapons and armour,
and part of a hoard of coins and
ornaments collected during a
raid.

105

perfected their skill in building ships that they made the best in the world, able to sail in any sea: in the cruel tides round Scotland, which even now can overturn a lifeboat, or in the huge Atlantic rollers. We know a good deal about these ships, because Northmen loved and cherished them, and often carved pictures of them in stone and wood, which you can still see in certain parts of Norway and Sweden. Better still, they sometimes buried them whole with their dead owners, and a few of these have been found, carefully dug up, and pieced together. One was at Gokstad in Norway, and the skeleton of the owner lay in it, a man about 5½ feet tall, well armed, and well supplied with goods that he might need in the next world—cups and candlesticks and a little sledge. This ship, superbly built, was 76 feet long, and had places for 32 oarsmen, 16 each side, but most ships were smaller than this—made for, perhaps, 20 oarsmen. In spite of the oars, they were first and foremost sailing ships, with masts of pine and square sails, striped or chequered in black and yellow, red, or blue. The oars were only used if the wind died away, or when the ship had to be manoeuvred up a narrow fiord or river. Because it was often difficult to turn round in such places, both ends of the ship, the prow and the stern, were pointed, so that it could move as easily backwards as forwards and would not need to turn. Often each end bore on it the strange head of a dragon or a bird carved in wood; this was partly because the Northmen were expert carvers and liked to use their skill on their cherished ships, and partly to give an extra look of strangeness and ferocity to depress their enemies as they neared the land.

These splendid ships moved fast. With a good following wind to fill the sails they covered 75–100 miles in a single day, and though such voyages were often exceedingly grim and perilous, the Northmen despised softness and had no fear of danger. When they quietly dropped anchor in some foreign river they quickly forgot the cold and wet, as they put on their nut-shaped helmets and coats of leather or mail, and pulled out the bright swords and axes which had been carefully stowed away to keep them safe from saltwater rust. Then they thought only of the pleasure ahead, the reddening swords and the spoils, the fame if they went home, the good land to be seized if they stayed.

They travelled immense distances, and you can see from the map on page 107 some of the places they reached: England, Scotland, Ireland and the outlying islands, Iceland, Greenland, and in 1005 even America, 500 years before Columbus. Some, sailing far to the south and raiding the coasts as they went, reached the Mediterranean Sea and fought the Saracens for the possession of Sicily. The Swedes turned east, mastered the Baltic Sea, and thrust overland into the heart of Russia. We actually know the name of

Above A strange bird head carved from the prow of a Viking ship, now in the British Museum.

Top right Invasions of the Vikings, Hungarians and Saracens in the 10th century.

Bottom right The famous Gokstad ship, Oslo, Norway.

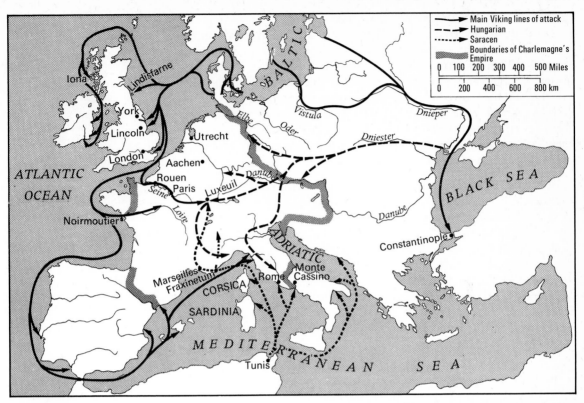

one leader who did this more than 1,000 years ago, for when 'all-powerful death' seized him and he did not return home his sons put up a memorial to him, and carved on it 'Retel and Bjorn raised this stone for Thorstein their father. He fell in battle east in Russia, leader of a host and the best of men from this land.' You can still see the stone in Sweden, and also another one which tells of a certain warrior called Rognvald who fought in 'Greekland': for some hosts, travelling many hundreds of miles by land and rivers, came at last to the great walls of Constantinople, and saw the marvellous dome of Sancta Sophia towering above them.

For long Europe lay almost defenceless before these tireless enemies. Charlemagne had fortified some coast towns before he died, but Louis the Pious was not a far-sighted person. For instance, quite early in his reign, 'because he enjoyed at that moment a deep peace and feared not the invasions of *any* barbarians', he gave leave for the stout walls built round the city of Rheims by the Romans to be pulled down, so that the stones could be used to rebuild the cathedral. This was very generous to the cathedral, but most unwise, and 50 years later the men of Rheims were forced 'in their great anguish' to rebuild their walls against the Northmen.

'Great anguish' afflicted countless others besides the men of Rheims. People who lived near the sea or near the mouth of a river were the first to suffer, but the Northmen had no fear of venturing on the land, and often one of the first things they did was to seize all the horses they could find. Then they rode very swiftly inland, usually by night, suddenly appearing out of the dark before distant villages, farms, and monasteries, to burn, kill, and rob, and return to load their ships with plunder and prisoners almost before the inhabitants realized what was happening.

During the summer months no place seemed safe from their incessant raids. The monks of Noirmoutier in France learned this only too well. Their abbey was on an island not far from the mouth of the river Loire, and when the dreaded square sails first began to appear round the coast, they prudently built a refuge some miles inland and spent the spring and summer there, returning to Noirmoutier when autumn came and the Northmen went home. But soon the island was so constantly ravaged that there was no food for them when they went back for the winter, and so they moved permanently inland, leaving the monastery empty and desolate. Even then they were not left in peace, and between 836 and 875 they had to move six times before at last they found a place of tranquillity. It is not at all surprising that the chronicles of the time, mostly written by monks, are full of misery and foreboding. One of them, written in a monastery which lay in the path of the Northmen by an unknown monk who must have seen with his own

This magnificent lion now sits outside the Arsenal in Venice. Venetians looted it from Piraeus, the harbour of Athens. It has a runic inscription on its shoulder carved by a Viking who reached Greece, and then served in the bodyguard of the Byzantine emperor.

Charlemagne's empire divided between his grandsons.

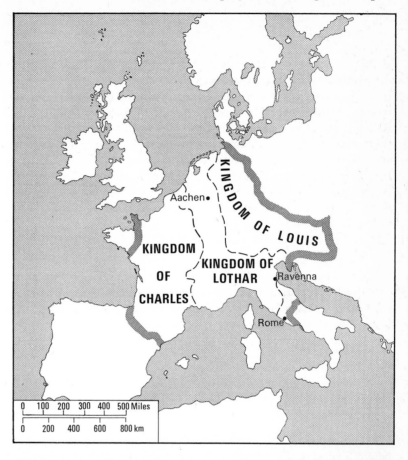

eyes the things he described, says 'Never do the Northmen cease to take captive and to kill Christian folk, to destroy churches and ramparts, to burn houses in flames. Through all the streets the dead are lying, noble and humble, priest and lay folk, women and men, youth and little children. Everywhere is tribulation and Christian folk brought to utter ruin and desolation.' To such writers the Northmen must have seemed nothing but blood-thirsty brutes, and yet it is wrong to think of them only so. Behind the fierce destroyers were sober hardworking forefathers, farmers, craftsmen, and shrewd traders, and when the turmoil was over and they occupied some of the lands they had raided, they settled down with their families into these occupations, solid, skilful, and business-like.

Before this happened, however, many things changed. After Louis the Pious died in 840 the last link which held the empire together snapped, and his three remaining sons divided it among themselves. The map above shows how it was done, and also shows how the shapes of France and Germany are beginning to

appear. The long narrow kingdom between them soon shrank until it was only a small state, one that has been fought and quarrelled over ever since. But even the other two were shaky and disorderly at the start. The strength of Charlemagne had ebbed away and his descendants were utterly inefficient. Occasionally some of them tried to oppose the Northmen, but others paid handsome sums of money to bribe them to go away, only to find, as Ethelred the Redeless found in England, that the money bought no more than a short breathing-space. One of them allowed Rollo the Northman and his host to settle permanently on some of the best land in France, soon known as the Land of the Northmen, and later as Normandy. This settlement took place in 912, and 154 years later Rollo's descendant set sail across the Channel from Normandy to raid England, and ended by conquering it. He was William the Conqueror, and you can read more about him in Chapter 11.

Yet the Northmen were not really invincible, as Alfred the Great proved. Most of their success and the helpless terror they caused was due to speed and surprise, and they were far less good at prolonged fighting, or at maintaining the dull patient siege of a town, and they could be very careless if taken by surprise themselves. One of their songs makes this quite clear.

> On we go in battle line
> Unarmoured against bright blades
> Helmets shine but I have none
> All our mail shirts are down at the ships.

The difficulty was to catch them and confront them at once with bright blades, skilful fingers on bow strings, the clash of spears, and all that they had taught men to fear so greatly. And this was difficult to do, because to alert the king was a slow business. Even if a messenger was sent off at once for help, he might have to ride to two or three royal estates before he caught up with the court, and by the time the king had thought and hesitated and at last decided— if he did decide—to come to the rescue, and had ridden back to the scene of disaster, the Northmen were miles away. People in trouble soon learned that nine times out of ten it was useless to seek help from the king. The only hope lay in the power of some tough man who was on the spot. Obviously such a neighbour would have to be a bold fighter, commanding plenty of equally bold and well-armed followers, and because it was very expensive to keep such men he would have to be wealthy himself. Nowadays wealth can come from land, or mines, or oil-wells, from factories or shops, but in those days almost the only source of wealth was land, and so a man's wealth depended on the amount of it he owned. Even the king depended on the soil to support himself, his family, and his court, and to pay for the business of government; and, as you know,

The 'bright blade' of a Viking warrior.

Charlemagne travelled continuously from one royal estate to another, using the produce of the soil, wheat, butter, cheese, eggs,
honey, wool, and linen, which was stored for him on each one.
Apart from the large royal share of the land, the fields and meadows
and vineyards, the forests, heaths, bogs, and hills were owned
almost entirely by two groups of people, the Church and the
nobility, or, as Alfred of England once called them, the men who
prayed and the men who fought. Alfred also mentioned a third
group, the men who worked, and you will hear more about them in
the next chapter. They owned no land and were very poor.

A good example of a man who fought in the dark years of the
tenth century, when the empire of Charlemagne had broken up
and the fury of invaders was terrible to endure, was Henry the
Fowler, Duke of Saxony, and he was exactly the sort of strong
neighbour to whom men turned when the king failed them. Indeed,
he grappled with both Hungarians and Vikings—and sometimes
with lawless men of his own Saxony too—, and defeated them by
hunger and by sword, or by wearing them down.

First of all he realized, as Alfred did in England, that open
villages and undefended towns simply asked to be attacked, and so
he used Alfred's plan of making fortified places—in England called
'burhs'—which people could reach quickly if news came to a
neighbourhood of an approaching enemy. Each burh was put in
charge of nine men, one of whom had to be always on the look-out
and busy building shelters for men and beasts inside the defences,
while the others farmed their own land and his, and then brought
one-third of the produce to be stored in the burh against the time
of need. Such places were reasonably safe as refuges, and their very
existence slowed down the dreadful swiftness of the Northmen,
who dared not leave an uncaptured stronghold between them and
their ships, and so had to stop and lay siege. This gave time for a
resistance-force to reach the spot and fight.

Henry the Fowler was often able to supply this, for he maintained
in his household a striking-force of fighting men—huge eaters,
deep drinkers, often bandy-legged from much riding. One of them
was well described in four lines of a contemporary poem:

> By God! fair sir! He's of your line indeed,
> Who thus devours a mighty haunch of boar,
> And drinks of wine a gallon at two gulps
> Pity the man on whom he wages war!

Hard and bold like their lord, they were a match for the Northmen
and the Hungarians in their speed and ferocity, and they went
everywhere with the duke, sat with him at table, guarded his
person, and fought at his will. In return Henry gave them food,

111

shelter, arms, and horses, and sometimes he dealt out a choice bit of plunder among them, gold chains and rings and good swords. Sometimes, too, he rewarded one of them with a parcel of land, and this was useful, for it meant that the man then had to keep himself and Henry saved the expense of his equipment.

These men were known as the vassals of the duke. They were all free men and well born, some were his young kinsfolk, and some had come to him simply because they lived entirely for hunting and fighting and knew that in serving Henry they were likely to get plenty of both. But some there were who joined themselves to him for a quite different reason, because in those perilous days they urgently sought someone stronger than themselves to aid and sustain them and were willing to pay a price for this. Imagine one such man, Bruno by name, a man of good birth, a man who fought, but not on a large scale. He owned only a modest amount of land, and though he lived in a house of good stone, with stables, a kitchen, a bake-house, a barn, and some huts for servants enclosed in a stout fence, the whole place was quite small, and it was in a dangerously lonely part of the country, surrounded by forests and, worse still, not far from a broad river. Lawless men and roving bands of Northmen frequently came out of the forests and from the river, and pestered Bruno to his great peril and dismay, for he and his fence and his handful of servants were little use against such marauders, and the time came when they hardly dared to work in the fields or drive the pigs into the forest to grub for acorns. His only hope was to get help from someone stronger than himself, and Bruno therefore presented himself to the great man Henry the Fowler to ask for it. Now Henry and men like him were always ready to grant such help—at a price—, and so Bruno the small man and Henry the great man made a bargain. Bruno had to hand over his house and land to the duke, and in return Henry promised to aid and sustain him. He might then join the duke's household as his vassal and a landless man, or he might hold and use during his life-time the land which had once been entirely his own; but in exchange he must turn up, fully armed, on a good horse, and carrying food for himself and fodder for his beast, wherever the duke needed him, and fight for forty days. Bruno became Henry's vassal, and Henry was henceforth his lord, and as lord and vassal they were closely bound together, each giving and getting something from their bargain. So that all might know of the bond between them, Bruno, on a certain day, came to do homage and swear fealty to the duke before his whole household. Then he put off his helmet, his sword, and his spurs, and knelt unarmed and in humble submission before the duke. He placed his two hands between Henry's, and in a loud voice, so that all should hear and bear witness, he swore the oath of fealty: 'I become your man from

Strongholds like the castle at Munzenberg above were built by lords to whom lesser men bound themselves as vassals.

this day forward, of life and limb and earthly worship, and unto you I will be true and faithful.' Then Henry kissed him as a sign of friendship, gave him back his sword, and ordered him to take again his helmet and spurs. In Bruno's case, because he was henceforth to hold his lands from the duke, Henry also put into his hands a small wedge of turf as a token of this, and the words 'for the lands I hold of you' were added on at the end of the oath. So a bond was made between them which could only be broken by death, a solemn thing in the eyes of all men, out of which there sometimes grew a deep devotion between lord and man, so that many vassals were quite ready to say:

> If my dear lord is slain, his fate I'll share;
> If he is hanged, then hang me by his side;
> If to the stake he goes, with him I'll burn;
> And if he's drowned, then let me drown with him.

The bargain seemed a good one. The face that Bruno looked up at as he knelt in submission, though a hard one and not particularly pleasant, was undoubtedly strong. He was now certain of this lord's aid, and he had the use of his lands and house. Henry for his part

113

The hall in Hedingham Castle. This was built more than 100 years after Henry the Fowler but it is the sort of hall in which a lord and his vassal would come face-to-face.

was lord of yet another estate, and had yet another man bound to give him military service, and this was the only way in which he could keep his power and his high name.

This kind of bargain, holding land in exchange for military service, was very old, so old that no one quite knows when it first began, but certainly it was before Henry the Fowler, and before Charlemagne too. You can imagine that it became much more common when men found their lands and lives threatened, for instance, by the Northmen, and at such times many were eager to commend themselves to a strong lord and become his vassal. It had such advantages that it spread all over Europe and became known as the feudal system, and because of it many vassals were able to frighten off their enemies by saying 'so long as my lord is safe and sound you can do no hurt to me', and many lords grew immensely strong and arrogant. Often, too, they became merciless and greedy, thinking more of their own profit than of the safety and well-being of their vassals, and as time went on it became the custom for them to demand a good deal more than military service in return for land. If, for instance, a vassal died and his son wanted to hold his father's land, he had, of course, to submit to his lord, do homage, and promise fealty and service, but he also had to fork out a 'relief'—a money payment—before he could do any of these things or have the land, and sometimes the lord demanded so much that he simply could not pay it. Then the land was utterly in the lord's hand to do with as he liked, and the heir became a landless man. If by chance the vassal left only a child as heir then the lord had the right of 'wardship', taking complete possession of the dead man's land and goods until the heir grew up. All the profits, after the child had been housed, fed, and clothed, went into his own pocket. Wardship over a girl had another advantage for the lord, because she was obliged to marry the man he chose for her, and this too he brought about to his own profit, even going so far sometimes as to sell an unhappy heiress to the highest bidder. So altogether it is not surprising that some feudal lords, with their lands, their armed vassals, their rights to reliefs and wardships, the strongholds they built for themselves, and so on, became as great as or greater than the king himself. This Henry the Fowler certainly was, for in 918, when the last direct descendant of Charlemagne lay dying, he ordered all his royal regalia, the gold ring and arm bracelets, the cloak, the sword, and the crown, to be sent to the duke, for he knew that there was no one else in the land strong enough to be called king. Henry knew well how to use the sword, and now he was able to wear the crown of Germany.

Chapter 8
The Manor

'God's house . . . is threefold, some pray in it, some fight in it, some work in it.' This is another way of saying what Alfred the Great thought—and other people in his day, and for long afterwards, too—about the way mankind was divided. We no longer believe in any such rigid classes, but it is important to realize that in the Middle Ages they were taken for granted, and also that two of them, the men who prayed and the men who fought, dominated Europe, and few people saw anything wrong in this. The men of prayer managed all through the darkest times to keep alive the love of learning, and continually taught the ways of holiness and salvation. The fighting men, from kings and dukes to simple knights, thought of war not as an occasional unpleasant necessity but as a worthy and essential occupation and their sole purpose in life. Both classes believed that they were absolutely necessary for the well-being of men in this world, and their salvation in the next, and that it was the will of God that they should continue and flourish. Between them, as you already know, nearly all the land of Europe was divided, and from land came wealth, but not automatically, as anyone who has a small back garden knows. Peas and lettuces will grow there if you cultivate it, but if you neglect it all you get is a crop of weeds, possibly beautiful to look at but not much use to eat or sell. This is true of any land at any time, and landowners in the Middle Ages knew quite well that, if they were to get the wealth they desired from their estates, someone had to work hard to produce it, some-one must plough, sow, and gather the harvest, make the hay, shear the sheep, milk the cows and goats, make cheese and lard, and do hundreds of other laborious jobs. This kind of work was thought vastly inferior to praying and fighting, and anyone who did it was regarded as inferior too. Knights never did menial work, and though the Rule of St. Benedict laid down that monks 'ought to be occupied at certain times with manual labour', the lands of the Church became so enormous that the labour of monks for 6 or 7 hours a day could never have cultivated more than a fraction of it; and, indeed, they became so wealthy that they did not need to. How were the two high classes to be supported in wealth and power? Who was to produce wealth from land? This is where the third class, the men of work, come into the picture; they were the peasants of Europe, whose lot in life, everywhere roughly the same,

The three divisions of 'God's house'. A medieval king dreams uneasily of the men who pray, fight, and work.

was to toil incessantly on the land of their lords, for the good of their lords, without praise or comfort, and often so near the hunger line that one wet summer and one bad harvest could bring them face to face with starvation.

Their work, the crops they grew, and the names given to their tools, their houses, and even to themselves varied with the part of Europe they lived in. In some places the most important crop was the grape-vine, in others corn; in France the plough was called '*araire*' or '*charrue*', in Germany '*pflug*'. Their lords varied, too, from great men with huge estates to poor knights with a few hundred acres. A lord could be a single individual, or the head of a community like the monastery of Saint Germain des Prés in France, whose estates were so vast that 10,026 peasants were working on them in the tenth century. It would be far too confusing to describe all the variations and give all the different names, and for that reason only the English names are used in this book; a landowner, for instance, is called the 'lord', his estate the 'manor', and the men working on it 'villeins', and only the commonest and most important things about the men of work are described.

Looking back a thousand years is always very difficult, and when it comes to trying to discover something about poor and illiterate men who could themselves leave no traces of their own lives, it is harder still. But fortunately some of their lords kept records which help us to a certain extent. Charlemagne, of course, did this on his estates, and a good many monasteries also kept estate books. Saint Germain des Prés was one of these, and from their careful records of their lands, the people who lived there, and the work they were expected to do (all written down by the monks), it is possible to piece together a good deal about the life of the villeins.

Actard, for instance, was a villein who lived at the end of the tenth century on one of the manors of Saint Germain des Prés, with his wife Erlindis and their two children. The lay-out of this manor was quite a common one. At the centre stood a small stone house called the 'hall' or the 'manor house' (names we still use for a country house of some importance), surrounded by an orchard and a garden, farm buildings, stables, barns, and workshops, all enclosed by a strong wooden fence. Here the lord of the manor usually lived, but as the monks could not leave the monastery this one was occupied by Nicholas the reeve, a hard-headed sharp-eyed person, who knew a great deal about farming and had been chosen to oversee the manor for the monks. Outside the fence, but clustered near at hand, was a collection of huts where Actard and the other villeins lived. There was also a tiny church, the only other building in the place that was made of stone.

Boothby Pagnall Manor House. A stone manor house of the early Middle Ages would look much like this except for the upper windows which are later additions.

Occasionally you can see the remains of an ancient manor house, much patched up, like the one on this page, because they were stoutly built, often of stone, and their owners could afford to keep them in repair and improve them occasionally. But you can never see a villein's hut, for the simple reason that they were built of materials which did not last, and so were destructible. Indeed, the poorest of them could hardly even be called a hut, and the best consisted only of a simple wooden framework, filled in with pliable twigs and strips of wood, called wattles, the gaps stuffed with moss or hay and daubed over with mud and clay. In winter they were unbelievably damp and cold, for the wind and the rain blew sharply in through many cracks and crevices. They were built by their owners, who were not all very skilled at the job, and were often so ramshackle that a few strong men could push them over, and a

119

moderate gale could whip the thatched roof right off. In 1202 a malicious Englishman living in Lincolnshire quietly cut through the posts of his neighbour's house and the whole place fell down.

The inside of Actard's hut was one little dark room. The only light came from the door when it was open, and from a very small window without glass. Glass was rare and expensive, only to be found in churches and in the halls of great men, and Actard closed his 'wind's eye' with a rough wooden shutter or a flap of cow-hide. You can imagine what the atmosphere inside was usually like, with door and window shut, the fire burning in the middle of the dirty earthern floor, its smoke curling out through a hole in the thatch, the family, also very dirty, squatting round it, together with several dogs, some hens, and perhaps an ailing piglet or a young goat, fleas hopping about and biting them all. Actard's hut, however, was reasonably free of animals and only a few shared it with the family. The rest, when not out in the fields, were kept in a lean-to shed joined on to the house, and there they added agreeably to the warmth and smell without actually getting in the way.

There was almost no furniture, just a clumsy bench, a few wooden stools, and a wooden box to keep food in. Earthenware or wooden cooking pots and bowls lay on the floor, or stood on a shelf along one wall, and there were some coarse blankets and sheep-skins in one corner for sleeping under. Bunches of dried herbs and onions, a few salt fish and a stringy ham, and all sorts of fishing lines, snares, and small tools hung on pegs driven into the frame-work. None of the family bothered to wash or comb their hair except Erlindis, who had a small wooden comb given her by Actard as a wedding present which she used occasionally, and as they had only the clothes they stood up in there was no need of places to keep them in. No artificial light was used; candles were for churches and the lord's house, and besides, the danger of fire was too great even for a torch of pine twigs. Actard and his family could neither read nor write, and had nothing to do after dark; they were content to go to bed with the sun and get up at first light.

Around the hut was a small piece of land enclosed by sharpened stakes and thorn bushes, which kept out wandering sheep and goats by day, and at night made a haven for man and beast against marauders—the hungry wolves for instance, that came slinking like gray shadows out of the forest in search of fresh meat, in the shape of a hen or a piglet or a lamb. Actard made spiked collars for his dogs, to protect them from a bite in the throat from these grim visitors. In this garden plot grew herbs and vegetables, parsley and mint, onions, garlic and cabbages, all rather measly versions of those we grow today. There were three apple trees and three beehives under them. The soil in this plot was usually very fertile, for all the

household waste was thrown out on to it, as well as the animal droppings, and being so near the hut it was easily dug and weeded.

Beyond his fence Actard looked over the big fields of the manor, and beyond them again to the dark encircling forest. As far as he could see all belonged to the monastery, and all looked utterly different from the same countryside today. Nowadays in much of central France and certainly in England the fields have a neat orderly look, and are usually grouped round farm-buildings and circled by some kind of boundary like a hedge, a ditch, or a wall. It is difficult to imagine how wild and empty Actard's surroundings must have looked, how dense the forests were, and how closely they pressed in upon ploughland and pasture. There were usually four huge fields on the manor, and each year two of them would be sown with food crops, such as wheat, oats, barley, rye, peas, and beans, one grew hay, and one lay fallow and rested. Each year the pattern of cropping changed round and a different field lay fallow, and this rotation was the only way men knew then of restoring fertility to the land and keeping it 'in good heart', as farmers say today, for there were no artificial fertilizers and very little manure; the crops were much thinner in the fields than in the garden plots, and very poor indeed compared with those of today.

Probably you already know something about the manor in the Middle Ages, and so will realize that the fields had no permanent fences round them, and were divided up into strips of about an acre apiece each strip marked off by means of an unploughed line of turf or an extra deep furrow. All of them belonged to the lord of the manor, but they were divided into two parts. One part was reserved for the lord and called the 'demesne', the other was let out to the villeins. Every scrap of produce raised on the demesne strips of Actard's manor was set aside for the monks of Saint Germain, or on other manors for the lord, and either carted off to the monastery or stored in the barn (or on the ground floor of the hall) for some future use. Seed for the next sowing would be kept there, and a supply of provisions in case the lord abbot should come, or some other important visitor arrive to break a long journey. Once when a bishop and his attendants stayed in the hall for a few days they disposed of 50 loaves of wheaten bread, 50 eggs, 10 chickens, and 5 sucking pigs, not to mention cheese, honey, and butter. The demesne provided the monastery with all the food, clothing, fuel, and drink for the monks, their guests, and their almsgiving; and if it was well managed it also gave a surplus of produce to sell. All this was the wealth of Saint Germain des Prés.

Apart from the demesne the land was divided among the villeins living on the manor. The amount each man had varied from place to place, but on the whole it was supposed to be enough to feed a

family on, and was sometimes written down as '*terra unius familiae*', the land of a family. No one had a compact block; the strips were scattered in the fields, as the demesne land was scattered. There were obvious drawbacks to this system of farming: much tedious tramping from strip to strip, and no choice of the crops a man could grow. In the cornfields all had to grow corn, in the hayfield all must take hay from their strips. But there were also advantages, one being that this was a rough and ready way of sharing out the good and bad land among all. Even the demesne strips were not confined to the good land.

Actard had 30 strips as well as his house and the garden plot round it, and he had the right, in common with his neighbours and the monastery, to graze his beasts wherever on the manor no crops were growing, and that meant (after the hay and harvest were gathered) on the fallow field until it was ploughed up, and on any odd pieces of uncultivated waste land. On this he and his family had to be almost entirely self-supporting, buying perhaps only salt and a few iron tools. Nowadays we live so much by buying and selling, and are so dependent on going to shops for food, clothes,

and furniture, and on lighting and warming our houses by the flick of a switch, that it is hard to realize what ceaseless effort was needed to grow or make everything necessary for day-to-day living, and just how simple and precarious a living it was. Actard built his hut from trees that he cut down himself and thatch that he collected, he made the crude furniture, and, what is more, he made many of the tools he used. Erlindis made their few clothes and the ill-fitting shoes they wore in winter, but before she could do so she had to clean and spin the wool cut from the sheep and weave it into coarse cloth, and she had to scrape and soften the skins of hunted and slaughtered animals to stitch into bristly boots (for the hair was left on the outside). All these were slow laborious jobs, taking hours of time, and there were many more to be done as well.

The staple food of the family was bread, and they grew the grain for it on their strips in the cornfield; not wheat, for that went into fine white loaves which only great men ate, but coarser grains which made a dark sour bread, distinctly unpleasant by our standards but very satisfying. Another important food was a kind of thick porridge made of oats and peas, and this was common enough in England to find its way into a rhyme.

> Pease porridge hot,
> Pease porridge cold;
> Pease porridge in the pot,
> Nine days old.

Actard's animals supplied the rest of the food of the family, for he owned a few sheep, goats, and pigs, some hens, and the three hives of bees. Sheep and goats gave milk as well as meat and wool. In the picture on this page you can see a villein's wife milking the

Milking.

cow. Milk, bread, eggs, cheese, bacon, lard, and honey, with vegetables from the garden and berries and nuts from the woods and waste—this sounds quite a good and varied diet, and no doubt stomachs were comfortably full in spring and summer, when hens were laying and milk was plentiful because the grass grew thick and sweet, and Actard and his son, when they set their night lines and snares, were sure of catching fish and rabbits. But things could be very different at other times of the year. It was rare for any household, except that of the lord, to start the winter with much reserve of food, and when the small stocks ran low, as they often did, there was no way of replenishing them. Because there was seldom enough fodder to keep all the animals going through the bad weather, many had to be killed off in the autumn, and those that were left grew miserably thin and certainly gave little or no milk. Often after the Christmas feast was over and in the first dark months of the new year the pangs of hunger bit sharply, and death thinned out the old and the very young from the families in the villeins' huts, especially if the last harvest had been poor, and spring was long in coming.

If Actard had been able to spend all his time and energy on cultivating his own land and tending his own few beasts, it would have been easier to supply the family with necessities, but he could not do this. House, garden, strips, and grazing rights—everything belonged to the monastery and he had to pay for them, not as a small farmer would today by a fixed money rent—money was scarce and little used on the manor—, but by service and dues. Just as the fighting men, the knights like Bruno, held their land from their lords by military service and dues, so too the men of work, also bound to their lords in the feudal system, held their land. But the service they had to give was not military, it was manual labour on the demesne, and through it the lord was able to live in plenty.

The service was usually of two kinds. First there was week-work, which meant that for about three days each week and all through the year a villein had to work from dawn to dark on the demesne at certain tasks allotted to him by the reeve. Year after year these tasks remained the same. But besides this he could be called on to give extra help—called boon-work—'at the lord's need', and the lord invariably 'needed' him at the busiest times of the year, at haymaking, harvest, or sheep-shearing, exactly when there was most to do on his own strips. These two kinds of service took up a large proportion of Actard's time, and when his share was multiplied by the number of other villeins on the manor the hours of work they were bound to do on the demesne obviously came to a considerable amount. Even so, it is astonishing to discover from the estate book of the Abbey of Prüm in Germany that the monks there were

supported by 70,000 days of service each year from their villeins. They must have been very comfortable!

In autumn and spring Actard's week-work was chiefly ploughing, because he owned two oxen. He had to be up at first light, take them into the cornfield, and join other villeins to make up a plough team of six or eight oxen. Then all day he ploughed the great field and afterwards sowed the corn. His own strips might want ploughing too, but work on the demesne came first. An Anglo-Saxon writer has described an imaginary talk with a villein like Actard, who says 'O Sir, I work very hard. I go out in the dawning, driving the oxen to the field, and I yoke them to the plough. Be the winter never so stark I dare not stay at home for fear of my lord, but every day I must plough a full acre or more.' In the summer Actard had to help cut the hay and corn, carry it to the manor yard, and stack it in the barn, and Nicholas the reeve kept a very sharp eye on the reapers in case they hid a sheaf or two for themselves, or tried to slip away and cut some of their own corn that was standing ripe and ready to fall. For the rest of his week work he had to help in keeping the hall, its out-buildings, and the fence round them in good repair; and each spring, as soon as the new grass began to grow and the young corn to sprout, he had to make and put up 22 yards of temporary fencing 'with little stakes' round the hayfield, to protect it from wandering animals, and round the corn *as much as necessary*. Those words usually caused argument and sullen anger from the villeins, for Nicholas was for ever trying to get as much work as possible out of them, and they always resisted if he put burdens on them which were not the custom of the manor. For instance, when the monastery ordered part of the forest to be cleared, ploughed, and added to one of the fields, Actard and two other men flatly refused to fence the extra bit, until Nicholas in return allowed them to take two bundles of wood for their own use.

Taking corn to the lord's mill. The reeve gets off his horse to extract payment for grinding.

Boon-work was not usually as heavy as week-work, but everyone detested it, because it was so unpredictable and so often demanded without warning. A man might be ordered to mend a road or a bridge, do guard duty at night in the manor yard, or even to escort a criminal to prison. Sometimes Actard had to fell trees on the edge of the forest for seven days, and cart two loads of the wood away to the monastery in his own cart. Sometimes the load was anything that Nicholas 'commanded', provided that all carting services did not add up to more than fifty leagues, but even so, a journey often took two days and a night, for the oxen moved so slowly and the roads were so bad; and though Actard enjoyed seeing the folk at the monastery, having a good gossip in the monastery kitchen, and telling tall stories of his adventures when he got back, he grudged the time. He was very careful to get his full allowance of bread, cheese, and ale for himself, and hay for the oxen, which Nicholas was bound to supply when a man did boon-work.

A villein's wife was also obliged to give service on the manor, and for Erlindis this meant going to the hall three times a week, and spending the whole day grinding corn by hand, or washing and spinning wool, and weaving it into a coarse white serge which was sent to the monastery to be made into habits for the monks. If all the demesne wool was finished before June, when sheep-shearing came round, she had to feed the poultry and do 'as she is commanded' by Nicholas before she could return home to her own work, and he usually managed to keep her busy for the whole day.

Besides week-work and boon-work Actard had dues to pay. Sometimes these were small sums of money, and were for special privileges, such as the right of 'pannage' or taking pigs into the woods in autumn to eat the acorns and beechmast, or the right to take 'house bote' and 'fire bote'. 'Bote' is an Anglo-Saxon word meaning 'wood', so you can guess what Actard took and how important this right was to him. But most dues were not in money, they were in kind, and they had to be taken to the hall on certain days of the year; so you could see Erlindis reluctantly giving the reeve a fat hen at Christmas, 15 eggs at Easter, and a measure of mustard in the autumn, while Actard had to supply oats for two horses, 10 brushwood torches, and 10 mats of straw made from his own scanty supply. These dues were a way of getting even more out of the villeins than their service; they were wealth for the lord extracted from the poverty of his men. At the monastery of Saint Germain dues added up to a fantastic amount of produce: in one year, among other things, 440 torches, 30,965 eggs, 5,818 chickens, and 46,903 hand-made roofing tiles were brought in. There were only 210 monks at the time!

Out of all these complicated arrangements between the lord—

whoever he might be—and the villeins on the manor it was invariably the lord who had much the best of the bargain. Of course, the villein got his home, his land, and his grazing rights, and out of these he could, by the sweat of his brow, scrape a living for himself and his family, but it was an exceedingly meagre one, and in return he bore the heavy burdens of service and dues. It is also true that he was generally protected from danger, for the last thing a lord wanted was a dead villein or one too badly injured to work, but he was not protected from the malice of a brutal lord, being his property and utterly in his power. Actard was better off in this respect than many, for the monks treated the peasants on their estates with charity and fed them if they were sick or starving, but most villeins could expect only hard treatment, contempt, and the absolute certainty that even when famine stalked among the huts on the manor, the lord in his hall would still eat as much as he wanted.

But perhaps the worst thing of all for the man of work to bear was that he had no freedom, and nothing to look forward to except absolute obedience to the will of the lord and endless toil for that lord's profit. No villein could leave the manor to which he was bound, and if he tried to run away he was usually brought back and punished. Some, of course, did manage to escape or disappear, perhaps to join a travelling pedlar, or a band of soldiers going to war, or a group of pilgrims bound for the Holy Land, sometimes to become simply a landless lordless vagabond. Occasionally, for some special reason, a lord would make a villein a free man; and then, as a symbol that he was free to go where he would, the lord placed in his hands the weapons of a free man and set him before an open door, so that he could see the open road, and know that he might leave the manor if he so desired. But a villein could not marry, nor could he allow his daughter to marry, without the lord's consent, for it might mean her leaving the manor and his service, and her children's service would be lost. No villein or villein's son could become a priest or a monk without permission, and this was not willingly given, for again it meant the loss of a man's service on the demesne. It must have been an awkward moment for the chapter of Saint Germain's when one of their villeins asked leave to enter the monastery. Should they allow a man of work to leave his class and become a man of prayer? or should they keep him bound to their manor and their service?

In spite of toil, hunger, cold, and the danger of living under a harsh unjust lord, life in the manor was by no means always unbearable. A man like Actard found comfort in his family, and from his religion too, even though that might only shoot a few gleams of light through the darkness of his superstitious fears. For the most part, he relied more on ancient charms and spells than on prayers

to ward off sickness, or ill-luck, or the malice of evil spirits; but when he heard the priest tell the story of the life of Christ, with its message of love and hope, when perhaps he saw it painted in bright colours on the walls of the church, he found some relief from his fears; and as he knelt at mass the coldness of life seemed warmed by the soft light of the wax candles on the altar, and the figure of the Man on the Rood brought him a strange solace.

Besides offering the spiritual comfort of these mysteries the Church made a very practical difference to his existence. There were the holy-days of the year, about 50 in number, when in many places no one did any work, or at least not after noon, and there were the great festivals of Christmas, Easter, and Whitsun, each of which brought him a week free from service on the demesne and the chance of a feast at the manor; similarly, there were the ale drinkings, allowed at the church after weddings and funerals. In summer there were games and dancing, or a day spent at the nearest fair, marvelling at jugglers and acrobats, making a few pence by selling some eggs or a spare bladder of lard, and drinking it all away before tramping back to the manor, to sleep off the effects ready for the next day's work.

By the year 1000 the worst of the invasions by Hungarians, Saracens, and Northmen were over, and in the next 300 years Europe, no longer overrun by ruthless hordes, gradually recovered from the destruction they had caused and became more settled and prosperous. Changes began to come in the life of the manor, though so slowly that in many places they must scarcely have been noticeable. For one thing, towns began to grow, and merchants moved actively along the roads, and this meant that more people were drawn in to work at crafts and trades, which left them little time to grow their food, and so they ceased to be self-supporting. Yet they had to eat and drink, which meant that the men who worked on the land had to produce enough for all. Any surplus food from the manor, over and above what the lord consumed, could promptly be sold to the townsmen, and even the smallest quantities that a villein might spare from his meagre supplies were in demand—a dozen eggs or a string of onions. Many a lord was shaken out of old habits as he saw his way to further wealth (and the villein to a few extra coins in his purse) and because of the hungry mouths of townsmen great efforts were made to bring more land into use. The ploughs gnawed into the wastes, the forests were attacked and cleared, and the fields of the manors grew bigger. Yet even this extra land could not grow the necessary food unless it was more skilfully farmed, and so tools had to improve. Instead of wooden ploughs that could only scratch the surface of the soil, heavier iron ones came into use, made to cut deeply into the earth and turn the furrows over. Another example of slow old methods giving way to

Man and Woman dancing.

newer ones was provided when lords built water-mills on their manors, and so did away with the tedious grinding of corn by hand, which wasted hours of time. Villeins were allowed to use these mills, but not free of charge, and before grinding, a proportion of everyone's corn was taken by the miller as payment. This was very profitable; the lord who had built a mill soon got his money back, and also had a steady flow of extra corn coming in to his barns. If at first there was grumbling at this new expense, especially when the lord forced his villeins to use his mill, it must soon have been obvious, even to the most sullen villein, that the new way of grinding his corn saved him a vast amount of time for other things. In these and other ways the poor man's work became more productive and his standard of living improved. One simple proof of this is that he began to eat better food. Once, a villein doing a day's boon-work had to be content with rye bread and ale, but in 1289 the villeins on a manor belonging to Battle Abbey in Sussex, who were doing carting service, not only expected cheese in the morning but meat or fish at midday; and on another manor in France in 1300 the men repairing the church as their boon-work, expected eggs, meat, and wine, as well as rye bread and bean soup. But although by 1300 the villeins might have more food, few of them had much increase in freedom; and in this side of his life it was not until the terrible catastrophe of the Black Death had swept through Europe that a great change for the better took place, and he began to escape from the bonds which tied him so closely to his lord's land.

Left *Killing a pig.*
Centre *Bees entering the hive.*
Right *Hay making.*

Chapter 9
The Empire of Otto

So far in this book we have given a good deal of attention to two empires, first the Roman empire and then the empire of Charlemagne. We have seen how the first was dismembered, the western part going down into the dark under the onslaughts of barbarian peoples, the eastern part, though often severely battered, remaining intact, imperial, and rich. We have also seen the second, Charlemagne's empire, collapsing because of the ferocious disagreements among his descendants, the equally ferocious attacks by Hungarians, Saracens, and Northmen, and the weakness of kings compared with the arrogant and growing strength of feudal lords. Now we must look at a third empire, which came into being in 962, and lasted till Napoleon brought it to an end in 1806.

The last kingly descendant of Charlemagne died in 918, and it was he who had sent his royal regalia to Henry, Duke of Saxony, knowing him to be the only man then capable of using kingly power. But even Henry, in spite of his reputation, had to face fierce opposition in order to become king in fact as well as name. At first he was really the master of only part of Germany. Outside his duchy of Saxony there were other very powerful dukes and counts to be confronted, and it was solely by iron strength and determination that he managed to subdue them. Gradually he forced most of these formidable men to acknowledge him as king, surrender the goodly portions of the royal lands they had swallowed, and give him the military service they owed for their estates. Henry's power and prestige were greatly helped because he won victories over Hungarians and Northmen. The German people, who have always understood the value of force, accepted him as a worthy king; and the proof of this came when he died in 936, and the crown, never his by right of birth, passed without commotion to his eldest son Otto, just as if it had been in the family for generations.

Otto was made king of the German people with splendid ceremony. The greatest of the feudal lords lifted him on to the throne, and all did homage to him. The high clergy anointed him and put upon him the symbols of royalty, the tunic and cloak, the bracelet and the baldric. They gave him the sword, the sceptre, and the crown, and then presented him to the people as 'Otto, chosen by God, appointed by Henry, and now made king by all the princes'.

As he sat at a great feast after the coronation he was waited on by the four most powerful men of Germany, and if they gnashed their teeth while doing so they did not show it. This feast took place in Charlemagne's palace at Aachen, and the coronation in the church where he was buried, and as Otto, a young man of 20, sat there in his place, beneath the pillars brought from the heart of the Roman empire, he undoubtedly had a vision in which he saw himself as successor to Charlemagne, an emperor reviving an empire. It was a vision he never for one moment forgot.

Charlemagne's throne at Aachen on which Otto I probably sat for his coronation.

But first he had to take firm hold of his realm, and in spite of his father's efforts, and the submissions and homage at his coronation, this was a daunting matter, since he could not trust any of his vassals and even members of his own family were at times very dangerous. These were the common hazards facing a king in the tenth century, and at one time or another Otto came into conflict with every German duke, as well as with two of his brothers and one of his sons. He endured many setbacks, but because he was not easily dismayed, and because he was distinctly wiser than many men of his time, he ended by being the real ruler of Germany and not just a great duke among other dukes. This finally came about after 955, when the last terrible scourge of Hungarians swept into Germany. In the face of such peril even rebel lords rallied to the king, and together they crushed the Hungarians so that their raids ceased entirely. After that Otto was nicknamed 'the Great', and men saw him as the most powerful ruler in Europe. It was largely because he was victorious over the Hungarians that he was able later on to become emperor.

But even so, he could never relax, he had to be ceaselessly alert for danger, and all his disloyal subjects did not disappear after one exhilarating victory. To guard his frontiers he appointed counts palatine, and for this he chose men who—so he hoped—would not plot against him or try to build up little kingdoms of their own. But to carry out day-to-day government of his realm he did not use the feudal lords at all if he could help it; instead, he turned to the Church and appointed clergy to be judges, counsellors, envoys, and ambassadors, in fact to do all the work that ministers and civil servants do today in a modern state. This plan had great advantages for Otto. The clergy were, of course, the only educated men in his kingdom, and in Germany at that time many of them were outstanding for learning and loyalty, and well able to show that there were other ways of settling disputes besides the use of the sword. Also, —and this perhaps was their greatest advantage in Otto's eyes—they were not allowed to marry, and so could not found important families. However much they enjoyed the rank, the wealth, and the power they might possess in this life, they could not at their death pass them on to sons and grandsons as a rich inheritance of wealth and power for some, possibly dangerous, feudal clan. Otto gave much land and money to archbishoprics, bishoprics, and monasteries, together with wide authority over people living in their territories, and some of the high clergy were indeed princes of the Church, as formidable and splendid as any feudal lords, but only very occasionally did one of them side with those lords or join in rebellions against the king. In any case Otto kept a tight hold over them in many ways. He treated the lands he gave the Church very much as he did his own; he made it plain

The wise men shown on this ivory-covered Gospel book are in Frankish dress. Ninth or tenth century.

that they were not to be sold or exchanged without his permission; archbishops, bishops, and abbots had to supply knights for military service, and some had to lead these vassals to war. The king demanded hospitality at will for himself and his court, and this could be very expensive for his host, since the court might consume in a single day 1,000 pigs and sheep, 8 oxen, 1,000 measures of grain, 2,700 gallons of wine, and the same of beer.

So Otto deliberately worked in close partnership with the Church and found it very useful. 'It is impossible to say', he wrote to one of his archbishops, 'how happy I am that we have always felt one and the same, and that our aims have never differed in any matter

of policy', their aims, of course, being always to maintain the strength of the king and the Church. But this meant that the king must be sure of getting the right men into the right positions, and he had to be able to control important appointments, such as those of bishops and abbots. There would be no difficulty in this as long as the king and the pope (as head of the Church) saw absolutely eye-to-eye at all times; but if they happened to differ, what then?

Now Otto the Great had never lost sight of the vision of himself following in the footsteps of Charlemagne. He knew well that Charlemagne had considerable power over the papacy, and in time he, too, was able to assert his authority in Rome and in very much the same way. During his reign Italy was in its usual state of turmoil, and in 951 Otto marched into the country to forestall other princes who were tempted by its beauty and the quarrels of its rulers to help themselves to portions of the country, and made himself king of almost all the land except for the independent

The church of S. Cyriakos, Gernrode, Germany, built in the reign of Otto I.

Empire of Otto I.

territory of the pope. Ten years later the Pope himself, almost overwhelmed by enemies in Rome, appealed to him for help, and Otto entered the holy city, subdued the Pope's enemies, and then naturally asked for a reward. He received it swiftly, for a request from a man who has just saved you is difficult to refuse, and on 2nd February 962 the Pope crowned him emperor in the church of St. Peter. The new emperor declared himself the protector of the papacy, but at the same time he extracted a promise that no pope should be elected without his consent, and this sounds rather more like control than just protection.

Otto had followed fairly closely in the footsteps of Charlemagne, and his vision had become a reality, in so far as his dominions were now called the empire—the Holy Roman empire to be exact—and he himself was emperor. But this third empire which now appeared was very different from the two that had gone before it. You have only to look at the maps to see that it was smaller than Charlemagne's

135

and very much smaller than the Roman world. Nearly all Otto's subjects were German; but Charlemagne had ruled over a variety of peoples, and Roman citizens belonged to almost countless races. Otto's empire was never assailed by barbarians, it did not fall apart when he died in 973, and in fact the German emperor remained one of the two most important men in Europe all through the Middle Ages. The other was the Pope, and before long these two rivals were locked in a long ruinous quarrel over their power and their rights.

Above *An imperial orb made about the time of the Emperor Henry VI, possibly for his coronation in 1191, now in the Kunsthistorisches Museum, Vienna.*
Left *Otto III, grandson of Otto I. The picture shows the ceremonial robes of the emperor and of the clergy and nobles.*

137

Chapter 10
Empire against Papacy

The two most important figures in Western Europe by the end of the eleventh century were the Holy Roman emperor and the pope. It was believed that they were ordained by God to rule and care for the Christians of the West. To the emperor had been given the duty of ruling over worldly matters, and to the pope belonged the duty of caring for men's souls. It was taken for granted that pope and emperor would work together in harmony, for the good of all Christians.

What happened in the late eleventh century was in fact a struggle between these two powers, in which men eagerly took sides, argued fiercely, wrote abusive pamphlets, and even fought wars. It resulted in such an upheaval of the old ways that Christendom was never the same again. How did this come about?

You will know from earlier chapters that the emperor was king of Germany and North Italy, and he only became emperor when he was crowned by the pope, as Charlemagne had been crowned by Leo III. Normally the pope did not make any difficulties about this, because he wanted the support and protection of the German king, who was also his close neighbour in Italy. Until the crisis of the eleventh century the emperor was the more powerful of the two, and from time to time he actually appointed the pope, but he did not always do so.

In the tenth and early eleventh centuries the position of pope was being fought over by two rival families of powerful Roman nobles. The men they chose were little better than successful gangsters. Sometimes son succeeded father in the pope's palace, and the head of the Church lived in an atmosphere of luxury, intrigue, and murder. One pope was strangled, another smothered to death. In 1046 there were actually three Roman nobles all claiming to be pope, and the pious emperor Henry III came himself to Italy to put a firm end to this scandalous state of affairs. He set all three aside and appointed one of his own German bishops instead, a man who was in favour of reforming the Church, as the emperor himself was. Unfortunately this pope and his successor both died soon after their appointments, for the heat and malaria of Italy often cut short the lives of men used to the cooler climate north of the Alps. A third German bishop was appointed by the

Empire and Papacy in the 11th century.

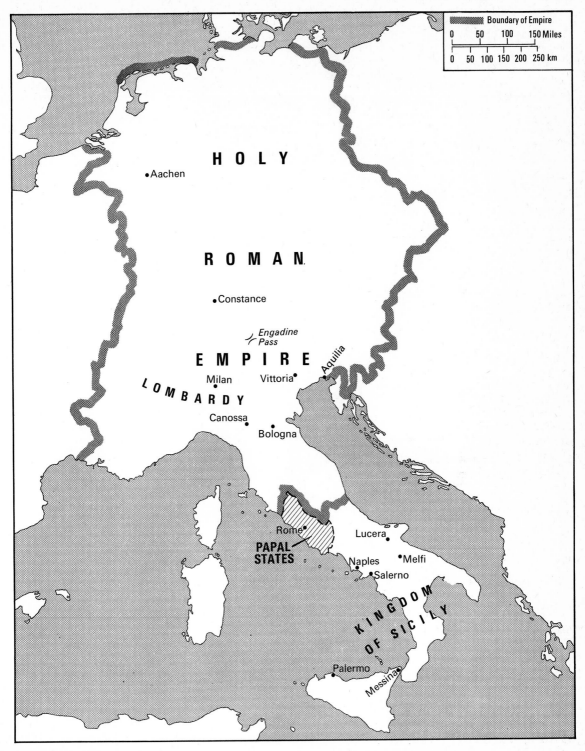

Boundary of Empire

0   50   100   150 Miles

0 50 100 150 200 250 km

HOLY

• Aachen

ROMAN

• Constance

Engadine
Pass

EMPIRE   Aquilia

LOMBARDY   Milan •   Vittoria •

Canossa •

Bologna •

Rome •

PAPAL
STATES   Lucera •

Naples •   • Melfi

• Salerno

KINGDOM
OF SICILY

Palermo •

Messina •

Henric̄ quartꝰ hen
rici impe ratoris filius
admocū̄ puer patri suc
cedens regnare cēpit
kxxxvij loco abau
gusto & regnauit
annis·L·

emperor in 1048, who proved tougher in every way. He took the title Leo IX.

Besides being a vigorous and effective man of affairs, and a warrior too, Leo was eager to remove abuses from the Church, especially among the bishops, and he determined to strike hard blows at some of the smug worldly bishops whom he knew about. He held a council in Rome at which he made severe rules against the sin of paying money to a king in order to get appointed to a high position in the Church. This custom was known as simony, and all those who wanted to improve matters in the Church looked upon it as one of the root evils. Most men would have left it at that, but Leo knew that no one would take a scrap of notice if he simply stayed in Rome making decrees. So he provided himself with an

impressive escort of bishops and Roman clergy, and set off on horseback over the Alps to the city of Rheims in France, where he called another council, of French bishops and abbots.

Officially Leo was in Rheims for the removal of the relics of the patron saint of the city, St. Remigius, to a new resting place in a church that had just been built for this purpose. The relics of saints were deeply venerated by medieval people, and the fine casket which held the body of St. Remigius was born round the town in solemn procession before it was brought back to the church for the pope to lower it reverently in front of the assembled clergy into its newly-prepared burial place. But Leo did not do this, or at least not straight away. He laid the box of relics dramatically on the high altar of the church, so that it was clear to all the bishops and abbots present that the council was going to take place actually in the presence of St. Remigius himself! A thrill of excitement and dread went round the audience. Leo alone was calm and stern. He turned to face those French clergy and one by one they were straitly asked whether they had paid money for their appointments. With terrible sinking of the heart each awaited his turn, excuses whirling round in his mind. They mumbled and stammered and muttered confessions and excuses, or remained miserably silent. One man was struck dumb when trying to bring himself to defend a guilty friend, and then the friend panicked and ran away from the town in the night. Punishments were dealt out, and at least one bishop was removed from his position entirely. In France at least, the churchmen now knew that the pope in Rome could strike at them and could strike very hard.

The council at Rheims was followed up by further ones in Germany and Italy, and more bishops were accused and were punished. Leo was working with the full approval and support of the emperor, Henry III, who had appointed him. A generation later things were very different. Leo had taken such firm action and given such a clear lead that some men were beginning to say that it was quite wrong that emperors should choose popes, for the pope was far greater than the emperor, and some thought that kings should not choose their own bishops either.

It happened to matter very much to the German kings that they should choose their own bishops, both in Germany and North Italy, because the bishops helped them a great deal in ruling their lands. Before a man became a bishop he went through a solemn ceremony in the king's court. Kneeling in front of the king, he placed his hands between the hands of the king and swore to be loyal to him as his *man* or vassal. The king in return placed a ring on his finger and a staff in his hand, for these were the special signs of a bishop's position. The ring showed his link with the Church,

as strong a link as that of marriage, and the staff or crook showed that he was the shepherd of his people. It was only after this all-important ceremony in the king's court that the bishop went off to his cathedral to get himself consecrated. There were men in Rome who now said that the king had no right to 'invest' bishops with the ring and staff, and that bishops should look to the pope as their superior and not to the king. These views were shortly to be thrust upon the world in their most extreme form by Pope Gregory VII.

Gregory became pope in 1073. When the Emperor Henry III had died in 1056 his heir was a little boy, six years old, and it had been very easy for the Roman clergy to make a ruling that in future they and not the emperor were to choose the pope. By 1073 the boy king was grown up, but he had many problems on hand, including some rebellious subjects, and he did not take any action when Gregory simply announced to him that he had been chosen as pope.

Two years later the clash came, over the archbishopric of Milan in North Italy. In that year Gregory had made a ruling that no king should invest a bishop with the ring and staff. Henry IV, coolly ignoring this, invested one Tedald as archbishop of Milan, brushing aside a man who had already been consecrated and recognized as archbishop by the pope. The whole question of royal power in the Church was at stake. Henry was determined to control his bishops as his forefathers had done. Gregory was equally determined that the holy Church must free itself from its slavery to kings. In Gregory's view the most humble parish priest was altogether greater than the most mighty king, because the priest had been specially set aside for the work of God, as one of the clergy, whereas the king, however powerful, was only a layman.

Gregory wrote sternly to Henry, threatening to excommunicate him, that is to expel him from the Christian Church. The king completely lost his temper, called together an assembly of German bishops, and with their support declared that Gregory was no longer pope. He sent a messenger to Rome with an angry letter, calling Gregory a 'false monk', and ordering him to 'come down, come down' from the chair of St. Peter. The royal messenger risked his life in delivering this letter to Gregory, for outside the pope's council chamber the crowd were ready to lynch him.

Emperor against Pope. In this drawing from a twelfth century chronicle there are four scenes. Top left: *Henry IV sits on his throne beside the 'pope' whom he has set up in place of Gregory VII.* Top right: *Gregory is driven out of Rome.* Bottom left: *Gregory consults with his advisers.* Bottom right: *Gregory dies and his bishops mourn for him.*

Gregory saved the messenger's life, but he now dealt with the king. The pope not only expelled Henry from the Church but declared that his subjects need no longer obey him.

If Henry's subjects had all been loyal, and if men had not by now got a new respect for the pope as head of the Church, Henry need not have worried. But times were changing. The German bishops became very uneasy at the idea of disobeying so confident and determined a pope. Worse still, in such a quarrel there are often some men who will take up one side for their own selfish purposes. The German dukes and counts did this now. Many of them had had an easy time while Henry was a mere child, and had grown slack in their duties. Henry had recently pulled them up sharply, and they did not like it. Now they rounded on him, cleverly pretending that they were eager reformers who supported Gregory. They told Henry that unless he was accepted back as a member of the Church by 22 February 1077 they would not have him as their king. Meanwhile they sent a friendly letter to Gregory, suggesting that he might like to come to discuss with them whether Henry was fit to rule!

No man could have been in a tighter corner than Henry at this moment. His only hope was to get Gregory to accept him back into the Church by the date in February that the German princes had set as the deadline. If he could do this, then many people would come back to his side, and the German princes would feel that Gregory had let them down and get angry with him. The question was, could it possibly be done? How was Henry even to get to Gregory, let alone persuade him to forgive him? The king's enemies would certainly try to stop his getting to Italy at all, for they guessed what he would be up to. They felt pretty safe, because it was the middle of a very hard winter, and no one in his senses would try the journey to Italy in that weather. Henry was desperate, but he had great pluck. Whatever the cost, he would cross the Alps to reach Gregory. It was intensely cold, the only passes he had a chance of crossing were thickly crusted with snow and ice, and it was still freezing hard. His small party set out on horseback. As they got higher the horses began to stumble and fall on the steep slippery ground. There was nothing else for it; he must leave the horses behind and carry on on foot, if some of the village folk of those bleak parts would turn out to guide him. Only they knew the passes well enough. A German monk writing a year or two later continues the story:

and so he hired natives, expert in the Alpine passes, to guide him up the steep mountain and over the drifts of snow. With great difficulty they reached the summit, but they could get no farther because the slippery ice seemed to prevent any possibility of descent. But straining every nerve,

now scrambling on hands and feet, now leaning on the shoulders of their guides, now staggering and slipping and falling, sometimes in great danger, they just managed to reach the plains below.

The moment that Henry was known to be safely down on the Plain of Lombardy he got a warm welcome from his own supporters there. But Henry knew that the stiffest job of all was yet to come. He learned that the pope, on his way to meet the German princes, had stopped at the castle of Canossa. Henry decided to prepare the way carefully. He sent ahead a small group of very respected people, including that old family friend, Abbot Hugh of Cluny, to plead his case with the pope. Gregory received this embassy with troubled feelings. It was he now who began to feel that he was being cornered. Journeying more slowly at this stage, Henry himself came to Canossa, a hill fortress protected by three encircling stone walls. Between the outer walls the great king stripped himself of all his royal robes and waited in plain woollen garments, barefoot, for three days, fasting and showing every sign of deep penitence.

Gregory still hesitated. He did not trust Henry; he knew that if he allowed him back into the Church the German princes would feel that Gregory had let them down, and he would no longer have them as allies. Yet Gregory knew too that churchmen, like St. Hugh and many others, would be deeply shocked if the head of the Christian Church refused to show mercy to the penitent king. Gregory hesitated, he argued, he tried to get Henry to give him all kinds of guarantees, but in the end he received him back into the Church. He had to.

We may well wonder which of them had won. In one sense Henry certainly had, for the German princes, once they heard the news of Canossa, threw Gregory aside, and themselves chose a new king for Germany in place of Henry. It was a revolt that Henry was able to put down, now that he was no longer regarded by everyone as an enemy of the Church. And yet there was triumph for the pope too. When we think of the way in which the Emperor Henry III had set aside three unworthy popes and appointed his own instead, the humiliation of Henry IV at Canossa seems scarcely believable. Canossa was a sign that the power of the Church was making great headway.

Gregory spent the rest of his life in a useless struggle against Henry IV. In order to fight Henry he had to ally with the Normans who ruled in Southern Italy; in the end, the Normans carried him off from his dearly loved city of Rome, leaving much of it in burning ruins, and Gregory died soon afterwards in Norman territory at Salerno. He felt that all was against him, and as he lay dying he exclaimed bitterly, 'I have loved right and hated evil, and therefore I die in exile.'

Gregory had claimed great power for the Roman Church; he said that the pope alone could dismiss bishops and kings, but that he himself could not be judged by anyone. Indeed there was no limit to his claims. The popes who came after him were more moderate and more careful in their claims, but they continued to fight to free the Church from the power of kings. In 1122 it was agreed between another pope and another emperor that bishops should no longer be invested with ring and staff by the king, but they were still allowed to do homage to the king for their lands and in practice the German kings still saw to it that the men they wanted as bishops were appointed. It was a compromise; each side gave way.

The pope who carried on Gregory's work most successfully was Urban II. In 1095 in the great Council of Clermont he preached an appeal to the knights of Europe to free the Holy Land from Muslims. From the pope's point of view it was a master-stroke. He had placed himself at the head of a great popular movement, and drawn towards Rome the loyalty and admiration of all Christian people. Gregory himself had dreamed of such a plan, and he would have rejoiced in Urban's triumph.

Gregory and Henry, by their quarrel, had broken for centuries to come the harmony between the popes and the Holy Roman emperors. Perhaps the struggle was inevitable once the Church had set itself on the path to reform.

Chapter 11
Norman Conquests

In the Anglo-Saxon Chronicle, against the year 900, the monk then responsible for keeping it up-to-date entered this short statement: 'In this year Alfred, son of Ethelwulf, died, six days before All Saints' Day. He was king over the whole English people *except that part which was under the Danes.*' Those last eight words are important, for they are a stark reminder that, before Alfred the Great, the Danes had very nearly subdued the whole of England, and that even in spite of his dauntless courage and effort, a formidable Danish kingdom still flourished in the land when he died. And although some of his descendants came to bear the title of '*Rex totius Brittaniae*', one of them, Ethelred the Redeless (978–1016), held his kingdom 'with great toil and difficulty' against fresh Danish invasions, and the year after Ethelred died Canute King of Denmark became king of England too. The Anglo-Saxon Chronicle here says that 'having won for himself all the English people . . . Canute was chosen king'; but as he was backed by a formidable army, which 'ravaged, burnt and killed all they came across', the English people clearly had no other choice. So at the beginning of the eleventh century Northmen (Danes) held all England, while just across the narrow strip of the English Channel some of their kinsmen, having invaded France, were settled in that part we now call Normandy. Fifty years later these kinsmen were to invade England too. How did this happen?

In 841, while Charlemagne's grandsons were quarrelling over the remains of his empire, and thirty years before Alfred began his long struggle, the black sails of Viking ships had appeared for the first time in the River Seine, and the Northmen started their merciless hammering of France. No Alfred appeared on the scene to resist them, and at last in 911 the Frankish king Charles, having tried to buy off the invaders without the slightest success, made a treaty of peace with Rollo, one of their leaders, and ceded him some land. Rollo, a giant of a man, did homage for the land in the Frankish fashion, placing his great fists between the hands of the king— something which 'neither his father, nor his grandfather, nor his great grandfather had ever done for any man'; but he could not bring himself to kneel before the king, and utterly refused to kiss the royal foot. He made one of his warriors perform that distasteful bit of the ceremony.

The Northmen quickly took firm hold of their new territory, enjoying the fat pastures, the clear placid streams, and the fair woods full of game. At intervals they went roving and raiding, the habit being very strong, and in this way they added to their lands, and no man could prevent them. They also added to their numbers from time to time by receiving fresh boat-loads of kinsmen from Scandinavia. But when Rollo died they had already settled deeply into France and so taken to Frankish ways that in some places they were even ceasing to speak their old Norse tongue and were using only the Frankish language. Soon they were known everywhere as 'Normans' and their land, Normandy, reached in the west to the coast; from there across 30 miles of sea they looked at England.

William the Conqueror, from his royal seal.

Through the years of settlement their leaders, Rollo's descendants, were tough ruthless men, called variously 'count', 'marquis', 'prince', or 'duke'. Indeed, they had to be tough if they were to have any control over their people, for the Normans could hardly live without war, and were proud, boastful, and greedy, most unwilling to serve anyone, and needing to be kept constantly under foot by their dukes. In 1035 Duke Robert I—the Devil—died while on a pilgrimage to the Holy Land, leaving only a small son of seven to follow him, and in those turbulent times it seemed most unlikely that the boy would escape a violent death, or live to keep anyone under foot. For the first ten years of his reign at least, this young Duke William was in daily peril from rebellious subjects, but because his father had left him in the care of a few faithful and tenacious men, who never deserted him, and because he himself turned out to be a true Norman, toughest of the tough and undaunted by any danger, he somehow survived. And at last, having crushed many rebellions, and warded off many attacks, he dominated Normandy, and was ready for a chance to extend his dominion elsewhere. The chance came in 1066.

In that year, in the first week of January, Edward, King of England, called 'the Confessor', died, a strange shadowy figure about whom we really know very little, although he wore the crown for 24 years. Someone who wrote a history of the reign soon after his death said that he was of outstanding height, had rosy cheeks, thin hands, and milky-white hair, but whether this means that all his life he was very fair, or whether only that he went white when an old man, we cannot tell. He was deeply religious, he was affable and gracious, and he had a habit of always walking with his eyes cast down and looking at the ground. He was the last of the old royal House of Wessex, Alfred's line, and he had no children. William, Duke of Normandy, was his cousin.

England was in an uneasy state when Edward died. His reign had been full of strife and anxiety, quarrels between the great men of

The reverse of the seal.

the realm, and threats of invasion. The people were much divided, and some must have known well that the next king of England could come from one of three places. Harold Hardrada of Norway might arrive with his host and take the crown, so might William of Normandy—who indeed swore that Edward had promised it to him—, or the English might choose an English earl for king. This last is what happened first, and the man they chose, Harold Godwinsson, earl of Wessex, was crowned at the end of January 1066 in the fine new church at Westminster, which the Confessor had built 'to the honour of God, Saint Peter, and all God's saints'.

Harold reigned for just nine months and 'enjoyed little tranquillity therein'. He must always have been aware of the dangers round him, from Norway, from Normandy, from his treacherous brother Tostig, from luke-warm friends and jealous rivals. All through the summer of 1066 news came to England of sinister preparations going on in Normandy. In May Tostig came out of exile with an army and landed on the east coast, but he was defeated and took refuge in Scotland. Early in September Harold of Norway arrived, also on the east coast, and Harold of England hurried north with the pick of his fighting men to face and defeat him, and to kill both him and Tostig, who had turned up again from Scotland. But of course neither of these two invasions is the one that has made 1066 the best-known date in English history. That one began on the night of September 27th, when the wind in the Channel shifted round from the north to the south, and William of Normandy with '700 ships save 4' set sail through the darkness for England.

He had been furiously busy preparing for this ever since Edward the Confessor died. He had sworn that he was really his cousin's chosen heir, he had denounced Harold as an unholy oath-breaker, he had sought the blessing of the pope in his enterprise, and he had been given it—with a silken banner as token thereof. He had recruited 7,000 men, chiefly from among his Normans, but some also from Brittany, Flanders, and even Spain and Sicily. Above all, he had carried out all the careful detailed planning which we can see so clearly in the Bayeux tapestry, a famous strip of embroidered canvas, about 18 inches high and many yards long, now in the museum at Bayeux in Normandy, which shows the building of the ships and the collection of food, drink, weapons, armour, horses, and men, as well as the events of the invasion itself. It used to be thought that William's wife Matilda and her ladies made the tapestry, stitching away at this astonishing record while the Conquest was actually going on, but now we believe that, though the great anonymous artist who designed it may have been a Norman, the actual stitchwork was done in England by English craftswomen not long after the events it shows.

HIC:NVN..TLATVM
WILLELM° + DEhA

William receives a messenger from Harold (the Bayeux tapestry).

In the morning of September 28th the Normans landed unopposed at Pevensey. Within the walls of the old Roman fort they hastily built a wooden castle, and then, leaving a strong garrison there, William moved his main army and his ships to Hastings, and settled down to wait for the English. The news of the landing took three days to reach Harold at York, where he and the remains of his fighting men were resting and feasting. He had lost many men, and the rest were very weary after fighting two battles in five days against the Northmen and the false Tostig, but he had to rouse them to ride off at once—first the 190 miles to London, and then 60 miles on into Kent. So it was not until October 14th that Harold and William, English and Normans, met. Then, on a bare hillside, seven miles from Hastings, after ten hours of terrible fighting, Harold was killed, the shield wall of his warriors wavered and broke, and the Normans 'gained the field of battle as God granted them for the sins of the nation', as the writer of the Chronicle smugly puts it. William, Duke of Normandy, had taken a long step towards the crown of England, and by Christmas Day it was his. At his hallowing at Westminster on that day 'he swore that he would so well govern this nation as any king before him best did if they would be faithful to him.' Englishmen noted those words and hoped for the best.

You can easily discover for yourself the full story of the Conquest, for there is a vast number of books on the subject. Since it happened, 900 years ago, historians have argued and poured torrents of ink on to paper about the Norman Conquest. Some have thought it a marvellous event, when 'those worthy ancestors of ours' (the Normans) overcame 'a gluttonous race ... lumbering about in pot-bellied equanimity' (the English). Others have believed it was a national disaster, 'a melancholy havoc of our dear country'. But without going to either of those extremes everyone agrees that it was of the highest importance. The question is, why?

It was most unpleasant for the English, who now found themselves very much the under-dogs, 'the low men', in their own country, for the Normans, 'the high men' who had entered the land, were a harsh and violent race. William their leader, the new master of England, was a stark stern person, who although, according to the writer of the Chronicle, 'a very wise men ... mild to those good men who loved God', was also 'severe beyond measure to those who withstood his will'. After the first shock of defeat some did resist his will. In the north, the east, and the west, at Exeter, York, and Ely rebellions broke out, and William, for his own safety, dealt with them severely. More than this, which was essential if he was not to lose quickly what he had won, he laid heavy taxes on the people, and when he went away to Normandy to deal with business there he was careful to take with him 'many

good men from England' as hostages: the Archbishop of Canterbury, the Abbot of Glastonbury, and certain important earls who might have dared to cause trouble behind his back. He left Normans in charge while he was away, and the Chronicle says 'these built castles far and wide throughout the country, and distressed the wretched people, and after that it grew much worse.' The last sad little entry for 1066 is 'May the end be good, when God wills.'

Norman soldiers, grim and fully-armed, look forward to their future conquests.

So, for the conquered, life grew worse for a long time, as William's will became clear. Englishmen were turned out of their lands and sank out of sight into the dark, Englishmen in high offices were replaced by Normans. At the end of William's reign there were very few who held more than insignificant parcels of land, but this was just what you would have expected. The 'new men' settled into the land and 'preyed upon the vitals of England', as William of Malmesbury wrote, although he himself was half Norman by birth; and he went on: 'at present there is no *English* earl nor bishop nor abbot, strangers all.' Another writer savagely attacked the Normans, calling them 'ignorant upstarts who gave rein to their pride and fury and thought they might do as they pleased'. There were very few of them like Gilbert de Heugleville, a kinsman of William, who did not find these things to his liking, and returned to Normandy because he did not wish to possess stolen property.

Of course, as time went on Norman brashness and English bitterness softened. The two races mixed, intermarried, and gradually became inextricably woven together, so that few could have told one from the other. But conquerors always leave some marks on the conquered, and the Normans have certainly left signs that in the eleventh century they were the masters of England. They came speaking Norman-French, and this was soon the language of the top people in the land, spoken in the king's court and by all who wanted to be fashionable. Though in the end it was the common English tongue that survived, there still remain plenty of reminders of the Norman Conquest in the common words and the many names of people and places derived from Norman-French that we use every day. For instance Osbern Gifard, one of the knights who we know came over with William, soon settled himself so firmly into his new estate of Stoke in Gloucestershire that in 20 years it had taken his name, Stoke Gifford; and the same was true of Stanton Harcourt, held by William de Harecourt, and of Kingston Bagpuize, whose new owner came from Bacquepuis in Normandy. Then there are personal names like Mortimer, Malet, and Beaumont, and plenty more that you can think of, which are Norman in origin; and, of course, words like 'beef', 'mutton', and 'pork'. And every time an Act of Parliament is given the royal assent today the old Norman-French *Le roi* (or *la regne*) *le veult* is used.

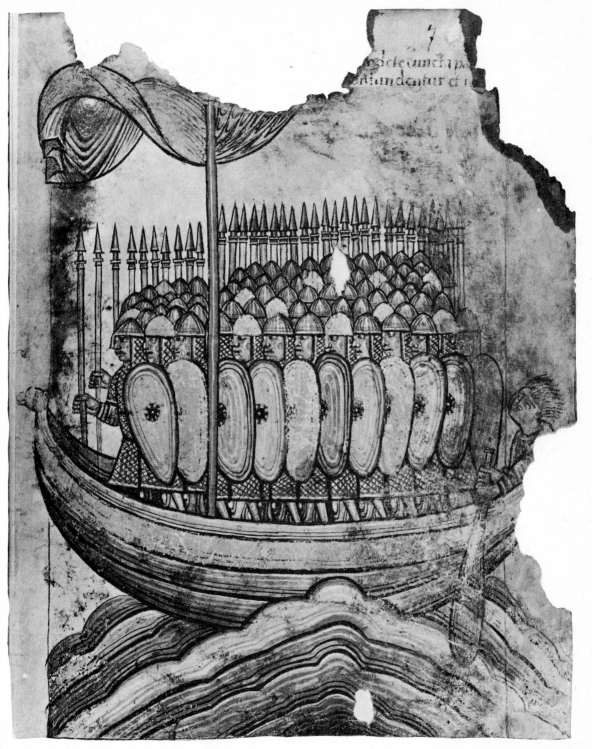

There were the other more solid results—castles and churches, for instance—, and these can still be seen by anyone who goes about with his eyes open. The Normans were great builders, and they found plenty of ways to use their skill in their new land. From the very first, castles were erected up and down the land, and for obvious reasons. Immediately after landing, William guarded his rear with castles, and by Christmas 1066 there were already five in use, Pevensey, Hastings, Dover, Wallingford, and Berkhamsted. Eighty-four others are mentioned by name in documents or chronicles written during his reign, and there must have been many more. Out of those 84, whose names we know, 71 were what are known as 'motte-and-bailly' castles, which consisted of a strong keep or tower, mounted on a high mound, which was either a natural one or artificial, and, of course, laboriously thrown up by the 'low men of England' out of clay, soil, and boulders. The first keeps were made of wood, partly because they were quicker to build, and partly because artificial mottes would not bear very heavy stone buildings until they had settled; but later, great stone keeps high on their mottes glowered down over towns like Thetford and Richmond and Oxford. Nothing was allowed to get in the way, and in the Domesday survey in 1086 it was reported that 166 houses in Lincoln had been destroyed 'on account of the castle', and there must have been many poor people there who cursed the owner; just as the Bishop of Worcester, driven beyond endurance, cursed Urse d'Abbetot for building a castle at Worcester that thrust into the very graveyard of the cathedral:

> Hatest thou Urs,
> Have thou Godes kurs.

Round the motte of these castles there was usually a ditch and a wooden stockade—later a wall—, and at its foot a large enclosed space for stables, barns, workshops, and dormitories, called the 'bailey'. Often a flight of steps led up from the bailey to the keep, and from some of the pictures of castles in the Bayeux tapestry it looks as if the Normans trained their horses to climb them.

William came to England with the Pope's blessing, and he was pledged to care for the English Church and bring new life into it. He was as good as his word. One by one, as English bishops and abbots died or resigned, they were replaced by Normans, till by the end of the Conqueror's reign only three Englishmen held high office in the Church, one bishop and two abbots; and the king's constant counsellor Lanfranc, abbot of Caen in Normandy, was made Archbishop of Canterbury in 1070. The Norman clergy were not much impressed by what they found. They thought the English churches were small and cramped, they were contemptuous of the way services were taken, and thought little of the scores of—

Above *The first Norman castles were of wood and stood on mounds like this one at Thetford. Mounds were often laboriously built by Englishmen.*

Right *Rochester castle frowns over the town.*

155

to them—unknown saints with unpronounceable names, like St. Cyneswide and St. Erconwald. But on the whole they did the work of bringing the Church up-to-date wisely and well. Only one arrogant Norman abbot, Thurston of Glastonbury, seems to have behaved with downright brutality, chasing the monks round the monastery with armed men because they did not like his new-fangled ways. They stubbornly refused to obey him and he was later withdrawn.

But the new brooms swept much away. 'He destroys well who builds better' was their motto, and every big church in the land (except Westminster and Waltham) and countless small ones were rebuilt in the Norman style. A Norman monk, who saw what the Norman bishop of Salisbury was doing to the cathedral there, wrote with approval, 'I would not allow buildings to stand unless they were according to *my* ideas, glorious, magnificent, most lofty, most spacious and most beautiful'; and there is no doubt that to this day the passionate energy and devotion of Norman priests and builders is written large across England in splendid cathedrals like Ely, Durham, Winchester, and Gloucester, and parish churches both large and small. Norman architects used a style which is sometimes called 'Romanesque', and this is because of the round pillars and round arches, which had been copied from the remains of ancient Roman buildings still standing in parts of Europe. Norman churches are not difficult to recognize if you look out for their thick walls, the massive round pillars carrying round arches just mentioned, and the round-headed windows and doors, some quite plain,

Ely Cathedral 'glorious, magnificent, most lofty, most spacious, and most beautiful'.

The church of St. Cataldo in Palermo, Sicily, was built by the Normans but has a distinctly eastern look.

Above *The Norman nave at Melbourne, Derbyshire.*

Left *The Saxon tower of Earl's Barton church which, fortunately, the Normans did not destroy.*

others elaborately decorated with patterns in stone; and when you have looked at a few you will agree that the monk of Salisbury was right. They are magnificent and most beautiful. Yet in the process of all this splendid building much that was ancient and beautiful too disappeared for ever. Some of the English churches were certainly small and cramped and some were ruinous and neglected, but not all were unworthy; and if you compare the two pictures on this page you will realize that English craftsmen had built well and decorated beautifully long before the Normans came.

So with their language, their buildings, their holding of the land, the Normans thrust themselves very deeply into England and English life, and for the first 21 years the great driving force behind all was William the king, the great strong burly man, with reddish hair, reddish face, and a guttural voice, a prince of proven worth and 'a very wise man', who, as you already know, was mild when men did his will but 'severe beyond measure' when they did not. Though he obviously could not oversee the building of every castle

159

and church, his influence was enormous and his hand was every-where. He owned all the land of England absolutely and un-mistakably, by right of conquest, and he was sovereign lord of all. No man was his equal in England, not even the very greatest of the warriors who had come with him, and in this way he was very different from the French kings. With the Conquest the feudal system of holding land, described in Chapter 6, was firmly planted in England, for William granted estates to his Normans as rewards for their help, and in return they gave homage, the oath of fealty, military service, and feudal aids. They in their turn sub-let parts of their land to other knights, this also in exchange for military service. All the details of service and dues were made very plain, and especially the fact that the king was supreme lord over every man, whether he held land of him directly or through another, and that loyalty to the king came before loyalty to any other.

William was a person who did nothing carelessly or without purpose, and he would not be deceived, cheated, or content with secondhand information. In 1086, so that he might know more about the land he had conquered, he 'held very deep speech with his council about the land—how it was peopled and with what sort of men', and the result was that he ordered the making of the Domesday survey. This was the greatest thing he left behind him, and is now one of our priceless possessions. It surveyed the land in every shire, and the property of every landholder, whether arch-bishop, bishop, abbot, earl, or knight; it laid bare how much everybody owned in land and cattle, and how much money it was worth. Slaves and free men, woods and meadows, mills and fisheries, everything was inquired into. 'So very narrowly did he have it investigated that not a yard of land, or one ox, cow or pig was left out.' So say the writer of the Anglo-Saxon Chronicle, and he adds 'Shame it is to relate it', but William thought it no shame. The survey told him much about the money and dues he could exact; but more than that, it told him what he certainly wanted to know about England how the land was peopled, and with what sort of men; nothing else could have done this so well.

To a great many people the words 'Norman Conquest' mean only what has so far been said in this chapter, '1066 and all that', and it is sometimes a surprise to find that William was not the only Norman to become the ruler of a foreign land, and that other restless descendants of Rollo and his Northmen invaded other places besides England, and this before William was old enough even to hold a sword. For one thing, the Normans were constant travellers and, for another, they were great pilgrims, much given to long journeys to holy places. But because they were a people in love with war, many of them went wearing a coat of mail under their sober pilgrim's robe, quietly carried a great sword as well as a pilgrim's

A page from Domesday book so clearly written that it can be read 900 years later. The list of tenants contains many Norman names.

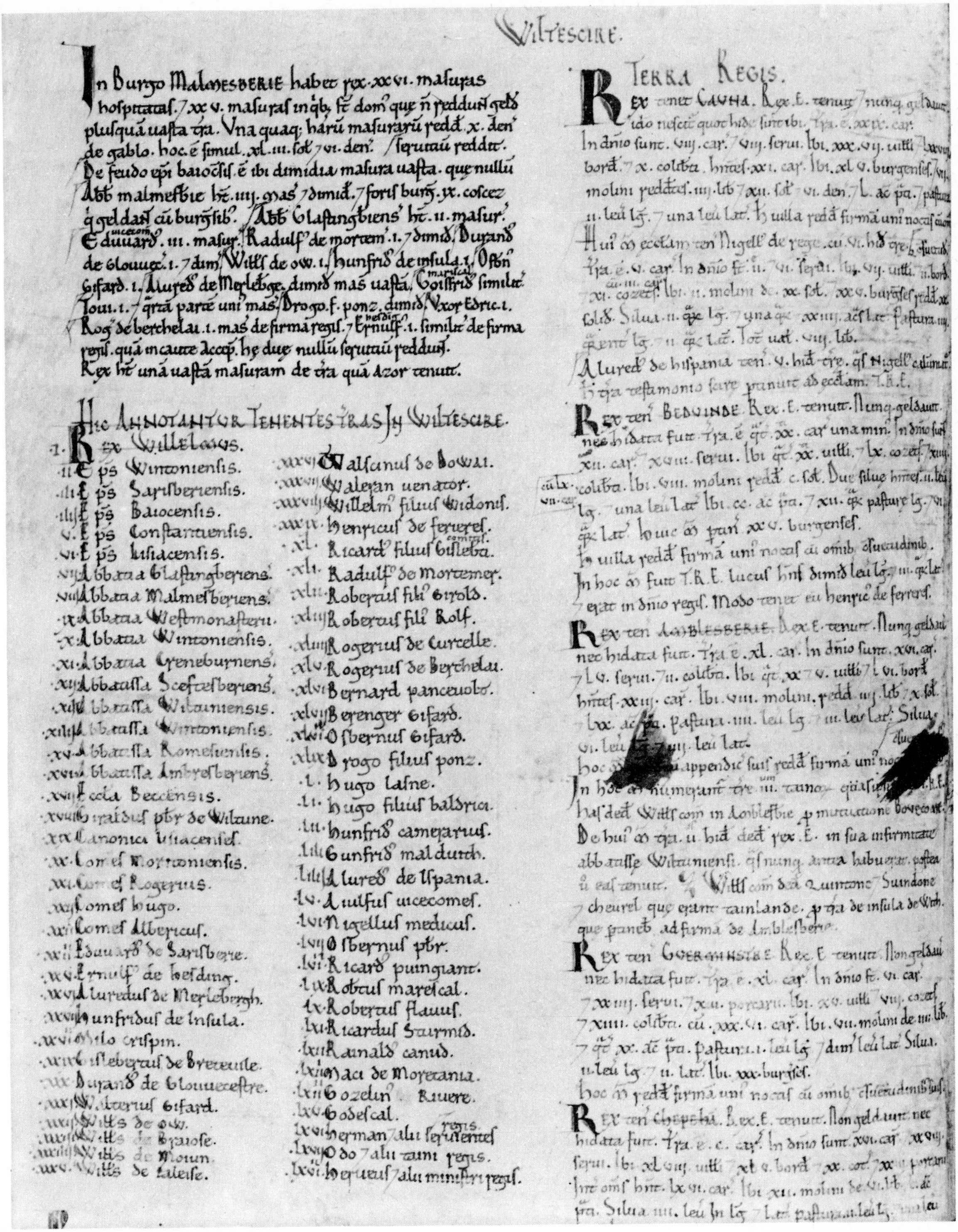
WILTESCIRE.

In Burgo Malmesberie habet rex .xxvi. masuras
hospitatas. 7 xxv. masuras in qb st dom que n reddunt geld
plusquā uasta tra. Vna quaq; harū masurarū redd .x. den
de gablo. hoc ē simul .xl.iii. sol 7 vi. den. 7 seruitiū reddit.
De feudo epi baiocsis ē ibi dimidia masura uasta. que nullū
Abb malmesbie ht .iiij. mas 7 dimid. 7 foris burg .ix. coscez
q geldant cū burgsib. Abb Glastingbiens ht .ii. masur.
Eduuard uicecom .iii. masur. Radulf de mortem .i. 7 dimid. Durand
de Glouuec .i. 7 dim. Witts de ow .i. hunfrid de insula .i. Osbn
Gifard .i. Alured de Merlebge dimid mas uastā. Goisfrid marescal similit.
Iou .i. 7 qrtā partē uni mas. Drogo f. ponz. dimid. Vxor Edric .i.
Rog de berchelai .i. mas de firma regis. 7 Ernulf de hesding .i. similit de firma
regis. quā in cautte accep. he due nullū seruitiū reddunt.
Rex ht unā uastā masuram de tra quā Azor tenuit.

HIC ANNOTANTUR TENENTES TRAS IN WILTESCIRE.

.I. Rex Willelmus.
.II. Eps Wintoniensis.
.III. Eps Sarisberiensis.
.IIII. Eps Baiocensis.
.V. Eps Constantiensis.
.VI. Eps Lisiacensis.
.VII. Abbatia Glastingberiens.
.VIII. Abbatia Malmesberiens.
.IX. Abbatia Westmonasterii.
.X. Abbatia Wintoniensis.
.XI. Abbatia Creneburnens.
.XII. Abbatissa Sceftesberiens.
.XIII. Abbatissa Wiltuniensis.
.XIIII. Abbatissa Wintoniensis.
.XV. Abbatissa Romesiensis.
.XVI. Abbatissa Ambresberiens.
.XVII. Eccla Beccensis.
.XVIII. [illegible]aidus pbr de Wiltune.
.XIX. Canonici Lisiacenses.
.XX. Comes Moritoniensis.
.XXI. Comes Rogerius.
.XXII. Comes Hugo.
.XXIII. Comes Albericus.
.XXIIII. Eduuard de Sarisbere.
.XXV. Ernulf de hesding.
.XXVI. Aluredus de Merleberge.
.XXVII. Hunfridus de Insula.
.XXVIII. Milo crispin.
.XXIX. Gislebertus de Breteuile.
.XXX. Durand de Glouuecestre.
.XXXI. Walterus Gifard.
.XXXII. Witts de ow.
.XXXIII. Witts de Braiose.
.XXXIIII. Witts de Moiun.
.XXXV. Witts de Faleise.
.XXXVI. Walscinus de Dowai.
.XXXVII. Waleran uenator.
.XXXVIII. Willelm filius Widonis.
.XXXIX. Henricus de Fereres.
.XL. Ricard filius Gisleba comitis.
.XLI. Radulf de Mortemer.
.XLII. Robertus fili Girold.
.XLIII. Robertus fili Rolf.
.XLIIII. Rogerius de Curcelle.
.XLV. Rogerius de Berchelai.
.XLVI. Bernard pancevolt.
.XLVII. Berenger Gifard.
.XLVIII. Osbernus Gifard.
.XLIX. Drogo filius ponz.
.L. Hugo Lasne.
.LI. Hugo filius baldrici.
.LII. Hunfrid camerarius.
.LIII. Gunfrid malduith.
.LIIII. Alured de Ispania.
.LV. Aiulfus uicecomes.
.LVI. Nigellus medicus.
.LVII. Osbernus pbr.
.LVIII. Ricard puingiant.
.LIX. Robtus marescal.
.LX. Robertus flauus.
.LXI. Ricardus Sturmid.
.LXII. Rainald canud.
.LXIII. Maci de Moretania.
.LXIIII. Gozelin Riuere.
.LXV. Godescal.
.LXVI. Herman 7 alii seruientes regis.
.LXVII. Odo 7 alii taini regis.
.LXVIII. Herueus 7 alii ministri regis.

TERRA REGIS.

Rex tenet Cauna. Rex E. tenuit 7 nunq geldauit
ideo nescit quot hide sint ibi. Tra ē .xxix. car.
In dnio sunt .viij. car. 7 .viij. serui. Ibi .xxx.vij. uitti 7 .xxvij.
bord 7 .x. colibti. hntes .xxi. car. Ibi .xl.v. burgenses. 7 .viij.
molini reddtes .iiij. lib 7 .xii. sol 7 .vi. den. 7 .l. ac pti. 7 pastura
.ii. leu lg. 7 una leu lat. H uilla redd firmā uni noctis cū om[illegible]
Hui m ecclam ten Nigell de rege cū .vi. hid tre. [illegible]
Tra ē .vi. car. In dnio st .ii. 7 .vi. serui. Ibi .viij. uitti .ii. bord
7 .xi. cozets. cū .iii. car. Ibi .ii. molini de .xx. sol. 7 .xxv. burgses redd .xx.
solid. Silua .ii. qrc lg. 7 una qrc 7 .xiiij. ac lat. Pastura .iij.
qrent lg. 7 .ii. qrc lat. Tot ual .viij. lib.
Alured de hispania ten .v. hid tre. qs Nigell calumniat.
H tra testamonio scire ptinuit ad ecclam. T.R.E.

Rex ten Beduinde. Rex E. tenuit. Nunq geldauit
nec hidata fuit. Tra ē qt .xx. car una min. In dnio sunt
.xii. car. 7 .xviii. serui. Ibi qt .xx. uitti. 7 .lx. cozets. 7 .xiiij.
colibti. Ibi .viii. molini redd .c. sol. Due silue hntes .ii. leu
lg. 7 una leu lat. Ibi .cc. ac pti. 7 .xii. qrc pasture lg. 7 .vi.
qrc lat. huic m ptin .xxv. burgenses.
H uilla redd firmā uni noctis cū omib consuetudinib.
In hoc m fuit T.R.E. lucus hns dimid leu lg. 7 .iii. qrc lat.
7 erat in dnio regis. Modo tenet eū henric de ferreres.

Rex ten Ambleseberie. Rex E. tenuit. Nunq geldau
nec hidata fuit. Tra ē .xl. car. In dnio sunt .xvi. car.
7 .lv. serui. 7 .ii. colibti. Ibi qt .xx. 7 .v. uitti 7 .l.vi. bord
hntes .xxiii. car. Ibi .viii. molini. redd .iiij. lib. 7 .x. sol.
7 .lx. ac [illegible]. Pastura .iii. leu lg. 7 .iii. leu lat. Silua
.vi. leu lg. 7 .iiij. leu lat.
Hoc [illegible] appendic suis redd firmā uni noc[illegible]
In hoc m nunquam tre .iii. taino[illegible] T.R.E.
has dedit Witts com in Amblesbie p mutatione [illegible]
De hui m tra .i. hid dedit rex E. in sua infirmitate
abbatisse Wiltuniensi. qs nunq antea habuerat. postea
n eas tenuit. Witts com dedit Quintone 7 Suindone
7 Cheuerel que erant tainlande. p tra de insula de Wiht.
que ptineb ad firmā de Amblesberie.

Rex ten Guerminstre. Rex E. tenuit. Nunq geldau
nec hidata fuit. Tra ē .xl. car. In dnio st .vi. car.
7 .xxiiij. serui. 7 .xii. porcarii. Ibi .xxv. uitti .viij. cozets
7 .xiiii. colibti. cū .xxx.vi. car. Ibi .vii. molini de .iii. lib.
7 qt .xx. ac pti. Pastura .i. leu lg. 7 dim leu lat. Silua
.ii. leu lg. 7 .ii. lat. Ibi .xxx. burgses.
Hoc m redd firmā uni noctis cū omib consuetudinib suis.

Rex ten Chepeha. Rex E. tenuit. Non geldauit nec
hidata fuit. Tra ē .c. car. In dnio sunt .xvi. car. 7 .xxviij.
serui. Ibi .xl.viii. uitti 7 .xlv. bord 7 .xx. cot. 7 .xx. porcarii
hnt omis hnt .lxvi. car. Ibi .xii. molini de [illegible]
pti. Silua .iiii. leu lg 7 [illegible] pastura [illegible]

staff, and on their way frequently put both to good use. If ever they saw a chance of profit or adventure by fighting they gladly lent a hand, joining in local warfare or taking part in a little enjoyable brigandage. One place where they frequently found both, and indeed visited often, was the south of Italy, a land much divided between many rulers and torn with strife, but always tempting and delectable. Here in the eleventh century came many Normans 'through the fields and meadows ... happy and joyful on their horses as they rode up and down to seek their fortunes'. Among the best known—and the most dreaded—of these Norman adventurers were the sons of Tancred, Baron of Hauteville near Coutances. The baron had twelve sons, and as his estates were not nearly large enough to support them, they naturally left home to seek land, booty, and renown: William the Iron Arm, Drogo, Humphrey, Robert, Roger, and the rest. The most famous were Robert (nicknamed Guiscard, the Wary) and Roger. Robert first arrived in Italy in 1046, when William the Conqueror was just 18, and for a time lived as a brigand, carrying off sheep and cattle and holding people to ransom. A Greek princess, Anna Comnena, who knew and hated him, described him carefully in her chronicle. She said he would never endure any control, and had come from Normandy with only five followers on horseback and thirty on foot. He was so tall that he towered above all others, his shoulders were broad, his hair flaxen, his cheeks ruddy, and his eyes of a dead blue like the sea (at moments, however, they all but shot sparks of fire). His voice was so terrific that it sounded like a multitude in uproar, and one bellow was said to have put thousands to flight. On his tomb are cut the words '*Hic terror Guiscardus*'.

It is not surprising that Robert Guisard 'grew daily in power and piled city on city and money upon money', until in 1071, just five years after the battle of Hastings, when his father's overlord William had begun his conquest of England, he was master of all southern Italy. Robert's conquest was recognized when he made a treaty with the pope and did homage for his great new domain; and so this Norman brigand became 'by the grace of God and Saint Peter, duke of Apulia and Calabria and, with their help hereafter, of Sicily'. Stories of his deeds rang through Europe, and William the Conqueror used to stir his own courage by thinking about them, for 'he thought it would be dishonour if he yielded in valour to a man whom he excelled in rank, for Robert was of middling birth.'

But Robert Guiscard did not become the ruler of Sicily. Instead, his younger brother Roger, who had followed him to Italy and fought along with him, did. No one knows exactly when the Hautevilles first saw the rich and beautiful island across the straits of Messina, but no member of their family ever saw a neighbour's lands without wanting them for himself. In this case the neighbours

were the Saracens, who had held Sicily for 300 years. The two brothers began the conquest of the island in 1061, intending to share it between them, but Robert Guiscard died before the last Saracen stronghold gave in, and Roger became 'the Great Count' and the master of Sicily. The island was a meeting-place of races, religions, and languages, for the people were mainly Greeks and Saracens, Christians and Muslims, and they spoke Arabic, Greek, and Latin. The Normans now added Western Christianity and French. It was a good thing that Roger was tolerant enough to let them all live together in peace, and did not persecute any of them for their different customs and faiths; and it is not surprising that when the Normans built churches there they gave them eastern domes as well as round arches, and that Roger's son, who first took the title of 'King of Sicily', dressed like an eastern monarch and kept a large harem.

So by 1066 the Norman William was King of England, the Norman Robert Guiscard conqueror of southern Italy, and the Norman Roger 'was the great Count' of Sicily. The descendants of the Northmen in their last invasions did not do badly.

Chapter 12
Cluniacs and Cistercians

In 1075, only nine years after William of Normandy's conquest of England, one of the energetic Norman adventurers who had shared in that expedition, William, Earl of Warenne, set off with his wife Gundrada on a pilgrimage to Rome. Rome, the sacred city of the apostles, the seat of the popes, with its 300 churches and its rich collection of relics, was deeply venerated by all Christians, and no doubt William of Warenne in his warrior's life had committed many sins for which he might think it good to do penance. Pilgrims to Rome from England followed the great Roman road which still cuts through France from Boulogne to Lyons, the Via Agrippa. As it reaches the southern parts of France it passes through the rich country of Burgundy, and here William and Gundrada met with a sharp setback. Other travellers warned them that they should take shelter quickly, as the war which had broken out between Pope Gregory VII and the Emperor Henry IV made it unsafe to go on. William was not the man to quail at the prospect of a skirmish, but we must remember that he had Gundrada with him.

They decided that it would be best to turn aside for a while from the main pilgrim route, and to ask for shelter at the great Benedictine abbey which lay about twelve miles away at Cluny. The thought of visiting Cluny must have roused their interest and excitement in any case, for Cluny was no ordinary monastery. As they rode forward they could see the towers of the church and the massive yet elegant buildings from some miles off, since Cluny lay among the pleasant vineyards of the broad fertile valley of the River Grosne, sheltered by the high limestone hills with their finely wooded slopes. It was a beautiful setting for a monastery of great dignity and splendour. At the towering gateway which led to the outer court of the abbey William was kindly and courteously received by the porter. The servants and grooms who attended him and his wife were taken away together with the horses, and looked after elsewhere in the various buildings of the vast abbey precincts, but William and Gundrada, having announced who they were, were treated with great honour and taken immediately to the monk who was appointed to look after the spacious guest-house. It must have been a relief to realize, as they could see at a glance, that they would be exceedingly comfortable and well looked after while they stayed there. There was plenty of room, for although there were

Entrance arches of the abbey gate at Cluny, with a view of the church beyond.

other guests, also people of rank, there was a dormitory for 40 men and one for 30 women, with a common refectory in which all the guests dined together, and talked of their adventures on the road, of the business of their journey, or simply, as one does, of the weather. The weather matters very much when you are travelling, and although Abbot Hugh of Cluny thought nothing of crossing the Alps in mid winter, to get to Rome, not all men were so fearless.

As they stayed on, William and Gundrada began to feel the spell of Cluny's charm. Abbot Hugh was away, but the monastery was

165

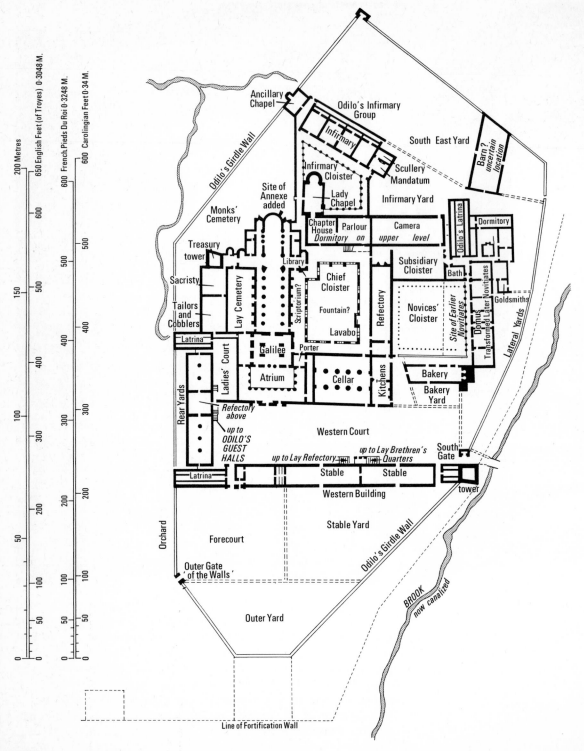

200 Metres

650 English Feet (of Troyes) 0·3048 M.

French Pieds Du Roi 0·3248 M.

600 Carolingian Feet 0·34 M.

Odilo's Girdle Wall

Ancillary Chapel

Odilo's Infirmary Group

Infirmary

South East Yard

Barn? uncertain location

Site of Annexe added

Infirmary Cloister

Lady Chapel

Infirmary Yard

Scullery Mandatum

Monks' Cemetery

Chapter House

Parlour

Dormitory on

Camera *upper level*

Odilo's Latrina

Dormitory

Treasury tower

Library

Subsidiary Cloister

Bath

Sacristy

Chief Cloister

Fountain?

Refectory

Novices' Cloister

Site of Earlier Novitiates

Domus

Transformed Later Novitiates

Goldsmiths

Tailors and Cobblers

Lay Cemetery

Scriptorium?

Lavabo

Latrina

Ladies' Court

Galilee

Porter

Cellar

Kitchens

Bakery

Bakery Yard

Atrium

Rear Yards

Refectory above

up to ODILO'S GUEST HALLS

Western Court

up to Lay Refectory

up to Lay Brethren's Quarters

South Gate

Latrina

Stable

Stable

tower

Western Building

Orchard

Stable Yard

Forecourt

Odilo's Girdle Wall

BROOK *now canalized*

Outer Gate 'of the Walls'

Outer Yard

Line of Fortification Wall

*Plan of the monastery of
Cluny about 1050.*

run with such discipline and precision that there was no slacking in
his absence. William saw almost the whole abbey under the guidance
of the guest-master, when the monks were in the church at Mass.
We can follow his tour with the help of the plan on p. 166. He was
taken first into the great cloister, a large rectangular garden with a
central fountain and round the sides a colonnade in which the
monks could sit and read or copy manuscripts. As he stood by the
door through which he had just entered, William was in the north
walk of the cloister, which ran alongside the church. The church
itself lay on his left, and the music of the service came faintly
through the door, adding to the peace of the beautiful quadrangle.
At the far end of the north walk, facing him, was the library. It was
a very fine library, looked after by the precentor, who also arranged
which monks were to read each day in the church and in the
refectory. He chose the ones with the best voices. The precentor had
his problems with that library, because some monks would borrow
books and forget to return them. There were lists of the names of
monks and the titles of the books they had out (one at least still
exists), but any librarian knows that it takes more than neat lists to
deal with the problem of missing books. Some had been lent from
Cluny's library to monks in other monasteries, but Abbot Hugh
strictly forbade this; he gave the precentor every support.

The guest-master did not take William along the north walk;
instead they turned right, down the west walk, and here they went
into the cellarer's store-house. It was a magnificent series of rooms,
built to store the food and wine for a community of some 300 monks,
and many others, servants and craftsmen who all made for the
smooth running of monastic life. William heard how the provisions
were brought here from Cluny's vast estates. The abbey owned
over a 100 properties in various parts of central and southern
France. Only the nearer estates sent in the actual corn, vegetables,
and dairy produce; on the more distant estates the produce was sold
and the money sent to Cluny instead. Cluny had valuable fishing
rights too, and the monk whom the cellarer put in charge of the
fishing was allowed special permission to ride out through the
monastery gates at night after Vespers, as this was the best time to
set the nets in the river.

Through a side door in the cellar they were able to walk into the
kitchen where the food was cooked. Monks themselves took their
turn at the kitchen work, as St. Benedict had expected them to.
The monks had three dishes at dinner, the main meal: first a dish
of dried peas, then fish, eggs, or cheese, and finally fresh vegetables
or fruit. It may sound rather dull, but the monks had in fact good
appetites; four or five eggs were allowed for each monk at this meal
and also a pound of bread.

Cloister walk at Silvacare, a Cluniac monastery. The capitals of the pillars are elaborate and beautifully carved.

When William and his guide stepped out again from the heat and bustle of the kitchens into the lighter and more airy cloister, they were standing at the head of the south walk, and on their right lay the refectory. As they entered this lofty dining room William was delighted by its fine proportions. It was very quiet for there was no one about at this time of day when the monks were in church. It was an elegant room, cool and gracious; the walls were covered with paintings, and the long tables were carefully laid out for the main meal of the day. By each monk's place was a drinking-cup into which his allowance of wine was measured, and each cup was covered over with a little sprig of box-wood to keep out the flies. There was another twig set in each place on the table too, a cutting of vine, dipped in glue, to act as a fly trap. The room had an atmosphere of great stillness as one entered it, perhaps because the monks never spoke during their meals. Instead of conversation they listened to one of the monks reading from the Bible.

From here the guest-master took William to another cloister, on the other side of the refectory from the great cloister. It was less imposing than the main cloister, but still spacious and pleasant, and round it were grouped the buildings where the novices slept and worked. These were the boys and men who wished to become monks, but who were still going through a time of testing and preparation. The novitiate should have lasted a year, but in Abbot Hugh's time it was sometimes cut down to a few weeks at Cluny, if the person concerned were very wealthy. The house was rather anxious to have the property that the monk would bring to it, and did not want him to have too much time to change his mind. As they returned to the main cloister, now strolling up the fourth side of it, the east walk, William may have seen some piles of washing being whisked off to the laundry, for this was a job done while the monks were at Mass. All the monks' clothes, which were in the care of an official called the chamberlain, were marked clearly in thread with the name of the individual monk, which greatly simplified matters of lost property and of returning the right clothes to the right monk when they came back from being laundered. The chamberlain was responsible for making the clothes too, and had a number of tailors working for him in a workshop on the premises. Each monk had a new tunic and a new cowl or hood each year, and a new sheepskin cloak every three years, and shirts and drawers when he needed them. He also had strapped shoes for day wear, and two pairs of night boots (summer and winter ones), which he would wear when he came down to the church for the night services.

As the two men approached the middle of the west walk the guest-master opened a door on the right and they climbed the staircase to the dormitory. Here were rows of palliasses filled with hay, each with its pillow, two blankets, and a sheepskin coverlet. The abbot slept here too, among his monks, as St. Benedict assumed that an abbot would. Later abbots, however, had their own separate lodgings. After they had come back to the cloister down the staircase, they turned right and the guest-master pointed out to William the door of the chapter-house, where the monks had their daily business meeting. They did not go in, because this room was not on the list for the guided tour. They had now completed their walk right round this immense cloister, and William perhaps turned round for a final admiring look at a place which, in the words of another visitor, was so beautiful that it seemed to invite monks to dwell there.

They left the great cloister by a narrow passage which led through to yet another whole set of buildings, grouped round a third cloister. Here was the infirmary, with its own chapel and store rooms. The sick monks were sent here, where they were allowed

food, such as meat, which was not permitted to the rest. The infirmarian, who was the monk in charge here, was chosen for qualities of gentleness and patience. In the evening after Compline he visited each sick monk and made every effort to give him whatever he needed. We know of Abbot Hugh's own deep concern for those who were ill. When one monk, Robert, was stricken with the terrible and incurable disease of leprosy, instead of turning him out of the monastery, Hugh ordered a little extra apartment to be made at the end of the infirmary, so that Robert should still be with them, although kept in some isolation. The infirmary was never empty, for many an elderly man who had led a full and active life as a feudal lord turned to Cluny when he felt death approaching, and wanted to become a monk there for the last days of his life.

We may imagine that William's mind had been working actively as he went round the buildings of Cluny, and as he saw evidence of the gracious, well ordered and holy life of the monks. He and Gundrada had both experienced by now the great kindness the monks showed to guests, and although they had not met Abbot Hugh they had met his deputy, the prior, and they had been impressed by him. We do not know just when William and Gundrada worked out their plan; it may have been in the monastery guest-house, or it may have been after they had left, on their journey back to their English estates in Sussex. Before ever they had gone abroad they had thought of founding a monastery at Lewes, in a niche of the South Downs, and now they were eager and determined that their new monastery should be Cluniac. William spoke of that memorable visit to Cluny in one of the documents drawn up in connection with the foundation of the new priory. He writes: 'And because we found holiness and religion and so great charity, and we were so honourably received by the good prior, and by all the holy convent, who took us into their society and fraternity, we began to have a love and devotion for that order and that house above all other houses that we had seen.'

This needs some explanation. William here refers to the 'order' as well as the house of Cluny. Cluny was not in fact simply a single splendid and wealthy Benedictine monastery; it was the head of a vast group of dependent monasteries or 'priories'. All were under the special protection of the pope, and all were subject to the abbot of Cluny. The order had spread to many parts of France, and also to Italy, Spain, and Germany. And in 1077, through William of Warenne and Gundrada, it came to England, when Abbot Hugh agreed to send three monks to start the little priory of St. Pancras at Lewes. You can visit the ruins today.

This great Cluniac order gave Cluny itself immense prestige, but it was an unwieldy affair. Monks in any Cluniac house, and there

were some 1,200 of these by the early twelfth century, were all regarded as monks of Cluny. Every monk had to take his vows in the presence of the abbot of Cluny, and at some time in his life he must visit Cluny itself. This huge order was a terrible strain on the energy of Cluny's own abbot, who was responsible for it all. It must have been rather like running a firm with 1,200 branches—but without a telephone!

Since Cluny was so popular, it is clearly important to understand what was special about her. Cluny based her way of life firmly on the Rule of St. Benedict, but over the centuries the tradition of Benedictine life had changed. Monks no longer spent much time in manual work, either in crafts or, still less, in agriculture. The emphasis had swung to the extremely elaborate celebration of the services in the church. At Cluny the services were longer, more splendid, more elaborate, more beautiful than elsewhere, simply because they aimed at the highest standards they could reach in the tradition they had inherited.

When we described Earl Warenne's tour of the monastic buildings at Cluny, we did not mention the church. This was not one of the places to which he would be taken by the guest-master, but in fact he would be allowed to see it and we may be pretty sure that he did. He may have been present at one of the services, watching the processions from the 'narthex' or vestibule at the west end. The church William would have seen was the second church at Cluny, but shortly after his visit Abbot Hugh began the building of a third church, which was the largest in the whole of Europe until the building of the present church of St. Peter in Rome. To the visitor it must have been a breath-taking sight, quite different from Justinian's St. Sophia in Constantinople, but not less fine. As you entered you could see the full length of the building, right up to the central eastern apse at the far end, where a hugh and magnificent wall-painting of Christ in Majesty dominated the whole church, a symbol of power and glory. To right and left down the centre of the nave three tiers of arches soared upwards to the lofty stone vault, and behind each arcade of arches were two side aisles, with their lesser arcades. Round these aisles went the solemn and spectacular processions of clergy and monks at the great festivals, the clergy resplendent in their beautifully embroidered vestments. Abbot Hugh had been specially permitted by the pope to wear the vestments of a bishop. As the processions proceeded up the church towards the choir and the high altar, covered by its sumptuous gold cloth, they passed through the 'crossing', where to right and left the greater transepts branched out, for the church was built in the form of a cross. Beyond these transepts as one went further east was a second set of smaller transepts. Radiating from the whole sweeping

curve of the east end of the church, and lining the eastern wall of each transept, were small chapels, each exquisite in its own way, each with its own altar, where the monks who were priests could celebrate Mass privately. The decoration of the church in wood and stone carving and in richly embroidered altar-hangings matched the splendour of the building itself. The service-books were in covers of gold or silver set with precious jewels. And above all these were the lights. St. Bernard of Clairvaux, a monk of whom we shall hear more later, resolutely opposed the Cluniac splendour. He happened to have a great gift for fine description, and as he rails against the fantastically beautiful devices for lighting the church we seem to glimpse their sparkling loveliness as William of Warenne himself must have seen them. 'The church', writes Bernard furiously, 'is adorned with gemmed crowns of light, like great wheels, encircled with lights which are scarcely more brilliant than the precious stones which decorate them. Moreover we see candelabra like great trees of brass, fashioned with wonderful skill and glittering as much with their jewels as with the lights they hold.' This is certainly a very good description of the seven-branched candlestick which Queen Matilda, wife of the English king, Henry I, had given as an offering to the church of Cluny. Indeed, all that could be done by a vast and highly decorated building, rich and dignified ceremonial, and fine singing, to give dignity and beauty to the worship of God was done at Cluny. In this respect it has probably never been equalled.

Such an ideal could only be achieved at a cost. St. Bernard, as we saw, thought that the cost was too great. The simplicity of early Benedictine life at Monte Cassino had been lost, and although the life at Cluny was still wholesome in Abbot Hugh's time, eventually the abbey was to sink beneath the distractions of her wealth and power. But that lay in the future. William of Warenne was not a man to be taken in by something fundamentally unsound, and Cluny stood for an ideal of the 'beauty of holiness' which has inspired many since that time. This did not mean that it was the right place for every type of man who wished to become a monk in the twelfth century. Clearly it was not the way for St. Bernard. Nor was it the way for a really great scholar such as St. Anselm, who became archbishop of Canterbury in William Rufus's reign. Anselm decided not to become a Cluniac monk himself, because he would not have had the time to give to serious study in the ceaseless round of church services. The only type of student who was perfectly happy in Cluny was one who simply enjoyed filling in odd moments with making extracts from other people's works. Such a one was the Cluniac monk Gregory, a man who would never have been known to us but for a chance remark of Abbot Peter of Cluny. He is now saved to us for ever as a real person. Gregory not only ferreted in the

library at Cluny, but managed to get permission to burrow in the dusty corners of libraries in other Cluniac houses. Abbot Peter, who also had to visit the other houses of the order on business, was always coming across Gregory. He is clearly amused and touched by the busy industry of this little old monk, and finally he sums it up: 'Wherever the business of the order calls me, in all our houses and even in their darkest corners, I find Gregory with his Sermons, Gregory with his Letters, Gregory with his treatises, with a pile of books and notes. I see you everywhere and everywhere in the same surroundings; the lap of your robe is full of books, your knees give way beneath their weight.'

Perhaps the only touch of disappointment that William and Gundrada had about their visit to Cluny was that they had missed meeting Abbot Hugh. Hugh had been abbot for nearly 30 years when their chance visit happened, but he was to rule Cluny for another 30 yet. The custom at Cluny was to appoint people to high positions not because of their age or experience but on sheer ability. Hugh was elected abbot at the early age of 24. He was a great man by any standards. He was of high birth, the son of a French count; one of his sisters became Duchess of Burgundy, and his nephews and nieces married into the royal families of France and Spain. He looked an aristocrat too, tall and well built, with a strikingly fine presence. Secondly, Hugh was great in the sense that he held a very powerful position. We have seen that the abbot of Cluny was in supreme control of the whole Cluniac order, and everywhere he went he was paid great respect. When his name was mentioned the monks bowed, and if he was attending service the bell went on ringing until he arrived, for it was unthinkable that he should be made to appear late. When he returned to Cluny after an absence he was met by a fine ceremonial procession of the whole community of monks.

Abbot Hugh was a truly European figure. He was well received at the papal court in Rome, for Gregory VII was a great admirer of Cluny and of Hugh personally. He was on friendly terms with the French royal family and with the imperial family in Germany too. In fact he was godfather to Henry IV. Since he knew both Gregory VII and Henry IV, we may well ask what his attitude was to their terrible quarrel. As Cluny stood for the purity of Church life, and had always been under the special protection of Rome, Hugh would certainly give wholehearted support to Gregory's zeal for the reform of the Church. Yet he was far more calm and detached than Gregory; he could see that Henry IV had a case too, and he hated to see pope and emperor, the two greatest leaders in Christendom, at war with each other. In his view they should have been working together in harmony, and so he did all he could for peace. Hugh was

present in the castle of Canossa in 1077. Perhaps his was the decid-
ing voice in persuading Gregory to receive back the penitent
emperor as a member of the Church.

Both pope and emperor would listen to Hugh, for he was a man
who commanded respect by the force of his own personality as well
as by his high position. Despite all the travelling to royal courts, all
the calls on his time in ruling the huge Cluniac order, and the
requests for his help in settling many disputes Hugh kept the inner
calm of a monk. As we have seen, he would concern himself with
making kind thoughtful arrangements for the poor leprous monk
Robert, even when great rulers were eagerly asking his attention for
their affairs. Hugh was the worthy abbot of a great monastic house
and we may end our account of Cluny with the words of Gregory
VII: 'Of all the houses north of the Alps there shines first and
foremost that of Cluny . . . . Without a doubt it surpasses all other
monasteries, even the most ancient.'

⋆ ⋆ ⋆

Perhaps any great movement produces in the end a man who
wants to rebel against it. So at least it was with Cluny. Romauld of
Ravenna, a Cluniac monk in the little Italian house of San Miniato,
somehow found the time to read deeply in the works of the monks
of the Egyptian desert, those solitary hermits who had lived long
before St. Benedict and had set out to endure a life far more severe
and harsh than anything St. Benedict had ever approved. The
desert monks believed in complete solitude, and the fierce repres-
sion of all their human desires for pleasure and comfort, as a means
to finding true contact with God. Romauld found these writings far
more inspiring than the orderly but comparatively quiet way of life
at San Miniato, and he founded two communities of semi-hermit
monks at places with romantic names in remote and lonely parts of
the Appennines: Fonte Avellana and Camaldoli. These were not
Benedictine monasteries at all, but drew their inspiration from the
writings of the Desert Fathers. Such ideas are infectious, and a
younger monk of San Miniato, John Gualbert, now founded a
monastery at Vallombrosa near Florence. This was different again.
The monks of Vallombrosa were not hermits, they were Benedic-
tines; but they wanted a much simpler life than that of San Miniato,
and to spend much more time in prayer and silence instead of in
lengthy, elaborate, church services.

It was not long before the stirrings of these new movements
began to be felt north of the Alps. Men became restless, impatient
of the traditional way of life at Cluny. They began to say that St.
Benedict had never intended all this elaborate ceremony and endless
church services, that he had not wanted monasteries to own vast

estates and control manors and serfs and mills. They had a great urge to get back to what they felt to be the *true* Benedictine way, a way of poverty and simplicity, in which men worked with their hands and had time to pray to God on their own. In Burgundy and also in northern France there appeared groups of hermits living in the woodlands and on the mountains in small huts which they made themselves of twigs and leaves. Often they were the followers of wandering preachers, who were giving a new call to a quite different way of monastic life. Many new orders of monks grew up. Since we cannot tell the story of them all, we will look more closely at the most famous one, the Cistercian order.

The founder of the little community in the forest of Cîteaux near Dijon was a Frenchman, Robert of Molesme, but by 1109 its prior was an Englishman, Stephen Harding, and three years later the little group of monks was joined by the young Burgundian nobleman who was to make Cîteaux known throughout Europe, St. Bernard. The community was very poor, and set out to follow the Rule of St. Benedict exactly and simply, but their numbers grew, and in 1115 Bernard was sent with a few monks to found a daughter house at Clairvaux. The site of the new monastery was not promising. The man who later wrote about Bernard's life called it 'a place of horror, a vast solitude, a den of thieves'. Here Bernard and his companions toiled away, cutting down wood, dragging it to the building site, and slowly putting up the walls of the rough little two-storey house in which they were all to live. In the lower rooms there were no floors, just the hard trodden earth. There was a small refectory with a simple table, and a little chapel, utterly plain, without even a lamp before the altar. On the floor above was the dormitory. The monks slept on bundles of straw, thrown down on the floor, with logs for pillows.

In the early days they were desperately poor. They often fed on coarse barley bread and beech leaves, and they possessed only one animal, a little donkey which had to carry the abbot on his journeys and also the wood for the fires. Several of the monks could stand this no longer; they begged Bernard to let them all go back to Cîteaux. Bernard would not give in; his great strength of purpose and tremendous will power eventually carried his monks with him. They stayed, they prayed for help, and in the end help came.

Within Bernard's life-time Clairvaux had struggled from these small and painful beginnings to become a great monastery of between 700 and 800 people, more than twice as big as Cluny. Many hundreds of Cistercian monasteries had been founded, in France, Germany, Italy, Spain, England, and Scotland. Cistercianism took Europe by storm. The way of life in all these monasteries was quite unlike that of Cluny. The Cistercian monks had firm

clear-cut ideas of what they were aiming at, and, with the help of Stephen Harding's gift for crisp exact expression, these aims were carefully written down, so that nothing was left in doubt. The Cistercians refused to allow themselves anything beyond what St. Benedict had actually mentioned in the Rule. They welcomed hardship. They would have no cloaks or shirts or warm hoods or bedspreads, and no extra dishes of food. Bernard was very scathing about the excellent food at Cluny, for although the Cluniacs did not eat meat they had deliciously appetising vegetarian dishes. Bernard demands angrily, 'Who may tell of the eggs alone, in how many ways they are cooked, tossed, beaten to froth, now hard boiled, now baked, now stuffed?' It certainly does sound delicious! The Cistercians would not allow themselves to own any manors or serfs, any mills, fairs, or bakeries, such as the Cluniacs had. Instead, they deliberately went out into remote uninhabited places and built their monasteries on wild uncultivated land. It was often very beautiful country. In England, Rievaulx and Fountains were built in the Yorkshire Dales, sheltered by the pleasant woods and gently sloping hills, with clear streams flowing in the valleys. Other houses were built in the hill country of Spain, Italy, and Germany, and Bernard was aware of the serenity that the beauty and the solitude could bring. 'Believe one who has proved it; you will find among the woods something you never found in books. Stones and trees will teach you a lesson you never heard from the masters in the schools.' Above all, almost in defiance of the splendour of the church at Cluny, they made their own churches as simple as possible.

Crucifixes were of wood instead of gold or silver; on the altars stood heavy iron candlesticks; there were no silk or embroidered vestments, only the plainest of linen robes, and even the chalices were to be of silver and not of gold.

In these plain churches there were simpler and much shorter services. Monks once again had time to work with their hands, and Cistercian monks ploughed the land, reaped the harvest, and tended the cattle, as well as doing the domestic chores inside the monastery. They had time too to step into the church for quiet private prayer. There was more time, more space, more fresh air.

Yet one wonders whether St. Bernard was demanding more than most monks could manage in setting such high standards. And, indeed, there were grumblers even at Clairvaux. Bernard, of course, knew how to deal with them. In one of his sermons he mentions to the monks some of their actual complaints that had reached him, so as to shame them into seeing how petty they were being. It was food, as usual: 'You plead that cheese burdens your stomach and milk gives you a headache, your chest complaint does not allow you to drink mere water; cabbages foster melancholy and leeks breed bile, fish from a stream or a muddy pond are utterly unhelpful to a man of your complexion.' He pauses. 'Here, brother, is no question of your complexion but of your calling. You are not a doctor but a monk.'

Yet the grumblers were very few, and those who found peace and happiness in this hard life were many. An English novice put it unforgettably: 'Our food is scanty, our garments rough, our drink is from the stream ... under our tired limbs is but a hard mat; when sleep is sweetest we must rise at a bell's bidding'; and yet 'everywhere peace, everywhere serenity and a marvellous freedom from the tumult of the world.'

The lands around a Cistercian abbey were worked as a huge ranch, and as there were no serfs all the hard manual labour had to be done by men from the monastery. The ordinary monks, even with a much reduced timetable of church services, could not long hope to deal with all the field work needed to provide food for a large community. The problem was solved by throwing open the Cistercian order to many thousands of peasants. This was a revolutionary step. The monks in the Benedictine houses of the eleventh and twelfth centuries were almost all men of the feudal knightly class, but every Cistercian house had a large group of 'lay brothers', men who spent most of the day ploughing, sowing, harrowing, reaping, tending livestock, as they had spent their days before they entered the order. They were attached in groups to 'granges', small farm centres scattered over the abbey lands, each with its little chapel for daily prayer, and here the lay brothers ate

and slept. But on feast days, from all the granges you might have seen them tramping back the weary miles to the monastery church, and at Rievaulx, 'You might see the church crowded with the brethren like bees in a hive, unable to move forward because of the crowd.'

Behind the startling popularity of Cistercianism stood the dominating figure of St. Bernard. We know him well, because he wrote hundreds of letters; he says that he never left a letter unanswered, and he often wrote them late into the night. He wrote letters to his friends, to his enemies, to abbots, bishops, kings, and the pope, and he pours out advice and rebukes and encouragement. Sometimes he would end a letter with amusing abruptness, like this: 'Please return as soon as you can those books of mine which you borrowed.' Bernard had a genius for making friends, and he cared enough to write to them often. Some who had been his monks at Clairvaux, and later rose to high office in the Church in distant lands, often missed him desperately at first; he gently teased and encouraged them, and above all kept in touch.

Bernard never seemed hesitant or in doubt. He took a firm stand on a question, and then acted vigorously. In many ways he was a fighter. When he heard of an unworthy man being appointed as a bishop he brought all the influence he had to get matters put right, writing forthright letters to the pope, the local clergy and the king. He usually won, though he made many enemies. When the rebellious young university lecturer, Peter Abelard, was writing about religion in a way that Bernard thought irreverent and wrong, he lashed out against him in letters to the cardinals at Rome. 'The faith of the simple is being held up to scorn, the secrets of God are being reft open, the most sacred matters are being recklessly discussed.' He did not rest until he had brought Abelard to be condemned by a great council of churchmen. Abelard's friends never forgave Bernard.

The splendour of kings held no terrors for Bernard, and a letter of rebuke to the young King Louis VII of France ends: 'I have spoken to you sharply because I fear sharper things for you, and I would not fear them so much were I not so fond of you'. He did not mince matters when warning a friend that he would be visited by a certain bishop, who was supporting the wrong cause in Bernard's view. 'It is not my habit to approach anything in a roundabout way', he starts. 'A deceitful man is coming to you, in order to deceive you, so I believe. May he not succeed! Do not let yourself be hookwinked by the man's sad appearance, mean clothes, pleading expression, humble words, nor even by his crocodile tears. All this is just appearances. . . . Pay no regard to what he says.'

It was not always the great affairs of Church and State that

roused Bernard to write so fiercely. On one occasion he was furious about some stolen pigs. The abbot of Chatillon, a good man, Bernard tells us, had gone on pilgrimage to Rome and had left his property in Bernard's care. . . . 'And now the servants of Simon, men of Belfort, have taken off his pigs.' Bernard is very angry indeed with the lord of the district who has done nothing at all to get those pigs back for Bernard's friend. Bernard rails against him for failing in his duty. 'I assure you,' he adds, 'I would rather have had my own pigs stolen.' He obviously feels upset about what the abbot will think when he gets back and misses those pigs.

Bernard's fighting spirit made him an eager supporter of the crusading movement. He preached rousing sermons in favour of the Second Crusade. Writing to the English people to stir them to action he exclaims, 'Your land is well known to be rich in young and vigorous men. The world is full of their praises and the renown of their courage is on the lips of all. . . . Now, O mighty soldiers, O men of war, you have a cause for which you can fight without danger to your souls; a cause in which to conquer is glorious and for which to die is gain.' Bernard also helped the young French knight Hugh de Payns in the founding of an order of crusading knights who were specially dedicated to protecting pilgrims. They were known as the Templars, and the Temple Church in London is one of their buildings in this country.

Yet Bernard was not all fire and righteous anger. Violence for its own sake he hated. A massacre of the Jews shocked him deeply: 'The Jews are not to be persecuted, killed or even put to flight,' he writes, and again, 'Is it not a far better triumph for the Church to convince and convert the Jews than to put them all to the sword?' Bernard could be very understanding too. When a very troublesome monk in a monastery at Dijon has run away for a third time from his house, it is Bernard who takes him in, and writes to his abbot urging still further patience in dealing with poor weak Brother Henry, who now wants to go back again. It is the finer side of Bernard's character that we touch in this letter.

> I appeal to your loving heart for this little sheep of yours, who has strayed from the fold. I beg you to have mercy and compassion on him after the example of the Good Shepherd. I know full well how capricious he is, I know that he has left his monastery twice before this and been received back. Nevertheless you know very well that mercy must be preferred to justice, and Blessed Benedict, who says that a monk is to be received back up to three times, is especially to be obeyed. It is for this that Brother Henry implores your kindness.

Clearly Brother Henry was enough to try anyone's patience to breaking point, but Bernard himself is infinitely patient with any man, however difficult, tiresome, and unlovable, who really wants to have yet another chance.

The tremendous success of Cistercianism, the founding of hundreds of Cistercian houses all over western Europe, was perhaps largely the result of Bernard's dynamic personality. But the success was made fast by the work of the Englishman Stephen Harding, the second prior of Cîteaux. The Cistercian order was even bigger than that of Cluny, but it was far better organized. Careful plans were made from the start for links between one monastery and another. When a Cistercian abbey founded daughter houses, the abbot of the mother house visited each of his daughter houses once a year to make sure all was well, and the abbot of each daughter house visited the mother house once a year. In addition to this, the abbots of all the Cistercian houses, however far distant, met at Cîteaux each year for an important meeting known as the General Chapter. Here the abbots who were inclined to be slack would soon hear of it; it was very hard to hide any really bad scandals for long with such a closely planned system. And there were scandals. One English abbot built a finely decorated church to adorn his abbey; it was clearly his pride and joy, but in General Chapter he was rebuked, and sent off home to pull it down. Worse things still were heard from the more distant corners of Christendom. In an obscure monastery in Poland there was an ugly incident of murder among the lay brothers. The Chapter got to know of it, and the severest punishment fell on the culprits. This elaborate system meant a great deal of travelling for the abbots, and they found it a strain, but it worked.

It may seem at first as though the differences and quarrels between Cistercians and Cluniacs 800 years ago are very far off from ourselves. We should be mistaken to think so. In every age there have been those who thought that God should be worshipped in buildings of impressive beauty, with fine music and ceremonial, and others who thought as Bernard did, that these things distracted men's attention from the true and simple worship of God. The Cavaliers and Puritans in the English Civil War were fighting partly over this very question. The question is with us still, and some of you may have strong feelings about it.

Chapter 13
The Rise of the Towns

One of the most remarkable things about the Roman empire was the number of cities and towns that flourished in it. The finest and the most admired was Rome itself, the capital of the world, but Alexandria, Antioch, Ephesus, Carthage, and Lyons were splendid too, and there were scores of others not far behind, from Constantinople in the east to London in the north-west. Although, of course, the cities varied in size and importance, all aimed at making life as comfortable as possible for their citizens, and indeed there were Roman cities of the fourth century which must have been quite as well planned and comfortable and hygienic as many cities of the twentieth century, and certainly much more beautiful. Almost all had abundant water, efficient drainage, and paved streets, often with covered ways running along the sides to give shelter from the rain and shade from relentless sun. There were shops and markets, temples, libraries, law courts, theatres, and triumphal arches, and nearly always large and beautiful baths, where, at little or no cost, any free citizen could go for his daily bath and exercise. Even now, when we can only see these imperial cities as ruins, they are still beautiful and impressive, and it is easy to understand how the first sight of them could quite take men's breath away: they stood unspoiled, spacious, and open—for originally few of them were confined by walls—, their buildings gleaming white and fresh, and so high that 'their tops seemed to pierce the soaring clouds', as one man wrote about his home town in Gaul. They were quite overwhelming to barbarians, coming from places outside the empire, where towns were non-existent, who had never seen tall buildings and certainly not temples and baths and fine statues, and even the most glowing reports of travellers could not altogether prepare them for the truth. A Gothic warrior named Athanaric realized this when he first entered an imperial city, and marvelled at it: 'Lo, now I behold', he said, 'what I have often heard of without believing, the wonder of so great a city.'

The barbarians, as they poured into the empire, did not deliberately set out to destroy it, cities and all. Their dream was to occupy it and settle down in it, to enjoy the sun of the south and the milder climate, to take possession of the fertile soil and the fine buildings. But of course in the grim struggle of their coming and taking possession they were terribly destructive, and by the end of the fifth

Above *The ruined city of Djem in North Africa, one of the places which must have impressed the invading Vandals.*

Right *The Pont du Gard is not a bridge but an aqueduct carrying water over the River Gard, Provence.*
Roman buildings like these astonished the barbarians.

century, when the whole of the western part of the empire had been invaded, a great deal of the glory and the wealth of the Roman empire was lost for ever, including many of the towns. Some of those which had lain in the path of advancing hordes of Goths, Huns, or Franks perished suddenly and violently, others crumbled slowly into ruins, deserted by their inhabitants, their streets blocked by fallen houses, their gardens and baths overgrown with weeds and brambles. A few survived, encircled by the stout walls which year by year had been raised against the barbarians, walls like those at Rheims, which stood till Louis the Pious so rashly allowed them to be demolished in 832, or those at Dijon which, even after the Franks had occupied Gaul, still stood 30 feet high, pierced by four gates facing the four quarters of the earth.

But those that survived no longer flourished. Inside their remaining walls they shrank till they seemed 'like dwarfs in the armour of giants', losing their vigour and the bustle of busy markets and streets. This decline came because, all over the western part of the Roman empire, the trade which had brought life to the towns gradually dwindled away till it became a mere trickle. This was not surprising, considering all that happened. For one thing, travelling became dangerous and remained so for a long time, and you can think of plenty of reasons for this. However keen merchants might be on making money by their trade, there was a limit to the losses and perils they dared to face, perils either from barbarians of every sort or from armed robbers lurking in forests, or later on from the truculent vassals of some greedy lord. Besides this, travelling became very difficult, for gradually the great network of Roman roads was allowed to go to rack and ruin, Roman bridges collapsed and were not often rebuilt, and there was no strong over-all government to put these things right. To travel in winter was nearly impossible, and even in summer men and animals moved slowly on the vile roads and rough tracks, and often had to go miles out of their way when a bridge that they had expected to cross had been swept away by winter floods and not replaced.

The third main reason for the shrinkage of trade—and so of the towns—was that in the seventh century the Muslim conquerors made themselves masters of the Mediterranean Sea, and cut the links between the lands which bordered on it and the west of Europe. The stream of trade which had poured into Europe from these parts, trade in silk, silver and jewellery, rugs, spices, wine, oil, wax, and corn, faltered and then ceased almost completely. Many of the merchants who carried and sold these goods were ruined, and over the years the towns they had traded with grew emptier and poorer, and most people were to be found in the country, where they could live, whether lords, vassals, or villeins, on what they grew or made on the manor, with little need of the towns.

Yet if you could have flown across the whole of western Europe on any spring or summer day, say between the death of Charlemagne and the year A.D. 1000, you would have realized that, in spite of all the difficulties, travel and trade had not utterly ceased, that certain ant-like figures were moving incessantly below you, and that the roads and tracks were in constant use. All sorts of travellers journeyed along them. There were the kings, who seldom settled for long in one place but moved from one royal estate to another (a French historian once said that the medieval kings positively killed themselves with travel), and the great lords, who did the same, because it was so much easier for them to make use of the wealth of their manors in this way than by staying in one place and having cartloads of produce laboriously collected and brought to them there. Yet in spite of the restless habits of great men there were always a certain number of people, like Actard and other villeins, plodding along the roads doing carting service for their lords, probably full of grumbles about the distance, the ruts and potholes, and the sins of the reeve, but most likely enjoying a change of scene and a break in the monotony of their other work on the manor.

Then there were always pilgrims on the move, those people who believed that by leaving their homes and families, and all that they loved, and going on a long uncomfortable journey to some holy place they would 'merit a warmer welcome from the saints in heaven', as Bede put it. The English were enthusiastic pilgrims. One sturdy old woman named Edwenna set off from London in the twelfth century with her son Godric to walk to Rome. 'They had scarcely departed when she took off her shoes, going thus barefoot to Rome and back to London.' Eventually she returned to her home in Lincolnshire, where no doubt she was much in demand for her stories of the journey, but one wonders if Godric was quite so enthusiastic as his mother about the bare feet, for the chronicle says he was obliged 'to bear her on his shoulders' for much of the way. People like Edwenna and Godric were by no means rare, and so many English people, 'noble and simple, lay folk and clergy, men and women', made the long journey to Rome that in A.D. 726 a hostel and a chapel were specially built for them near to the church of St. Peter, and you can still see the place where it stood if you go to Rome today.

Kings, lords, men of work, pilgrims, all these travelled, and so, of course, did many merchants, who moved from place to place in search of customers to buy their merchandise. And these men toiled up hill and down dale on their business all over Europe, the solitary pedlar with a heavy pack on his back, and the richer men on their horses, with full saddle-bags and laden mules, travelling in companies for safety's sake. Such merchants would arrive dusty and travel-stained at a fair or a market, undo their bundles, and sell as

much as they possibly could before sunset, when they packed up and went to find a meal and a bed. They stayed, perhaps, at the nearest monastery, hoping no doubt that their goods would not be stolen, and that they themselves would be 'well and clenly lodged', and sleep in a bed free from certain insects that 'scapeth peril with lepynge and not with runnynge, and spareth not kynges'.

Merchants managed to carry an astonishing number and variety of goods about with them; the bundles of one man travelling through France contained, among other things, '12 dozen woollen belts, 1 dozen leather ones, 7 fleeces, 300 brass thimbles for cobblers, 1 dozen garlands for girls, a certain box full of combs, and a certain small basket full of iron trumpets'. Sometimes merchants made great profits, and even solitary pedlars rose to be rich men employing servants and armed guards. But it was always a hard life, with little rest or comfort, and when you think of the hazards they faced it is astonishing how far they travelled about their business. About A.D. 650 a dauntless merchant brought some silver bowls of great beauty, which had been made in Constantinople, to a remote corner of England, selling them there to a Saxon king, who prized them so greatly that at his death they were put in his burial mound at Sutton Hoo in Suffolk. In 1939 they were dug up, and you can now see them in the British Museum among all the other treasures found in the mound, a memorial of the unknown king who owned them 1,300 years ago, and also of the intrepid merchant who bore they safely to England.

Other traders went in the opposite direction, carrying the produce of England across the Channel, dogs and horses, cheese and fine woollen cloaks. Charlemagne himself knew some of these merchants, and once when they had sold inferior cloaks in his kingdom he wrote sharply to Offa, King of Mercia, to complain, and said that the cloaks must be the same length as before. In 1010 English merchants, arriving at the frontiers of Lombardy, were furious because their packs were all undone and they were forced to pay customs duty to the King of Lombardy amounting to 10 per cent of the value of their goods. 'They poured out abusive words and struck blows', and altogether made such a fuss that in order to keep the peace—and the English trade—, the king agreed to free them from paying duty in the future, if in return they brought handsome gifts for himself and his officials every third year. The gifts were always to include 2 fur coats and 2 greyhounds, 'hairy or furred, with silver collars covered with gilded plates sealed with the arms of the king'.

From the end of the tenth century, and especially after the Viking raids ceased and life became more peaceful, every kind of traffic on the roads increased, merchants prospered, new towns grew up, and

old ones revived. This did not happen suddenly or by chance. If any town was to grow and flourish certain conditions were absolutely necessary, and it is not difficult to work out what these were. First of all, the site of the town had to be easy to reach by road or by water or both, and so towns tended to grow in sheltered harbours, on navigable rivers, and where important highways met. Oxford, for instance, came into being because roads from north, south, east, and west met there, dropping down from high ground into the valley to reach the fords which crossed the Thames and its many feeder streams, and because the place could also be reached by boat up the river all the way from London.

Another necessary condition was safety for men and merchandise, and therefore places which were strong and fortified often grew into towns. Some of these were the burhs which had been built for defence against the Northmen, even if they were originally very small like Chichester which, in Alfred's reign, you could walk across in five minutes. Some, of course, were the old Roman towns whose walls could be repaired.

And thirdly, if merchants were to sell their goods they had to find customers to buy them, and therefore any spot where people had a reason for collecting together, for a weekly market or for a fair, or at some holy or exciting place, was likely to become the site of a town in the Middle Ages. A castle or a monastery, for instance, nearly always attracted hangers-on to settle outside the walls, and these in their turn attracted pedlars and merchants. A Flemish chronicle of the fourteenth century described very clearly how the city of Bruges first began to grow round the castle of the Count of Flanders. 'In order to satisfy the needs of the castle folk there began to throng before the gate near the castle bridge, traders and merchants selling costly goods. Then came inn-keepers to feed and house those doing business with the count, who was often to be seen there, and these built houses and set up their inns . . . and the houses so increased that there grew up a town which in the common speech of the people is still called Bridge, for in their patois Bruges means bridge.'

In England at Bury St. Edmunds the shrine of the martyr-king Edmund, killed by the Danes in 868, drew pilgrims from far and wide, and even before the Norman Conquest there was a busy little town round the monastery where the precious shrine lay. Many of the 300 inhabitants were originally servants of the monastery, but when you read the list of them it is clear that they would also serve the pilgrims, who would bring much profit to them. There were bakers, cooks, washerwomen, tailors, shoemakers, robe-makers, ale-brewers, porters, and agents, as well as the poor people who earned a living by daily praying for the king and all Christian souls, and the

13 reeves in charge of abbey lands who had houses 'in that same town'. And when the Domesday survey was made in 1086 'that same town' had grown so much that it had begun to spread out over land that once had been ploughed and sown.

The remains of medieval towns in Europe are now so often embedded in large sprawling cities that it is not easy to get a clear idea of what they really looked like, but there are some, like Aigues Mortes and Vezelay in France and Rothenburg in Germany, which, having for some reason been left high and dry by the tides of growing trade and industry, probably look very much as they did in the Middle Ages. Towns were then very small and compact. They

The roof-tops of Perugia. Houses in medieval towns were crowded inside the walls although there were gardens, orchards and fields too.

188

were usually defended either by walls, or by a ditch, a bank, and a palisade of strong stakes, which had to be kept 'good and whole' by the townsfolk, and at first hardly any houses were built beyond these defences. The little towns would seem very countrified to our eyes. Beyond the walls the fields lay so close that the sights and sounds of the country were never very far away, and on summer days a man could still hear the musical rasp of a scythe being sharpened and smell the sweet hay as it lay drying, and he only had to slip through the gate to be at once in the fresh air and among the green fields and woods. Inside, too, there were plenty of open spaces, not the neat parks and play grounds that we call open spaces, but large gardens, orchards, and small fields, where cattle and sheep were pastured when they were brought into the town at night for safety. There are still a few places where you can understand how closely knit together the life of town and country were. At Vezelay, for instance, although the houses have long ago spilled out beyond the old limits of the town, the little fields creep up very near to the ancient walls, and if you go out into the streets early in the morning you will see cows being driven out through the gates to pasture, and meet sheep pattering over the cobbles on their way to the fields. It is still quite common there for a man to keep a shop and be a farmer too, and in the Middle Ages this was the usual thing, for there was no sharp dividing line between trade and farming.

Gradually, as population grew, the orchards and fields inside the towns began to disappear, and the houses were packed closely together. They were built of whatever materials were easily available, stone in some places, wood, wattle, and daub in others. Many at first would be hardly better than the villein's huts on the manor, but others were bigger; these fronted onto the streets, and were narrow and tall, with one or two floors above the ground level. None had many rooms; on the ground floor there might be one in the front, used as a combined work-room and shop, with a store-room at the back. Above these would be the 'solar', or living room, of the owner and his family, and perhaps a small bedchamber as well. On the second floor under the roof were the attics where the rest of the household slept. The two upper storeys often projected out beyond the ground floor, darkening the rooms there and narrowing the streets.

If the owner of the house was a merchant or a craftsman, he worked in his shop and displayed his goods for sale to the passers-by by hanging them round the doorway (some shops still do this), or by laying them on a wooden trestle, which at night acted as a shutter to close the window, and by day was let down and supported on wooden legs to make a small counter. Besides selling from his shop a man might also rent a stall in the market place, for nearly every town had some open place, either in the centre or just outside

the walls, where the weekly market was held. Today you can almost always discover in an old town where this place was; it may have changed into a permanent covered market-hall, or just been left as a wide street called Market Street. The photograph on this page of the market square at Beaumont du Perigord was taken only a few years ago, but the place must have looked much the same in the thirteenth century; and perhaps the stallholders there still grumble when the rain comes through the canvas awnings, just as, in London, the merchants grumbled in the reign of Edward I. 'All the merchants exposing their goods for sale', they complained, 'were put to great inconvenience, for they had no shelter but canvas tents, and owing to the changeable gusts of wind assailing them they were cold and wet . . . and their feet were soiled by the mud, and their goods rotted by the rain.'

The market place in Beaumont du Perigord which has changed little in appearance since the Middle Ages.

190

A medieval street in Vence, France. Except for the drain-pipes, this also looks much as it did in the Middle Ages.

Merchants were important people in any town, and their complaints and requests likely to be listened to. Sometimes they were men who had been born and bred in the place, sometimes they had first been travelling merchants and then, finding a good spot for business, left their journeyings and settled down. Some were entirely their own masters, others worked for another man. A wealthy merchant family named Datini, living in Florence, had several branches in other towns, and also agents who travelled widely in France, and they expected their employees to send them frequent reports at their headquarters in Florence about the state of trade. One of their agents wrote back saying 'We have sent to Pisa four sacks of another lot of woad and told them to send two sacks to you. The lambskins are all sold out. We are informed about the little slave girl you need and about her features and her age. We

shall see if there is anyone we consider suitable and we shall get her . . . but keep in mind that *little* slave girls are as expensive as grown ones!'

The agent of another Italian merchant was sent to France for the great annual fair at Troyes, and dispatched a letter to his master 'by the first messenger of the fair of Troyes' (the posts were well organized for the merchants coming to the fair) 'in the year 1265 written on Sunday, the day before the last in November'. He was in rather a gloomy frame of mind: 'Messer Tolomeo,' he wrote, 'I would have you know that goods here are selling so badly that it seems impossible to sell any and there are plenty of them. Pepper does not sell well and Scotto's partner has a lot of goods and cannot turn them into cash. He is trying to send them to sell in England.' Then comes a few notes about prices.

Ginger 22–28 deniers depending on quality
Wax of Venice 23 deniers the pound
Wax of Tunis of $21\frac{1}{2}$ deniers the pound
Saffron much in demand and there is *none*.

He obviously wished he had taken more saffron and less pepper with him!

Some merchants were undoubtedly dishonest in their dealings, gave short measure, and charged monstrously high prices, but many had very high standards, and these were probabaly the ones who bought and read very carefully some of the books which were written for their guidance. 'Be courteous to everyone,' says one of these, 'making nice manners and a cheerful pleasant appearance part of yourself. Pay on the day . . . and make your weighing so accurate that you may never be caught in error.' And in another part of the book young merchants are advised to 'look carefully round by night and by day . . . and see to it that your doors are well bolted early.'

Merchants were nearly always treated as free men and under no lord. In any case, when a man travelled from place to place, or came from Italy and settled himself in France, it was quite impossible to prove that he was anything else. But of course there were many other people who lived in towns, the inn-keepers, messengers, porters, and above all the craftsmen of every kind, as the list from Bury St. Edmunds shows. In towns which had some speciality, Bruges or Perugia, for instance, which were famous for making cloth, there were spinners of wool, weavers, carders, fullers, and dyers. These workers were sometimes runaway villeins who, if they lived undetected in a town for a year and a day, could not then be seized by their lords and taken back to the manor; or they were landless men whose lords for some reason no longer wanted them.

But there were many who were still bound to a lord and could be compelled to do service and pay dues to him; and if it was hateful to be a villein in the country, it was far worse in the town—for a weaver, for instance, or a shoemaker, or a man who had set up a small inn—to be called off to work in the harvest field, or compelled to cart loads of wood, or fish, or salt for the lord on whose land his house stood. In the growing towns the thing a man desired most passionately was to be free to spend his time and skill as he wanted. It was often a long hard battle to achieve this, but as towns began to develop a community spirit and townsfolk began to act together, they also began to bargain with their lords for freedom and other privileges. Where this spirit grew quickly and the towns prospered they became very powerful, and their authority often included not only the town itself but some of the country round. In Italy and France such places were called communes, and you can easily see the reason for the name. Milan, for instance, was a very important commune; it kept a list of all its tradesmen and merchants (there were 300 bakers and 440 butchers), appointed its own doctors, judges, and other officials, employed '6 honourable men' as trumpeters for special occasions, and if necessary could call up 40,000 men against its enemies. Milan called no man its master, for it was a proud and powerful city. But in other places, far smaller and humbler than Milan, the townsmen, after many checks and struggles, won their freedom; for always they were willing to pay for it, and many lords were shrewd enough to make a bargain with them, realizing that it was far better to get a regular rent for a dwelling house and garden than to try to extract service from a most unwilling and resentful tenant. So the process went on steadily, and when in 1193 the Earl of Leicester quietly agreed to release 'the burgesses of that same town from ploughing and other servile customs that they were wont to make', he was only doing what many other lords, whether kings, earls, or abbots, were doing all over Europe.

Besides freedom townspeople everywhere wanted safety and peace. Stout walls and massive gates were some protection against outside interference, and powerful communes had their armed men, while others were like Bury St. Edmunds, where 8 gatekeepers were employed to guard the gates and watchmen patrolled the streets. Careful citizens bolted their doors in good time at night, and hoped the watch would keep a sharp eye open for those who prowled in the dark for no good purpose.

Protection was also needed against dishonest traders, men like John Russell of London, who tried to sell 37 pigeons which were 'putrid, rotten, stinking, and abominable to all the human race'. Seven worthy citizens—'2 pye-bakers and 5 cookes', who certainly knew a putrid pigeon when they smelt one—sat in judgement on

John, and decided to put him in the pillory and burn the pigeons under his nose. It was a sharp punishment, a warning to others who might be dishonest.

All these—walls and gates, watchmen, and the overseers of trade who caught men like John Russell, and who supervised the markets —had to be paid for, and the townsfolk had to raise the money among themselves. This they did in various ways; they charged for the right to put up a stall in the market, and this fee fell alike on local men and on foreign merchants, and they also levied taxes on themselves—we still do this, and call them rates—, according to the size of their houses. All the householders met together once a year to choose a council of, perhaps, 12 or 24 men, to see that the money was collected and properly spent, to keep order, safeguard property, punish the dishonest traders, and altogether 'to cherish the honour, the good and the welfare of the town and to devote their property and person to the same'. This sounds a good deal to expect of men who had to run their own businesses as well as the town, but there were always some who were prepared to take it on, just as there are today: those who enjoyed the honour and importance it brought to be chosen out by their fellow citizens, those who saw in it a way of profit for themselves, and also those who really believed they had a duty to the town, and took to heart the Italian song about worthy conduct, which said: 'A merchant wishing his worth to be great must always act according to the right. Let him be a man of long fore-sight and never fail his promises to keep. He will be worthier if he goes to church, gives alms for the love of God, and clinches his deals without a haggle.'

The author of another book of advice wrote, 'The dignity and office of merchants is great and exalted in many ways, they must have respect for the common weal, for the advancement of public welfare is an honourable purpose.' There were many merchants in the medieval towns of Europe, sparing, temperate, solid, and upright men, who believed this and steadily laboured for the common weal as well as their own pockets.

Solid they might be, and no doubt sometimes stodgy, yet there were many highly adventurous spirits among them. The Datini family were bold enough to set up branches of their business in places far from Florence, but their boldness was nothing compared with some. The great city of Venice, for instance, lying in the Adriatic Sea 'like a ship moored to the land', bred merchants famous for their toughness and enterprise, men who were a byword for their long journeys, amazing endurance, and hard bargains. Venetians could be ruthlessly greedy and unscrupulous, but there was no denying their courage, or their love of adventure. In 1268 Martino da Canale, a clerk in the customs house there, wrote a chronicle about his beloved city. He said it was the 'farest and pleasantest in the world, full of

194

beauty and all good things . . . and the salt water runs through it, around, and in all places save the houses and the streets'. At its centre lay the great church of St. Mark in its huge paved square, and high up on the church there pranced the four magnificent horses of gilded bronze which the Venetians had looted from Constantinople during the Fourth Crusade. The 'good things' he mentions included spices of every kind, ginger, pepper, cinnamon, cloves, and nutmegs, sandalwood and ebony, silks and pearls and perfumes. Some of this merchandise came from lands round the Mediterranean Sea, but some reached Venice from the mysterious East, and found its way into the towns of Europe.

Venice must have been full of travellers' tales, which passed from sailor to sailor and merchant to merchant, tales about far-off places like India, Cathay (China), Cipangu (Japan), and Ceylon, rumours about the Great Khan, or the strange shadowy figure of Prester John, the priest-king who, somewhere in Asia, ruled over vast lands and was said to be a Christian. But no tales were more amazing than those told by the three Polos, Nicolo, Maffeo, and Marco, son of Nicolo, themselves merchants of Venice, who had twice, in 1265 and again in 1269, struggled over mountains and rivers, plains and deserts, bearing 'the extreme cold, the snow, the ice and the flooding of rivers', and reached the palace of the Great Khan in China, who eagerly welcomed the travellers. Marco Polo spent 17 years at the court of the Khan, and visited places where no European was to set foot again until the nineteenth century. When at last he returned to Venice he was a rich man, having prudently brought back a great store of precious stones sewn into the seams of the coarse skin coats he wore. Later he dictated his experiences to an Italian writer, and the *Book of Ser Marco Polo the Venetian concerning the Kingdomes and Marvels of the East* became exceedingly popular, and spurred on still more the merchants of Europe to seek to trade with the East by sea and land. But when the Great Khan died, the door to China was shut, the rulers refused to admit any foreigners, the Muslim conquerors blocked the routes, and it became impossible for Europeans to reach the East overland. Yet men still continued to read of Marco Polo's adventures, and 220 years later one such man set out again to find Cathay. But he decided to sail west across what was then called the Sea of Darkness (the Atlantic), for he said 'The world is round, and may be I shall come to Cipangu, and somewhere in those great seas must lie Marco Polo's rich Cathay.' His name, of course, was Cristoforo Columbus.

Chapter 14
Crusaders

In 1101 a monk called Ekkehard, on pilgrimage to Jerusalem, found there 'a little book' that told the story of the capture of Jerusalem by Christian knights two years earlier, and of the adventures of these crusaders during the three years before 'the joyful victory of the taking of Jerusalem'. The 'little book' was later rewritten by an archbishop, who felt that its style was so simple and unpolished that it was unworthy of so magnificent a story. In fact the archbishop's version was rather dull, but the little book itself, written while the events of the journey to Jerusalem and its capture were actually taking place, by a man who was in the crusading army in the thick of the fighting, is exciting and moving. Its short direct sentences are written by a soldier and a man of action, who does not care about using long words and elegant phrases; he writes at resting-places on the march, or in a besieged city, and the cause he fights for is one for which he may have to die the next day. He simply wants the world to know about the fighting and the sufferings of the army and the final victory. He cares so little about his own reputation that he never tells us his name. We can only do as others have done and call him 'the anonymous', the writer without a name.

First, we must find why he was there in the Holy Land at all. Jerusalem, along with the whole of Palestine and Syria, had, of course, been wrested from the emperor of Constantinople and overrun by the Muslims in the seventh century, and those armies of Muslim horsemen had swept on beyond Syria to master the whole North African coast. The fleets of Islam had followed up this attack until the Mediterranean was controlled by Muslim ships, and Spain and Sicily were wrenched from their Christian rulers and swallowed by the power of Islam. Today tourists admire the remains of their beautiful mosques, which are still to be found in these countries, reminding us of this conquest by the followers of Muhammad.

In the ninth century Western Europe lay almost stunned by repeated attacks from Muslims from the south and Vikings from the north. Pillaging, looting, and burning brought religious life, trade, and even farming to such a low point that people had scarcely energy to do more than struggle for survival. Men have rightly called this period the Dark Ages. It did not end in disaster; it led to new life. Gradually, in the tenth century (it was the century in which

Duke William of Aquitaine founded the abbey of Cluny), the force of the raiders was spent; men took fresh courage, more people survived, and the population figures rose. They brought more land under the plough and hacked down the trees on the edges of the forests; merchants ventured further afield now that their goods were less likely to be plundered, and great lords founded and reformed monasteries, as they now had time to aim at more than barely keeping alive. Like some great wounded beast, battered and torn in a fight, Western Europe licked its wounds, stretched, rose, and turned again to face its enemies. The chief enemy was the Muslim world, which had pushed the boundaries of the Christian West further and further in, seizing every tempting outlying district. Now came the turning point, the time to push back against the Muslim invaders and reclaim land and sea for Christians. It happened in Spain, where Christian rulers, starting from tiny states, steadily pushed harder and harder against the Muslims and drove them further south. The Spaniards were helped by men from France, young knights seeking adventure in a holy war. It happened in the western Mediterranean too. The merchants of Pisa and Genoa had never quite stopped slipping furtively round the coast line from North Italy to the French port of Marseilles, bringing spices and silks from the East, hoping to avoid the notice of the terrible Muslim fleet, which would cut them to pieces if it should spot them. Now the Genoese and Pisans built fleets that sailed out boldly to attack the Muslims; they snatched Corsica and Sardinia back from Muslim clutches, and by the early eleventh century the western Mediterranean was once more free and safe for Christian shipping. The third place where the Christians rounded on the Muslims was Sicily.

The story has already been told (in Chapter 11) of the daring exploits of the sons of Tancred of Hauteville, who seized lands for themselves and built strong castles in southern Italy and Sicily. Among the brothers the two who stood out for their cunning and leadership were Robert Guiscard and Roger, who was the conqueror of Sicily. And it is here at last that we find our anonymous crusader, the writer of the little book. He was a knight attached to the company of Bohemond, eldest son of Robert Guiscard, a magnificent figure of a fighting man, tall, broad-shouldered, and immensely strong, driven on by the fearless energy that had already done so much for the rest of his remarkable family.

A generation before the Crusades began, when the first Norman adventurers had stepped ashore in southern Italy they were on their way back from a pilgrimage to Jerusalem. Pilgrimages were tremendously popular throughout the Middle Ages, and we cannot hope to understand the Crusades unless we realize why this was so, because pilgrimages and crusades were very closely linked. Most

people thought about religion simply, starting with places and people. They had a deep respect and reverence for saints, and every saint had his own church or churches with which he had very clear and useful links. At the abbey of Bury St. Edmunds in East Anglia the monks were happily convinced that St. Edmund looked after them every minute, and was ready at a moment's notice, if his attention was drawn to it, to bring terrible punishment on any one who did any harm to his church or one of his monks. St. James, who was remembered as a warrior, was honoured in a large and very beautiful church at Compostella in the north of Spain, and thousands of pilgrims journeyed to this remote spot on the Atlantic coast to pray to a man whom they thought of as a patron saint of those fighting against the Muslims. Thousands too, and among them William of Warenne and his wife Gundrada, as you will remember, made the long pilgrimage on foot or on horseback to Rome, where the tombs of the apostles Peter and Paul were to be found in magnificent churches. But the most holy, most sacred place of all for pilgrimages was Jerusalem, the very spot where Christ had preached and had been crucified. It was the most dangerous to reach, especially since it was in Muslim hands, but the power of its many links with the earthly life of Christ compelled men to risk everything to reach it. It drew our anonymous writer, and at the end of his little book he describes the places that he had so often heard about and had now at last seen and walked round, so that other pilgrims might be sure to find them. Just a brief quotation may bring back to us the picture of him, trudging the dusty roads, climbing little hills and pausing to look into buildings, feeling a nearness to Jesus and his family and his disciples that he could not have known before, and for which he had specially come.

Nineteen miles out on the Jericho road is the sycamore tree up which Zacchaeus climbed so that he might see Jesus . . . . To the south of Jerusalem, about a bowshot south of the wall, is Mount Sion, and there is a church which Solomon built. Our Lord ate the Last Supper there with his disciples . . . . A thousand paces away is Sychar, where Our Lord talked to the Samaritan woman. There too is Bethlehem, the City of David, where Christ was born, and it is four miles southwards from Jerusalem; and there in the place where Christ was born is a church built with marble columns.

The new readiness to fight against the Muslims, wherever they were to be found, together with this deep veneration for the city of Jerusalem, which was in Muslim hands, helped to prepare the way for the Crusades. The actual call to arms came from the emperor of Constantinople. The Turks, a fierce warlike race who had become Muslims, had swept over the emperor's lands in Asia Minor. In 1081 a new emperor, Alexius Comnenus, seized power. He was a much more determined and firm ruler than the men who had come

before him, who had given in to the Muslim Turks, and he fought sturdily against all his enemies. Apart from the Turks he had a tiresome Christian enemy who was attacking his Greek lands, none other than the Norman adventurer Robert Guiscard from southern Italy, who was now helped by his dauntless son, the formidable Bohemond, in penetrating ever deeper into the Emperor's lands. In 1085 Guiscard died, but Alexius still had reason to hate and fear the name of Bohemond.

Alexius knew that he could not hope to win back the lands he had lost to the Turks without outside help, and so he appealed to Pope Urban II to arrange for some hired soldiers to be sent to Constantinople to strengthen his army. Pope Urban felt the cause to be a good one, for he would always wish to strengthen the hand of a Christian ruler against a pagan one. Then as he began to think how he could best organize some help for Alexius, another far greater plan began to form in his mind, and he turned it over again and again as he journeyed over the Alps to France, for he had decided that he would make his appeal first in the town of Clermont. First Urban held a council of clergy in the church at Clermont, and then he called a great public meeting, and preached to hundreds of people from a platform set up in the open fields outside the city gates. His message was unexpected, and inspired. If he had simply asked for men to volunteer to fight in Alexius's army to recover the emperor's lands, it is doubtful whether more than a few hundred altogether would have been interested. Urban was now inspired by a far more exciting and ambitious aim than this. He preached fervently for men to go out to the East, wearing the sign of the Cross on their clothes, to fight the Muslim armies and recover Jerusalem and all the land around it for the Christians, as well as to help the emperor. He urged men to think how shameful it was that the sacred places where Christ had lived as boy and man, where he had preached and taught with his disciples, where, finally, he had been crucified and had risen from the dead, should be in the hands of pagans. The crowd were so moved and excited that they could scarcely let the pope finish his speech. They interrupted him with loud shouts of 'God wills it!' As soon as he had finished, hundreds crowded round and offered themselves as crusaders, that is men marked with the sign of the Cross. It was not only the people who had heard him at Clermont who were affected. The news spread like wildfire; bishops, clergy, and wandering preachers all over Europe urged men to join the Crusade and risk everything for Christ. Their lands were to be protected while they were away; if they died on the journey or were killed in fighting they were assured of forgiveness of all their sins. In France, Germany, and Italy especially men eagerly rushed to join this expedition. They quickly made arrangements for their families, attached themselves

to a great lord and set off for the grand meeting-place, the city of Constantinople itself.

The kings of England and France, and the Holy Roman emperor were all in disgrace with the Church at this time, and did not go, but some very powerful French and German barons did go. There were three main groups. The first came from the Rhineland and were led by Godfrey of Lorraine, later to become a ruler in Jerusalem, and his brother Baldwin. The second was led by Raymond of Toulouse from the south of France, and with him was the official leader of the whole Crusade, the pope's special representative, Adhemar of le Puy. But the third group may interest us most, for it is here that we should have found the writer of the little book. This was a very big group, including Robert Duke of Normandy, Count Robert of Flanders, and all their followers, and from southern Italy the Lord Bohemond and many of Bohemond's knights, whose names our author knew and mentioned, for they were his closest companions on the journey and in the fighting.

Alexius was horrified when he heard what was happening, and that these three armies were bearing down on Constantinople. He had asked for extra soldiers whom he could pay as his own troops. Instead, as his daughter Anna put it, 'He heard a rumour that countless Frankish armies were approaching. . . . What actually happened was more far-reaching and terrible than rumour suggested for the whole of the West and all the barbarians who lived between the Adriatic and the Straits of Gibraltar migrated in a body to Asia, marching across Europe, country by country, with all their households.' No wonder Alexius was alarmed, for he and his daughter, like the other citizens of Constantinople, thought of the westerners simply as uncouth barbarians, and Alexius must have been particularly disturbed to learn that his old enemy Bohemond was one of the leaders. In fact, Bohemond, who was no fool, knew this too, and was being very careful indeed to behave quite correctly, and would not let his men plunder at all on the way through the emperor's territory to Constantinople.

While these three groups were pushing ahead to reach Constantinople by the spring of 1097, another very different group of crusaders had already arrived there. They were the first to arrive, yet they had not come on horseback, but on foot; they were the 'People's Crusade'. Under the leadership of a fervent wandering preacher called Peter the Hermit, a strange rough-looking man who usually rode on a donkey, a band of some 20,000 crusaders, most of them poor peasants or townsmen, came to the gates of Constantinople. Peter had preached in many parts of Europe and had stirred up wild enthusiasm. Some of these people were ruffians out for all the plunder they could get, but some were simple and

ignorant peasants, caught up in the whirl of a movement which was to drag them to ruin. A Frenchman writing at the time describes some of these people as they had first been seen, setting out from their homes, perhaps hoping to escape from bad harvests or a harsh landlord to the delights of this beautiful city of Jerusalem which had been described to them by the preachers. Whether 'Jerusalem' was in heaven or on earth they did not quite know, but they were absolutely sure that it must be a far kindlier and pleasanter place then their own village. 'There was nothing more touching than to see these poor crusaders shoe their oxen like horses and yoke them to a cart on two wheels, on which they put all their scanty possessions and their little children. At every castle and at every town they saw along the road the children would stretch out their hands, eagerly asking whether this was not already that Jerusalem which they were looking for.'

Alexius, hardened politician as he was, was touched with pity by these poor folk, especially as many were half starving by the time they reached his capital. When he sent for Peter the Hermit, he gave him clear, urgent, and sensible advice. 'Do not cross the Hellespont until the great army of the Christians arrives, for there are not enough of you to fight against the Turks.' But then the rougher elements among the crusaders got the upper hand; Peter could not control them, and they sacked and burned the palaces of Constantinople and ran riot through the streets. Alexius would not have this. His first duty was to his own subjects, and the crusaders were ordered across the Hellespont immediately. The tragic end came quickly. They were little more than a huge unruly mob, split into gangs, and once the well disciplined Turkish troops fell upon them they were cut to pieces. Only a few, including Peter himself, struggled back alive to Constantinople to tell the shattering story.

By now the various parties of knightly crusaders were assembling. Duke Godfrey of Lorraine came first, and then the party from the south of France with Bishop Adhemar and Raymond of Toulouse. The Lord Bohemond's party was now a little way off, and Bohemond came into Constantinople alone in the first instance, leaving his army some distance away; and the author of the little book tells us that 'when the Emperor had heard that Bohemond had come he ordered him to be received with proper ceremony, but took care to lodge him outside the city.' He explains to us with pride that the emperor 'was much afraid of the gallant Bohemond, who had often chased him and his army from the battlefield.' Alexius' daughter Anna was present when Bohemond visited the emperor's palace, and she was both horrified and fascinated by him. She describes his broad shoulders, deep chest, and powerful arms, and the fact that he wore his hair short, unlike the other barbarians, who had it hanging down to their waists. He had piercing blue eyes and a

savage glance, and she sums up: 'A certain charm hung about this man, but was partly spoilt by a general air of the horrible.' That was the view of an elegant cultured princess, but to the author of the little book Bohemond was more simply a gallant lord, a great fighter, and a brave leader of men.

Before the knights left Constantinople, Alexius insisted that the leaders should do him fealty. This meant their promising that Alexius should be the feudal lord of any lands that they conquered from the Turks. Only Raymond of Toulouse, who seemed to treat the oath more seriously than the others, finally refused to take it and would only make a general promise of loyalty to Alexius.

The crusaders now set off from Constantinople on the road for the wealthy city of Antioch in the north of Syria, which was, of course, in Turkish hands at the time. There is no doubt that Bohemond had his eye on Antioch and the land around it as a lordship for himself. It is at this point that one begins to doubt the motives of some of the leading crusaders. Had they come for Christ or for gain? Before they even reached Antioch, Baldwin, brother of the Duke of Lorraine, branched off from the main route and settled himself comfortably in the district of Edessa, where he became lord, and only left it to succeed his brother Godfrey and become king of Jerusalem itself in 1100. The main army struggled on to Antioch in the teeth of sharp Turkish attacks and very bad conditions; many of the pack-horses that carried their equipment died, and they had to use wretched dogs and even sheep as pack animals. Just north of Antioch they had to get through the high passes of the Anti-Taurus mountains, and the author of the little book describes vividly their bitter experiences:

We who stayed at Coxon set out and began to cross a damnable mountain, which was so high and steep that none of our men dared to overtake another on the mountain path. Horses fell over the precipice and one beast of burden dragged another down. As for the knights, they stood about in a great state of gloom, wringing their hands because they were so frightened and miserable, not knowing what to do with themselves and their armour, and offering to sell their shields, valuable breast plates, and helmets for three pence or five pence or any price they could get. Those who could not find a buyer threw their armour away and went on.

Our own knight, the author of the little book, got through and came with the rest to Antioch. Here Bohemond put all his strength into a mighty effort to capture the city. He urged his men on to tremendous exertions, with rousing commands: 'Charge at top speed like a brave man and fight valiantly for God. . . . Be very courageous as becomes a champion of Christ.' The author describes Bohemond himself in battle as being 'like a lion which has been starving for three or four days, which comes roaring out of its cave,

A crusader doing homage. This illustration comes from a thirteenth century psalter, now in the British Museum. Notice the symbol of the cross on the surcoat worn over the knight's chain mail. He kneels as he puts his hands together in the act of homage.

thirsting for the blood of cattle, and falls upon the flock careless of its own safety, tearing the sheep as they flee hither and thither'. How far Bohemond was inspired by the cause of the Holy War, how far he was desperately determined to win Antioch for himself, we can only guess. Our knight trusted him, fought alongside him, and eventually scaled the walls in hand-to-hand fighting, until the city was in Christian hands. He was close to his lord Bohemond in the next stage too, when a huge Turkish army closed in on the city

203

and surrounded the Christians for weeks, until the crusaders, again under Bohemond's masterful leadership, made a vigorous sortie from the city and put the enemy to flight. Bohemond had set his heart on Antioch and would not now give it up. Raymond of Toulouse was very angry, but in the end he could only give way to Bohemond's strong will, and left him behind in possession of Antioch, as he had left Baldwin behind in possession of Edessa. Raymond and the crusading army set out once more on the long weary road to Jerusalem.

You might think that at this point the writer of the little book would have complained bitterly of Bohemond's selfishness. He makes no whisper of complaint; he was a loyal knight, Bohemond was his hero, and whatever secret sadness and disappointment he may have felt he never wrote it down in his little book. But he at least had come for Christ and not for lands or gain, and so he quietly joins the followers of Raymond of Toulouse and journeys on towards the great goal of Jerusalem, leaving his old lord Bohemond behind, putting things to rights in his hard-won principality of Antioch, and following his new lord, Raymond.

More hardship came upon the crusaders as they trudged down the Palestinian coast, many of them now having lost their horses and being reduced to the rank of the foot soldiers. In June 1099 they arrived at last before the walls of the holy city of Jerusalem and besieged it for a month, suffering great anguish from lack of supplies, and above all from lack of water. Relief came from Genoese trading ships, which sailed into the nearby port of Jaffa bringing supplies. The Genoese merchants had their own reasons for wanting to get a foothold in the ports of the Syrian coast, for it was to these ports that the silks and spices of the East were brought, and the Genoese, as you know, were great traders.

It was on 15 July 1099 that Jerusalem fell. The fighting was ruthless and horrible. The Muslims were slaughtered without mercy as the Christians established their control. They chose Godfrey of Lorraine as the ruler, but he would not take the title of king in so holy a place, and he was called the 'advocate' or protector of Jerusalem instead. His brother Baldwin, who had fewer scruples, succeeded him in 1100 with the title of king.

In 1099 Bohemond's unknown knight finished his little book. He adds a guide to the Holy Places, and we may believe that he saw them all before he died. We know no more. After following him through the grim sufferings of a journey that had lasted for over two years, we might expect that at the end he would be a bitter man, disappointed in his own beloved lord, Bohemond, shocked by the selfishness of some of the other leaders, cruel and hardened as a result of his hand-to-hand fighting with the Turks. In fact, he was

Krak des Chevaliers. This massive crusader fortress, dominating the desert, was never captured.

simply overcome with joy at the recovery of Jerusalem for Christ, and this is how he ends his book:

> Then our men came back to Jerusalem rejoicing, bearing with them all sorts of provisions which they needed, This battle (a victory at Arsuf, outside Jerusalem) was fought on the 12th August by the mercy of our Lord Jesus Christ, to whom be honour and glory, now and for ever, world without end. May every soul say 'Amen'.

High in the black barren mountains that rise on each side of the 'Homs Gap' stands the magnificent crusader castle of Krak des Chevaliers. As you can see from the picture on this page it is a massive stone fortress, with two rings of mighty walls and nine solid stone towers. The walls enclose a space of five acres. At one time in the Crusades it housed 2,000 soldiers and many refugees from the surrounding countryside as well. Krak was superbly equipped. There was a great hall, 390 feet long, opening onto a cool covered gallery. The remains of a chapel, storehouses, stables, windmills for grinding corn and sugar, an oven for baking the bread, and a wine press are to be found within the ramparts; most important of all were the wells, 84 feet deep, from which to draw up the precious water supplies in those intensely hot summers.

In the high summer of 1163 Krak was besieged by the Muslim leader Nureddin, a soldier of fine reputation. At the time it had only a very small garrison of Christian knights, and Nureddin felt confident that he would soon force it to surrender. Weeks had gone

by. It was midday and the sun was scorching; most of Nureddin's army were resting, and only a few men were on the watch for signs of movement on the castle ramparts. Suddenly the Muslim guards leaped up and seized their weapons, shouting in alarm to their fellow soldiers, as the castle gates swung open and the knights of the garrison, mounted, and fully armed in their chain-mail hauberks and metal helmets, thundered down the slope and scattered the Muslim troops, driving them off to the shores of the lake of Homs. The knights of the garrison returned, the gates closed behind them, and the hot eastern sun blazed down silently on Krak des Chevaliers.

The victory that time lay with the Christians. It was not always so, and we must look more closely at what this battle represented if we are to understand what was happening to the crusading movement in the twelfth century.

Krak des Chevaliers belonged to the Knights Hospitallers. Like the Knights Templar whom St. Bernard helped to found, the Hospitallers were an order specially dedicated to the defence of the Holy Land. Their castles and those of the Templars and of the great barons of the Kingdom of Jerusalem were dotted all over Syria and Palestine. Without them the Christian settlers would have been forcibly driven from the Holy Land. They were a tiny minority amid a hostile population of native Muslims, and outside the Kingdom the Muslim armies hovered, ready to pounce on any weak point in the Christian defences.

Not only in the mountain passes but in the coastal towns the crusader castles were the signs of the Christian army of occupation. Beneath their walls were the homes and warehouses of the Italian merchants, who settled themselves quickly in these wealthy ports, as soon as most of the men of the First Crusade had left again for their homes in the West. The people who really counted now in the Holy Land were these Italian merchants, single-minded in their pursuit of wealth, and the barons who were usually the descendants of the leaders of the First Crusade. Since the settlers were so few, they needed to keep in close touch, and when danger threatened, flaring lights could be seen at night flashing signals from one castle to another, from the coastal plain to the mountains, and back again to the castles of the plain, throughout this conquered country.

The hold of the Christian settlers was constantly threatened or openly attacked. In 1144 the province of Edessa had been pulled back into the Muslim grasp by Nureddin, and Western Europe had sent out the Second Crusade, for which St. Bernard preached so urgently. It was a failure, wrecked by the quarrels between the crusaders and the Christian settlers. Far worse was to come. The Muslims had now found a leader who could unite them in a far

The Crusades.

more powerful attack, a man so outstanding that even his Christian enemies could hardly help but admire him: Saladin.

On the death of King Baldwin of Jerusalem in 1185 Saladin took full advantage of the petty jealousies and quarrels that broke out among the barons of the Kingdom and attacked sharply. In 1187 he won a great victory over the Christians at Hattin, and in 1189 he recaptured the holy city of Jerusalem itself. The little Christian army was shattered by the disaster and the splendid castles fell one by one into Saladin's hands. The settlers were forced back to the coast, and group after group of them rode into the city of Tyre, seeking the safety of a walled town. Here they waited in confusion and dismay, until an Italian adventurer, Conrad of Montferrat, arrived to organize their defence, pending the arrival once more of help from the West.

The terrible news of the fall of Jerusalem had meanwhile reached Europe. At first people would not believe it; but as the grim truth gradually bore in on them, their violent anger produced a further rousing call to a new crusading effort that should hurl the hated

Muslims back once and for all, and avenge this insult to Christ. This Third Crusade was to be led by three great rulers of the West, the German emperor, Frederick Barbarossa, and the kings of England and France.

Frederick was an old man nearing seventy but he had been a vigorous and active soldier and an able ruler, and men respected him. He led his German army along roughly the same route that the First Crusaders had taken, and he kept up its morale despite lack of supplies, lack of water, and hostile attacks. His men appreciated Frederick's strict discipline, even though they grumbled about it; they realized his devotion to the crusading cause and his concern to protect them from hardship and danger. Saladin was deeply depressed when he heard of the steady advance of this well disciplined German army. His fears were cut short. As Frederick and his army reached the River Saleph in Asia Minor, the emperor's horse slipped, his rider plunged into the river, and was dragged down by the weight of his armour. In a matter of minutes the emperor's body was dragged ashore: he was dead. The men were so shattered by the loss of their leader that they seemed quite unable to rally. Most of the army returned miserably home, and those who did press on had lost all their zest and confidence. After a long and wearying march they finally buried the emperor's corpse in the cathedral church of Antioch, and they played only a small part in the rest of the Crusade.

The other two leaders of this Crusade were much younger men, and they disliked each other intensely from the start. Richard I, king of England, had just succeeded his father as ruler of a vast collection of territories, which stretched from England in the north, down through Normandy, Maine, Anjou, and Aquitaine to the Mediterranean coast. Philip Augustus, king of France, had in fact less of France under his direct control than Richard had. This in itself would have made for bad feeling, but they also hated each other just because of the kind of man each was. Let us watch them.

The two kings had agreed to travel by sea from the south of France to the Holy Land, rather than to take the land route of the Emperor Frederick. Their first port of call was the town of Messina in Sicily, and we happen to have a lively description of the entry into the port first of Philip and later of Richard. It is written by one of Richard's own men, Geoffrey de Vinsauf, a passionate admirer of the king, and therefore it is extremely biased against Philip. First he describes the French king's arrival. We are told how all the men, women, and children of Messina rushed out to watch. People are always ready to gather to watch a show, even if it is only a bride coming out of church, and certainly the people of Messina expected Philip's arrival to be much more grand than that. They were

dreadfully disappointed. 'Content with a single ship,' writes Geoffrey de Vinsauf scornfully, 'as if to avoid the sight of men, he entered the port privately.' The crowd naturally felt thoroughly cheated and 'returned indignant to their homes'.

They soon rushed out again. Rumour had now reached them that King Richard of England was about to arrive with his crusaders. They hurried out to the quayside, pulling their children along, and pushing their way to a good position, for this time as soon as they got in sight of the sea they knew that it was going to be a superb display. There were dozens of galleys approaching, their standards floating in the breeze, prows gaily painted, and the shields of the knights on board glittering cheerfully in the bright sunshine. More and more people joined the crowds on the shore, the sounds of trumpets were heard, and the crowds jostled each other to make room for the small party of Richard's knights who had been sent ashore early, so that they should be ready to receive their king. Richard himself was now sighted, standing on the prow of a specially large and richly decorated galley, smiling contentedly at his reception party. He was in his element, and he looked the part of a great king too, tall, well built, handsome, and splendidly dressed. As he landed, the citizens of Messina cheered and acclaimed him. The arrival had been really worth seeing.

This little incident shows something of the characters of the two men. Richard loved pageantry; he was a natural leader, and he wanted people to like him and think well of him. Philip, by contrast, hated display and had only come on crusade because he knew that if he did not men might think so poorly of him that it might hinder his plan of driving the English king out of France. For that was what really interested Philip, to make his kingdom strong, and gain for himself those parts of France that Richard held.

The citizens of Messina could not have known on that sunny morning of Richard's arrival that he was a very quarrelsome man, but before he had left Sicily he had stirred up trouble there because of a grievance he had against the Sicilian ruler, Tancred, as well as made clear his contempt for his fellow crusader, Philip. Richard's mind was busy with his personal plans too; he was not simply thinking about the Crusade. He arranged for his mother to bring to him in Sicily the girl whom he had chosen to be his bride, Berengaria, princess of Navarre. Richard had originally been engaged to the French king's sister, Alice, but he now made it quite clear that he did not want Alice and that he intended to marry Berengaria. Philip was very angry at the insult to himself and his sister.

When the weather was fit to put to sea the two fleets set out from Sicily, Philip to sail straight to the Holy Land, Richard to sail first

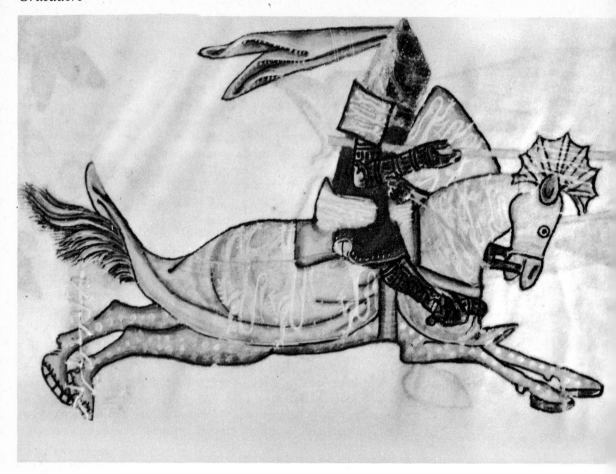

to Cyprus. The ruler of Cyprus was foolish enough to ill-treat some of Richard's sailors when they had been forced to put ashore on the island in heavy seas. Richard would stand no such insults. He landed on Cyprus, attacked the ruler, Isaac's, troops, and then announced his terms—that Isaac should swear fealty to Richard and send 500 knights to the Crusade. Isaac was later to lose the whole island to Richard through trying to break his bargain. At the meeting with Isaac, Geoffrey de Vinsauf tells us, Richard was mounted on a fine Spanish charger, the horse's saddle glittering with gold and red spangles and little gold lions. The king wore a rose-coloured tunic, ornamented with silver crescents, and his spurs and his sword-hilt were of pure gold. This love of display found splendid scope in the arrangements for his marriage to Berengaria, which also took place in Cyprus, with a magnificent banquet. One cannot help feeling that Richard showed no sense of urgency about his journey. Surely he must have known how desperate the Christians in Palestine were. The main army was

Richard I and Saladin in combat. This is how an artist of the fourteenth century imagined the two leaders.

210

now encamped outside the port of Acre. Inside Acre was a strong Muslim garrison, and camped around the Christian army was a large Muslim army, commanded by Saladin. Yet Richard still lingered in Cyprus, while King Philip, who had sailed straight for Acre, was giving practical advice on the making of siege-machines, ready for a big Christian offensive. The Christians round Acre were eagerly looking forward to Richard's arrival and sent messages urging him to hurry.

On 8 June 1191 Richard came. The weary soldiers in the Christian camp forgave him all his delays; they lit bonfires and blew trumpets, and many instinctively looked to Richard as their real leader. If they were looking for a fine soldier they would not be disappointed, for Richard was not only personally brave, he could inspire and control men in battle far better than any other leader in the crusading army. A big attack on Acre was launched, and on 12 July the town surrendered. Richard took prisoner the members of the garrison with their families, and held them as

hostages. Saladin, deeply distressed at the surrender of the city, but honourably determined to stand by the garrison which had fought so valiantly, promised Richard a very large sum of money in return for the freeing of the hostages.

Meanwhile Philip, anxious about affairs in France, and far from well himself, was eager to go home. He very much disliked the cool way in which Richard had taken the lead and the contempt that he had shown for Philip and for some of the other crusaders. When Duke Leopold of Austria, now the leader of the German crusaders, put up his standard beside those of Richard and Philip on the walls of Acre, Richard simply seized it and hurled it into the ditch below. Leopold never forgave him, and he was later to have an unexpected chance of revenge.

Once Philip had left for France, Richard wanted to start off south to Jerusalem without delay. Saladin had paid an instalment of the money for the hostages, but since it had not all been paid Richard declared that the bargain was broken, and cruelly ordered the massacre of the 27,000 survivors of the garrison of Acre. This was brutality of a kind that Saladin on his part never showed, and it is a sharp warning against too romantic a view of Richard Coeur de Lion.

The march down to Jerusalem was hard and dangerous, but Richard kept rigorous control of his men, and when the moment came for an open battle at Arsuf he kept his army in strict formation until they were all assembled, in spite of heavy shooting by the Turks. Then Richard's knights in one tremendous movement thundered down on the enemy, and the Muslim soldiers broke their ranks and fled. Richard now came within a few days' march of Jerusalem. The supreme goal was at hand, and the men were full of excitement and eager to press on. They were to be bitterly disappointed.

Richard did not take Jerusalem. The Christian settlers advised him not to attempt it, as they thought it could not be held once the crusading army had gone back to the West. Richard himself was ill by now and anxious to get home. After one further victory, the capture of Jaffa, Richard made peace with Saladin. The coastal cities were left in Christian hands, and Christian pilgrims were allowed to go in peace to visit Jerusalem. Richard himself did not go up to Jerusalem, though most of his soldiers did. The king stayed in his camp. He had had so many brilliant successes, but he knew that in the end he had failed, for the holy city was still in the hands of Saladin, and would remain so.

To hurry home was now Richard's main concern, and he went off ahead of his army. By ill luck he was shipwrecked and fell into the hands of that very Duke Leopold of Austria whose flag he had

The tomb of a crusader in the Temple Church, London.

torn down at Acre. Leopold handed his prisoner over to the German emperor, who kept Richard prisoner for a further year, and only released him on the payment of a large ransom. It was a wretched ending to an enterprise which Richard had begun in fine spirits and high hopes. Yet he had had some success, and he had shown a gay and colourful personality that has made him for us one of the most real and lively people of the twelfth century. A recent writer has said of him, 'He was a bad son, a bad husband and a bad king, but a gallant and splendid soldier.'

The Third Crusade is partly a story of human weakness. The fervour of the early crusading movement had given way to quarrels and self-seeking, and so it was to continue to be. For another two centuries men used the call to a Crusade to cloak their own selfish aims to get wealth or power for themselves.

The movement left marks on Europe. Trade increased, there were new fashions in castle building, new ways of collecting taxes were thought out to provide money for the crusades, and, as we saw in another chapter, the pope gained firmer power over the Church as leader of the first Crusade of all. It is true, too, that among the crusaders there were men like the anonymous writer of the little book, whom we are bound to admire. Even so, when we think about the crusading movement as a whole we find ourselves looking into one of the darker stretches of history.

Chapter 15
Feudal Monarchy in England and France

The summer of 1137 was scorchingly hot and sultry. In a hunting lodge at Béthizy King Louis VI of France lay dying. He felt the heat and the noise so much that he had been moved here away from the stifling air and the street clatter of his capital city of Paris. At Béthizy it was more airy and it was quiet. Louis was very ill, but he was struggling hard to pull himself together and concentrate, because he knew that there were important decisions to be made, decisions which only the king of France could make.

If you look at the map on this page you will see the kingdom over which Louis ruled. At first glance it seems much the same shape and size as the France of today. Over the whole of this area he was

England and France in the 12th century.

recognized as king and feudal overlord. That sounds impressive, but from a lifetime of very bitter experience Louis knew just how little power this position gave him. In practice, since the break-up of Charlemagne's empire the real power in France had been grasped by the king's great feudal vassals, the dukes of Normandy, Brittany, Burgundy, and Aquitaine and the counts of Anjou, Blois, Champagne, and Toulouse. You can find their lands on the map. These great vassals had been able to build up their power in their own fiefs, because at the time of the Viking invasions the king of France had not been able to defend his subjects in the outlying parts of the kingdom, and men had turned in desperation to the local count or duke and had put themselves under his protection, and his control. Not one of the present dukes or counts would have denied that Louis was his feudal overlord and king; there was no need to; it meant so little. These men scarcely ever bothered to attend the king's court, and within their own fiefs they acted as they chose, built castles, appointed bishops, minted coins, and collected feudal armies with which to fight each other.

The king himself had his own small area, round the cities of Paris and Orleans, which he ruled directly, in the same way that the duke of Normandy, for instance, ruled his own duchy. This area under the king's direct control was called the 'royal demesne', and it is marked on the map as the Île de France. Here there were lesser feudal lords holding their lands from the king, men not nearly so powerful as the dukes and counts but on the same level as the dukes' and counts' own vassals. Yet the power of the king under Louis's predecessors had become so very weak that even those lesser lords of the Île de France were out of control and defying the king under his very nose.

From time to time as he lay in that room at Béthizy, thinking rather feverishly, with the sun beating down and the flies buzzing, he just had to let his mind take its own course, and when he thought of the Île de France he did get some comfort. There he really had made a difference. Despite his nickname 'Louis the Fat' (and he was too heavy now even to get on his horse), he had been an energetic and determined king. From the first he had set himself to hammer away at those petty lords of the Ile de France until he could force them to obey him. He would never get anywhere in attempting to control the counts and dukes if he could not set his own house in order first. He thought of some of them now, Thomas de Marle, for instance, that 'ravening wolf', as his neighbours called him, perhaps the worst of those cruel brigand lords. He had terrorized the countryside round Orleans, burning, looting, killing; he was a man who took pleasure in cruelty and devised horrible tortures for his victims, hanging them up by their thumbs and

showering blows upon them until they died, tearing their eyes out, or starving them to death in his beastly dungeons. Louis had summoned him to the royal court to answer for his crimes. Thomas no doubt laughed out loud at that. The king rallied other lords and the Church too to support him, and Thomas was shocked to find that his castle of Marle was surrounded by a royal army. This king evidently meant what he said.

Then there was Hugh of le Puiset, as ruthless as Thomas de Marle, and perhaps even more wilful and determined. Complaints had poured into Louis's court about Hugh's brutal attacks on villages and monasteries. Louis repeatedly summoned Hugh to his court to answer for these, and Hugh contemptuously tossed aside the summons and led his robber troop out of the castle of le Puiset on the next plundering raid. Louis was not to be mocked, and he decided on stern swift punishment. The royal army rode out to le Puiset and battered at Hugh's fine fortress, of which he was tremendously proud, until only the foundations and piles of rubble and stone remained. The culprit himself was captured and imprisoned. At that point in his recollection of the story Louis recalled his own mistake. He had later released Hugh, feeling certain that the man had now learned his lesson. Not at all. Within a few months Hugh was committing worse atrocities, 'as a dog that has been chained up too long will bite and tear at everything that comes his way'. The castle of le Puiset rose from its ruins strongly rebuilt. Louis was extremely angry. Out came the royal army to punish this impudent defiance, and this time it did its work more thoroughly. The great earthen ramparts which lay underneath the stone defences were levelled to the ground, and the soldiers toiled away at shovelling soil into the moat until the whole site was flattened. They went off with a sense of grim satisfaction. Louis was not an unduly optimistic man, but when the news reached him barely a year later that a third castle had risen on the site of le Puiset, even he was near despair. The king might have given up the struggle, but this was just where Louis showed his fibre. The soldiers, the siege experts, the engineers, and the workmen were all got together for a third time. Again the walls of le Puiset were encircled, were undermined, the stones hurled down, the earthworks levelled. The lord Hugh realized at last that he had met a man more patient and more grimly determined than himself. There were no more castles built at le Puiset. The other lords of the Île de France took heed. Law was now respected, and if a man needed protection against a greedy land-grabbing neighbour he turned to King Louis's court, for there he knew he would get justice. Other men farther afield were watching too, The dukes and counts knew what a stiff job it could be to bring these lesser feudal lords to heel. They regarded the king with a new respect.

As Louis turned on his bed and dozed or brushed away the flies, he made a big effort to rouse himself. He knew that he had put in some hard work during his reign on that royal demesne, but it was not enough. The Île de France was smaller than Normandy, smaller than Aquitaine. If the king were ever to make his will felt throughout France, as the king of England did in his kingdom, he must add more land to the royal demesne, a great deal more land. That was it; that was why he *must* make himself think and plan and force others to act now. Duke William of Aquitaine had died. The great opportunity had come.

Duke William X of Aquitaine had died very unexpectedly on pilgrimage. He was only 38, and he had left no son to succeed him. His wealthy duchy would now pass to his daughter Eleanor. She was just 15, a lively, wilful, pretty girl, and now a great heiress. Eleanor had been brought up in a very different way from that in which young noblewomen in the north of Europe were often reared, in convents. Eleanor had lived at her father's court at Bordeaux, gay and carefree. Bordeaux still kept something of the glory of the old Roman civilization in its villas and schools, and in the ducal court itself. Her family was distinguished. They had founded the great abbey of Cluny. Her grandfather Duke William IX had been a poet and song writer, one of the first troubadours; he read widely in the poetry of ancient Rome and he learned the verses of poets from Muslim Spain as well. His culture was far broader than that of the king of France. The court of Aquitaine was full of civilization and warm southern sunshine, and Eleanor grew up eagerly believing that life was meant to be enjoyed and that it was full of limitless possibilities. As well as being pretty she was healthy and energetic, and very intelligent too.

None of all this was of any interest to King Louis. He had his eye simply on the young girl's duchy, which now seemed within his own grasp. It would more than double the royal demesne. The old king on his bed was surrounded by his advisers, the good Abbot Suger among them. Suger would be a loyal servant to his son; there was no doubt of that. Among them stood the young Prince Louis, a good-looking, very solemn young man of seventeen. He had been brought up in a monastery and would have preferred to become a monk rather than a king, but he was the key to his father's present plan. Louis listened obediently as his father told him plainly that he must set off immediately on the road for Bordeaux. He would be provided with an escort of knights, and on his arrival he must take possession of Eleanor, marry her without delay, and then get the Aquitanian vassals to do him homage. As a gesture towards courtesy and something of an afterthought, the old man thrust upon his son a handful of jewels. It was only right that Louis should give Eleanor a present! If the young prince felt that there was a slightly indecent

haste in all this, he fully realized the need for it. If he did not marry Eleanor some other great lord would undoubtedly get there first, and to marry Eleanor meant to add her duchy to the French royal demesne.

Louis was an efficient boy; the journey was made, the jewels delivered, and Eleanor felt that the future king of France was a fitting husband for one of her high birth. They were married in the church of St. André in Bordeaux; the housefronts were hung with tapestries and decorated with leafy green boughs, and gay processions led by minstrels playing the flute and the tabor brought an air of festive gaiety to the cobbled streets and squares of the old city. The lofty church was ablaze with hundreds of tapers and echoing with the chants of the choristers as the young prince and his charming duchess entered at the head of the bridal procession.

Louis had still only accomplished half the task his father had set him. He must next get the feudal lords of Aquitaine to do homage. Some had already come, but there were stragglers. Louis rounded them up. It was late summer before he could return north with his bride, but as soon as he could he set off towards Paris. They travelled speedily despite the heat, but before their journey ended, messengers came riding out from Béthizy to bring them news that King Louis VI was dead.

Eleanor found Paris a restless city. It was already famous for its schools, which were later to develop into a university. There were students from England, Italy, and Germany, as well as from all parts of France. They drank and argued in the noisy taverns, and they rushed off in scores to hear the lectures of the popular young master Peter Abelard. The city always seemed to be full of students, and there were merchants and tradesmen too, pushing and jostling in the narrow streets, where you had to watch your step lest you trod in the rubbish or were knocked down by a horse-drawn cart tearing round a sharp corner. The city seemed cramped, with its steep gabled houses huddled together under the shadow of the dark churches. The ancient palace tower where the king and queen lived, which went right back to Merovingian times, depressed Eleanor by its cold and gloom. The walls were so many feet thick that only chinks of light struggled in through the narrow window slits, and the corridors seemed like long dark hollow tunnels, echoing to Eleanor's step. While her young husband was busy at his studies she would often look out through the narrow window of her room, over the mean streets and the grey River Seine to the flat countryside beyond, and long for the warmth and comfort and light of her southern city of Bordeaux.

In 1149, when Eleanor had been queen for ten years, her life was suddenly touched with adventure. The king decided to go on

crusade. He was a deeply religious man and he had now come closely under the dynamic influence of St. Bernard of Clairvaux. It is to be feared that Eleanor, who heartily disliked St. Bernard, was attracted to the Crusade much more by its promise of adventure and romance than through devotion to the cause of Jerusalem. She thoroughly scandalized St. Bernard by insisting on taking troubadours with her, to make things more pleasant.

The Second Crusade was a failure. For a long time the French army was held up in Antioch, a city of Syria which is marked on the map on page 207. This was the centre of one of the small Christian states which had been set up after the First Crusade. The leaders could not decide on the next move and there was grumbling among the troops, but Eleanor did not mind in the least. Her uncle Count Raymond was prince of Antioch, and in him she found a pleasant companion who could talk to her of her beloved Aquitaine. He was not much older than Eleanor and he set out to be a charming host. His palace was surrounded by pleasant gardens and terraces, where they were free to walk, sit, and talk, and the luxurious style of living reminded Eleanor of the splendours of Constantinople, which had impressed and delighted her as the crusaders had passed through on their way to the Holy Land. The whole tone of Antioch was intriguingly oriental. The Christian community was small; Muslims worshipped freely in their mosques, and the little bells rang out their call to prayer from the tall minarets. The port was bright with strange ships carrying colourful cargoes, and cheerful bronzed sailors shouted directions in many strange languages, for Antioch was one of the greatest of all the markets for exchange of merchandise between eastern and western worlds. Eleanor was stimulated and fascinated by it all, and Prince Raymond was delighted to talk to her and answer all her eager questions. In fact, he was very anxious that she should persuade her husband to concentrate on helping Raymond in his own political plans and an attack on Aleppo, instead of pressing on to Jerusalem as Louis felt he should do.

The visit to Antioch ended in violent quarrels. Louis would not let Raymond beguile him into giving up his original purpose, and Raymond flew into a rage. He was convinced that an attack on Aleppo was by far the most statesmanlike plan, as well as being in the interests of his own state of Antioch. Worse still, Louis had become jealous of Raymond's courteous attention to Eleanor, and was very far from soothed when Eleanor not only supported Raymond's policies but, in the course of the quarrel, reminded her husband that he and she should never have married in the first place, because, according to the laws of the Church, they were too closely related. Louis brooded miserably on this, and wondered whether the fact that he had had no son by Eleanor after ten years

of marriage was indeed a judgement of God on an unholy union. Yet he loved Eleanor passionately, 'almost beyond reason', as some one said at the time. Louis took his wife away from Antioch by force, marched south with his troops, took his part in a wholly unsuccessful attack on the Muslim city of Damascus, and returned sadly to France.

Much damage had been done. Louis was tormented with doubts about his marriage. St. Bernard urged a divorce, because he saw Eleanor as a wicked, worldly influence on Louis; and meanwhile at the French court there appeared a man who saw something to his own advantage in this situation: Geoffrey Plantagenet, count of Anjou. Geoffrey had come to court to get Louis's assent, as king and overlord, to the investiture of Geoffrey's young son Henry as duke of Normandy. Henry was 18 and as yet unmarried. Geoffrey's quick mind fastened on an ambitious plan. If Louis were to divorce his queen, Eleanor would be free to marry again. Why should she not marry Henry? If you look at the map you will see what this would mean on Geoffrey's death. Henry, already duke of Normandy, would then inherit Anjou, and if he could add Aquitaine as well then he would be in control of a solid block of land stretching from the English Channel to the Pyrenees; he would in fact be far more powerful than the king of France, his overlord.

Young Henry Plantagenet saw the force of his father's arguments. Eleanor was ten years older than he, but she was still a lively and attractive young woman. Events moved swiftly. In 1151 Geoffrey died suddenly, and Henry inherited Anjou. In March 1152 King Louis, after much troubled discussion, divorced Queen Eleanor. The events of the next few weeks read more like a romantic novel than sober fact. Eleanor was obviously a splendid match for any French lord, and it was a good thing that she could look after herself. As she made her way south to Aquitaine, she first fell into an ambush laid by Henry Plantagenet's younger brother, aged 16, who thought he would capture Eleanor and marry her himself! Eleanor just managed to escape this, only to hear that the younger son of the count of Champagne had planted a force of armed men near Tours to capture her as she crossed the River Loire. Eleanor had no wish to marry any one's younger brother; she had other things in mind. She took a roundabout route to avoid Tours, rode fast, with her small but faithful escort, and arrived safely in the courtyard of her own strong castle of Poitiers. There she drew breath, for she could fight off unwelcome suitors if they arrived. However, the next suitor to appear did not come as a brigand, and he was admitted, welcomed, and accepted. It was Henry Plantagenet. Eleanor no doubt had a certain pleasure in marrying her former husband's great rival. Henry was now lord of Normandy, Anjou,

and Aquitaine. Two years later he succeeded to the throne of England as well, for he was the grandson of the English king, Henry I, and the great-grandson of William the Conqueror. If you look again at the map on page 214 you will see what a vast stretch of land Henry Plantagenet now controlled. He was suddenly the most powerful ruler in Western Europe. And he was just 21.

The Great Seal of Henry II, showing the king enthroned, crowned and holding orb and sceptre. The king's chancellor took care of the seal, and its imprint on wax was attached to all the most solemn and important state documents.

In appearance Henry was healthy and vigorous rather than handsome. His sturdy broad-shouldered figure gave an impression of power and energy, and he had a rather harsh voice. What you could not tell at first sight was the quality of his keen, clear, original mind. Eleanor's second husband was in fact one of the great men of the twelfth century. His genius showed itself in a strongly practical way. He was not a man of learning, he was not a poet, he was certainly no saint; he was a man of government. To Henry the great challenge of his life was the actual ruling of the lands he had gained through inheritance or marriage. As a vassal of the king of France Henry knew how the government of a country could be pulled to pieces by feudalism. The great French dukes and counts, of whom he was now the greatest, could almost ignore their king. Within his own dominions Henry was determined that this should never happen. No vassal of his should ignore his authority; he would find ways to prevent it, though he did not yet know what they were to be.

The first need was to get round all these lands. This may sound simple. It was not. Henry knew that royal officials, if left to themselves, got lazy and slack and sometimes even disloyal. To keep them up to the mark you had to shock them by arriving unexpectedly and catching them out. Henry was for ever on the move, and so was his household. In England he was to be found at any one of a number of castles: London, Winchester, Wallingford, Nottingham, Oxford, Lincoln, Marlborough, the hunting lodges at Clarendon or Woodstock, and sometimes in more outlying places too, the Scottish or Welsh borders, or the Peak district of Derbyshire. The royal household who travelled with him sometimes numbered as many as 200 people. There were Eleanor and the children, of course (for by her marriage to Henry she had seven children), but there were also the chancellor, chamberlains, marshals, stewards, butlers, clerks, chaplains, knights, ushers, watchmen, serjeants, huntsmen, hornblowers, and scullions. Everything had to be loaded on to pack-horses and carts: all the equipment of the king's chapel, candles, portable altars, silver plate; all the eating equipment and kitchen utensils, the bed furnishings, the clothes, and above all the royal documents and the king's great seal. These last were the special care of the chancellor.

You can imagine the commotion that these moves caused, the

grumbling among the courtiers and servants, the shouting of orders, the general bad temper; and Henry often made it worse by clearly announcing that he would stay in a place for a day, and then suddenly ordering a very early start. Quite clearly he sometimes did this simply to keep his men alert for a change of plan! Peter of Blois, who was frequently at court, describes what happened next:

As a result you see men dashing around as if they were mad, beating their pack-horses, running their carts into one another—in short giving a lively imitation of Hell. If on the other hand the King orders an early start, he is certain to change his mind, and you can take it for granted that he will sleep until midday. Then you will see the pack-horses loaded and waiting, the carts prepared, the courtiers dozing, traders fretting, and everyone grumbling. When our couriers had gone ahead almost the whole day's ride, the King would turn aside to some other place, where he had, it might be, just a single house with accommodation for himself and no one else. I hardly dare say it, but I believe that in truth he took a delight in seeing what a fix he put us in.

All this would have been tiring enough in England, but at short notice the king would be off to Rouen, Angers, Poitiers, or Bordeaux. Normandy played a big part in Henry's plans and his government there was very strong. At the Norman town of Caen, as in London, there was a great Exchequer Court. It was partly a court of law, and Henry's chief official for Normandy presided there and dealt out justice in the duke's name. It was also the place where Henry's bailiffs brought the money they had collected for the duke, and had their accounts sharply checked. It was called an 'exchequer' because when the accounts were checked it was done by moving counters on a chequered cloth, like a chess board. That is where our words 'check' and 'cheque' come from, and it is also why we still have a 'Chancellor of the Exchequer' in England, who deals with our government's money. The exchequers at Caen and London were there already when Henry came to the throne, but he used them far more than other dukes of Normandy and kings of England had ever done. We shall see more of this later.

Henry went to out-of-the-way places too—to take his stewards or the keepers of his castles by surprise. He would then jump down from his horse and stand talking for an hour or so to one of his officials, who had to stand too. It was all very exhausting, for the king was asking detailed questions and expecting prompt and detailed answers. Henry himself seemed tireless. To relax, he went hunting or hawking. The first scientific treatise on hawking came from his court, and he once spent over £56 on sending a ship to Norway to buy falcons there (this would be several hundred pounds in modern money). He hardly ever sat down, except at meal times or when he was in the saddle, and even in church his glance would

rove, he would shift about restlessly, scribble notes, pull his neighbour's sleeve and whisper to him on matters of business, or even pace up and down the church, impatient for the service to be finished. No wonder that at the end of the day he had to have his swollen feet rubbed, and before he went to sleep listen to a musician or have a book read to him to relieve the tension of his mind. Walter Map, one of the courtiers, thought that it was even worse for Henry's companions: 'We wear out our clothes, break our bones and our beasts, and never find a moment for the cure of our sick souls.'

These ceaseless journeys were vital to Henry's task of government. But they were not enough. The truth was that no one man could possibly tackle this huge task of government alone. Where then was he to turn? Perhaps he might look for help to his feudal vassals. Certainly Henry believed in using the feudal bond between lord and man in his own interests. He would not let his vassals pull apart from him; he exacted to the full the services they owed him. Each vassal had the duty of bringing a certain number of knights to fight for Henry when asked to do so. Henry enforced this service rigorously, especially in England and Normandy, where he kept careful records of exactly how many knights were due from each vassal. Sometimes he called his English vassals to a Great Council meeting and discussed his plans with them to be sure of their support, and he encouraged them to seek justice at his court. Yet the help of his vassals was not enough either.

Henry needed men to help him who would make the work of government a full-time career. Such men were more reliable than feudal vassals, because they owed their position solely to the king, and they were prepared to give their whole energy and attention to serving him. There were already some men of this kind in all feudal governments, but usually very few. Henry wanted a great many. Some of them were needed for key positions such as that of Chief Justiciar in England or Normandy, or for the office of Chancellor, which was very close to the king indeed. Thomas Becket, who held the post in the early part of Henry's reign, became a great friend of the king. Henry discussed much of the day-to-day business with this lively, intelligent, and ambitious servant. It was Becket who helped Henry to restore order to England after the chaotic reign of King Stephen.

Richard Fitznigel, the king's treasurer in England, took such pride in his work that he wrote a book about the Exchequer, and dedicated it to Henry. It begins like this:

> In the twenty-third year of the reign of King Henry II, as I was sitting at a turret window overlooking the Thames, I was addressed by someone who said very earnestly, 'Master, why do you not teach others that

knowledge of the Exchequer for which you are famous, and put it in writing lest it should die with you?'

Richard really did not need much persuading, and thoroughly enjoyed writing his book. There was no other country in Europe in which that book could have been written.

Henry needed men with expert legal knowledge too. His court was immensely popular, and if a man had a really tricky lawsuit he would literally chase the king from one end of his dominions to the other to get justice. We know this from the story of Richard Anstey, who believed he had been cheated of the lands of his dead uncle William. Richard started the case in England, then had to rush off after the king to Aquitaine, and back again to England—first to Romsey, then to Windsor, across to London, over to Reading, back again to London, and finally to Woodstock, where the royal court gave its final verdict on uncle William's lands. Richard was triumphant: 'At last by the grace of God and the King and by judgement of his court my uncle's land was adjudged to me.' From the relish with which Richard tells how much money he spent and how many horses he killed in this enterprise, I suspect that he rather enjoyed it.

In England the sheriffs looked after the king's interests in each county. There had been a sheriff in charge of each county since Anglo-Saxon times. They presided in the county courts and collected the money due to the king, as the bailiffs did in Normandy. Twice a year they rode off to the Exchequer in London, to take the money, in large bags of silver pennies, and to present their accounts. Each sheriff was interviewed separately in the great hall which had the Exchequer table. Round the table sat important royal officials, perhaps discussing points about the account of the sheriff who had just gone out. Clerks were writing down all the details on long parchment rolls, called 'pipe rolls'. They wrote quickly but very carefully and neatly, and were trained in a special kind of handwriting, so that you cannot tell the difference even if one clerk goes off for his lunch and another takes over from him. We have all these rolls from Henry II's reign in the Public Record Office in London, just as they came fresh from the clerks' hands, and you can see a photograph of part of one on the page opposite. It was a terrifying moment for the sheriff when he came into this room and was asked to sit down at one end of the long table. Facing him, far away at the other end of the table, was the most imposing royal official of all, the king's Chief Justiciar. The sheriff was closely questioned about all his receipts and payments, and the least slip was pounced on by the officials. It was bad enough if you were capable and honest, but if you were in the least inefficient those royal officials could reduce you to a state of gibbering foolishness in a few minutes, and then you

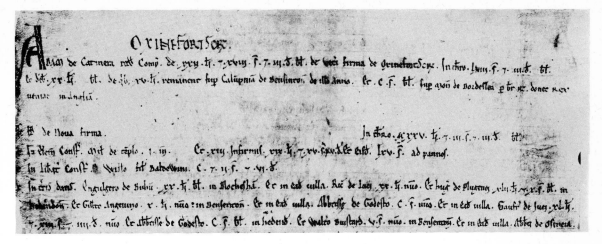

Membrane of a Pipe Roll of Henry II's reign.

might be dismissed from your post, or at least be made to pay a very heavy fine.

Perhaps you might think that no dishonest sheriff could slip through this system. Some did. In 1170 Henry returned to England after four years in France. Complaints had reached him about corrupt sheriffs and other officials. He was grimly determined to root these men out. An inquiry was launched, and Henry's English subjects were deeply impressed when many sheriffs were dismissed.

With Henry justice was a passion. To give justice to his subjects he was prepared to wear himself out; he was prepared to see any man who came to him and begged for a hearing; he was prepared to ride thousands of miles to catch out royal stewards, sheriffs, bailiffs, or keepers of castles, in slack or dishonest deeds, and he would reward honest and hardworking officials generously. Yet there was still crime and disorder that went unpunished; there were both vassals and officials who escaped his watchful eye. Henry was not satisfied.

If the king was going to experiment, perhaps England was the most promising place to do it, because here there was a tradition of strong government going back to Anglo-Saxon times, and there was something in the make-up of the Englishman that made him take to the law with a sureness that Henry liked. Painfully, by means of long hard discussions between the king and his ablest advisers, often going on late into the night, a system was gradually battered out over the years: an exciting experiment that stood the test of time, and long outlasted feudalism. The system was built on ancient customs, but as a *system* it was new. It meant the sure discovery and punishment of crime; it meant putting the king's court at the service of every ordinary freeman who wanted to use it; above all—and most revolutionary—it meant that the king called

on the ordinary freemen of his kingdom, along with the knights and nobles, to co-operate with him in bringing about justice and good government. Through the courts they were to help in governing themselves. This system was so sound that it has been studied since then by lawyers in all the English-speaking countries in the world, and much of it remains the basis of our own system of law today.

If we were to choose one key document in this programme of change it would undoubtedly be the Assize of Clarendon of 1166. Henry laid down that from every 'hundred' (a division of the county) twelve lawful men were to come to the county court and be put on oath to tell the truth. They were then to name in front of the sheriff which of their neighbours were reputed by everybody to be criminals—robbers, murderers, or thieves. They were to name these men not only in front of the sheriff but also in front of judges sent out by the king into that county from his own court. The royal judges then dealt with the criminals. By sending out his own judges Henry was really opening up local branches of his royal court in the countryside. The jurymen (the men put on oath) were simply respectable law-abiding freemen, who were being used by the king to help him in keeping order. Such men still do this duty today; you may easily be called on to do it yourself when you are a little older. Juries now actually decide whether the man is guilty or not, instead of just telling the judge what people they suspect, and the daily newspapers are full of verdicts brought in by juries. You will find that these juries are still summoned by a sheriff and that the court is still presided over by a royal judge. Henry II had built a system that was made to last. When America was colonized by Englishmen in the seventeenth century, the colonists took the jury system with them, and cases are still dealt with by juries in the United States as well. I wonder how many American businessmen, called upon for jury service, know that an English medieval king was originally responsible for putting them to that inconvenience!

Henry went still further. As well as using the jury system himself, he let his subjects use it. If a man was unlucky enough to have his land forcibly seized by a greedy neighbour, he could ask for a royal 'writ', that is a letter from the king which told the sheriff to summon a jury to look into the matter. There came to be more and more cases for which juries could be summoned, and more and more freemen had to sit on juries. It was often a thorough nuisance to be summoned to sit on a jury, as it still is, and there was a lot of grumbling about it, but men saw how useful it was, and so they were prepared to do it—unpaid.

You will have noticed that Henry was now getting into touch with

men who were not feudal vassals and not royal officials. just ordinary freemen. In fact his reforms in a sense bypassed the feudal system. This was typical of him. He thought about his *subjects*, as a modern government does, not merely about his *vassals*, as most feudal kings did. In 1181 he made arrangements that all freemen were to be equipped to fight for the king, not only the barons and knights. The better-off freemen were to have a shirt of mail, a helmet, a shield, and a lance, and even the poorest must still have a padded coat, an iron cap, and a lance. I expect they looked an ill-assorted lot when called out, and Henry would only use them in an emergency, but it was important that they should feel that, as subjects of the king, they had a duty to fight for him.

Henry's greatest achievements were in the closely-governed lands of England and Normandy. In Anjou and Aquitaine he had to be content with a looser control. The nobles of Aquitaine were particularly restless, and as soon as Henry's son Richard was old enough he was sent there to represent his father on the spot. Richard was Queen Eleanor's favourite son, and when relations between Eleanor and Henry grew very cool in 1169 Eleanor went south too, and set up her own gay court at Poitiers. Here she worked against Henry rather than for him, and eventually stirred up Richard to rebel against his father. But meanwhile Poitiers became one of the most brilliant centres in Europe and added to the glory of the Angevin Empire.

Eleanor gathered round her a sparkling company of young women of high rank and fashion. The countess of Blois and the countess of Brittany, princesses of the French court, and Eleanor's own daughters, the queens of Castille and Sicily, were all visitors here. Above all, Eleanor had with her her eldest daughter, Marie de Champagne, who shared eagerly in all her mother's plans. The brilliance of beauty and wit and grace at Poitiers began to draw young knights from all over the West; they came to joust and tourney, and they came to find a bride. Above all, they came to learn the rules of courtly love, how to write songs for the minstrels to play, and how to pay homage to a high-born lady. They revelled in stories of King Arthur and his Knights of the Round Table, and they vied with each other in writing elegant verses and in winning the favours of their mistresses. In this gentle company their rough manners became gallant and refined, for no boorish, uncouth behaviour was ever allowed. The knight must be generous, courteous, and considerate, as well as being a brave warrior. Eleanor had found her own road to power and influence, but her methods were very different from those of her husband.

Henry hated war, but it was only by force that he could keep

The castle of Angers, capital of Anjou. This fortress would withstand almost any attack.

control of his lands in France. As well as feudal knights, he had about 6,000 mercenaries, paid soldiers who made fighting their job. They were often rough and sometimes brutal men, but they obeyed orders and they would fight for as long as Henry needed them. He could march them quickly from one part of his dominions to another. This force and his network of strong stone castles meant that Henry could hardly be defeated.

England and Normandy already had strong royal or ducal castles and Henry improved and extended them. The castle of Tours, which guarded the passage of the River Loire, was made into a fine strong fortress. To feel the immense strength and bulk of these castles, look at the picture on this page of the entrance to the fortress of Angers, the capital of Henry's native Anjou. You can also see at Angers and Le Mans the stone hospitals he built, and a great dyke that runs for many miles along the Loire still holds its flood waters in check, protecting the valley road.

Wide as Henry's territories were, he planned to stretch out his hand still further. He led expeditions to Wales and Ireland and against the king of Scotland. In France he claimed Brittany for his

son Geoffrey, and in the south he forced the count of Toulouse to become his vassal. He married one of his daughters to the Spanish king of Castile, and another to the king of Sicily. His ambitions were never foolish. He always aimed at the possible, but he thought and planned on a grand scale.

Had this great man any weaknesses? Henry made some bad mistakes, and they were nearly always mistakes about people. He chose his friend and chancellor, Thomas Becket, to be archbishop of Canterbury, and Becket turned against the king in order to defend the Church. The quarrel ended in the tragic murder of Becket in Canterbury cathedral. Henry failed badly too with his own family. At first he and Eleanor worked hard, with a common purpose, but when he made clear to the whole court his love for his young mistress Rosamund Clifford, Eleanor would not stand it, and withdrew to set up her own court at Poitiers, feeling very bitter towards her husband. Among his sons the king had favourites, and showed it. Prince Henry, the eldest, was never on good terms with his masterful father; Richard was his mother's darling, and was deeply jealous of Henry's favourite son John. The jealousies among the sons and their resentment of their dominating father flared up into open rebellion in 1173. Henry crushed it, brought his sons to heel, and had his wife, who had supported them, confined in one of his castles for the next 15 years. The danger remained. If anyone were to appear who could play on the bad feelings and fierce tempers within Henry's family, he might bring disaster to the Angevins yet.

There was such a man. As Henry's sons made their peace with their father in 1174, a little boy of 8 years was learning his lessons in one of the castles of the French king. He was clever but restless at his studies, and he longed impatiently for the time when he would be king of France. The young Prince Philip was King Louis's only son, and there were strange stories told of the events in Paris at his birth. There was a large group of English students in Paris at the time, and they were far from popular with the French citizens. One of these students was woken up on the night of Philip's birth by the joyful pealing of bells and the blaze from lighted candles which shone in through his bedroom window from the street below. Thinking that there must be a fire, he leaped out of bed and rushed across the room to open the casement window. People were rushing through the streets in great excitement, and he called out to two old women who were running along with lighted tapers. One of them recognized him as a student from England, and she shouted up: 'By God's grace we have an heir to the kingdom now, and through him your king shall suffer dishonour and defeat, punishment and shame, confusion and misery.' On she ran past the house, shaking her fist; she hated the English king who ruled half

Plantagenet tombs at Fontevrault

of France; her own sons would fight for King Philip. This feeling of belonging to France or belonging to England was eventually going to help to destroy not only the empire built up by Henry II but feudal society itself.

When Philip became king of France he was to play off father against son and brother against brother in Henry Plantagenet's family, until the Angevin lands were aflame with war. In 1189 Henry was to die fighting against his own son Richard, who had become Philip's ally, and as he lay dying he was to learn, to his terrible grief, that his favourite son John had secretly plotted against him too. The struggle did not stop with Henry's death, and King Philip did not rest until he had driven the Plantagenets out of both Normandy and their native Anjou, and had added their lands to the demesne of the king of France.

King Henry II

Yet Henry II's achievement remains immense. He was a great king. What did Queen Eleanor really think of him? He had humiliated her, and she had wronged and betrayed him. It is interesting, then, to come across this story in a chronicle of the abbey of Bury St. Edmunds. King Henry, the chronicler tells us, had once given the monks 'a great golden cup worth a hundred marks'. Some time after Henry's death, when his son Richard was on the throne, the monks sent this cup to the Queen Mother, Eleanor, in payment of a debt that they owed her. She was not pleased; she returned it to the monks 'on behalf of the soul of her Lord King Henry, who had first given it to the abbey'. Later King Richard was imprisoned on his return from the Third Crusade, and the great golden cup was taken again from Bury to help to pay for his ransom. Queen Eleanor found out, 'and bought back the same cup for a hundred marks and sent it back to us, receiving a charter from us in token of our promise on the word of truth, that we would never let go that cup from our church under any circumstances whatsoever'.

Queen Eleanor

A few years later Queen Eleanor was buried beside her lord King Henry in the abbey of Fontevrault. Opposite there are photographs of those royal tombs.

King Richard I

Chapter 16
Pope Innocent III and St. Francis

One day in the summer of the year 1210, in the audience chamber of the papal palace in Rome, two of the most remarkable men of the Middle Ages came face to face for the first time. Pope Innocent III was engaged in what was always—and still is—part of the pope's regular routine, the giving of audiences to some of the thousands of people who wanted to see him, kings and nobles, soldiers and statesmen, priests, monks, nuns, and many others; some who themselves had sought his presence, others who, for reasons of his own, the pope desired to see. On that particular day Innocent III received a very curious little group of twelve men. He was not particularly anxious to see them, but had been urged to do so by one of his cardinals, Ugolino, and he was not at first much impressed by what he saw. They were a very shabby-looking lot, who had clearly done little or nothing to spruce themselves up for such a great occasion, for they were dressed in coarse woollen habits, much patched and mended, and tied about their waists with bits of cord, their feet were bare and no doubt dirty, and they had not shaved or cut their hair. In fact it was surprising that they had ever managed to get anywhere near the presence of his Holiness. Their leader was just as unkempt as the rest. He was a small spare man with dark hair and bright dark eyes, and someone who knew him well said that he was 'not at all prepossessing, his habit dirty, his face far from handsome'. His name was Francis of Assisi.

The contrast between the two men was extraordinary. On the stately throne sat one of the most important men alive, the great prince of the Church, well-born, well fed, well groomed, surrounded by all the outward signs of power and ancient ceremony, believed by himself and many others to be 'set in the midst between God and man, below God but higher than all men'. Before him stood Francis, the 'Poverello' (the 'little poor man'), who owned nothing but his tattered habit. When Innocent went about he travelled in state, sometimes carried shoulder high in a golden chair. Francis and his companions, as they always did, had tramped the long miles from Assisi to Rome along the dusty summer roads, sleeping rough and eating only what scraps of food they could beg as they went. What had brought these two opposites face to face? And why is it that now for one person who has heard of Pope Innocent III there are perhaps a dozen who know something about St. Francis?

Pope Innocent III looking young but determined.

Innocent was twenty years older than Francis, and had been Pope since 1198. He was a man of great energy, courage, and persistence, at times adding to the discord of Europe by his demands and actions, at times making men obey him by persuasion as well as by the special threats he could use. Again and again he asserted his power, as Head of the Christian Church, over kings and rulers, because, as he said, 'just as the moon receives its power from the sun, which is the greater by far . . . so the royal power receives its renown and prestige from the papal power.' This idea, as you can imagine, was not popular with the 'royal powers', especially as Innocent believed he had a special duty to watch over their behaviour. During his reign he punished two emperors and seven kings for various crimes with his terrible weapons of excommunication and interdict, among them John Lackland of England, who was only forgiven when he humbled himself to become the pope's vassal and to pay him a yearly tribute of 1,000 marks.

But in spite of his power and his success in humbling the mighty, Innocent III was often almost crushed by his responsibilities and deeply depressed by what he saw going on in the world around him. For it was not only that great men, in their arrogance, flouted his power and disobeyed his instructions, spending their time locked

233

in combat and intrigue, but it seemed that there were terrible evils everywhere, and three of them specially haunted him.

The first was in the Church itself, which, though outwardly great and strong, was inwardly corrupt in many ways. Although the clergy still overawed people by instilling a kind of superstitious fear of what might happen to their souls and bodies, they were not loved or respected, and this was not surprising, for so many of them led scandalous lives that the good ones were hardly noticed. Such men had low standards, they spent their days in hunting, drank too much, wore gay bright clothes, and disobeyed the rule that clergy might not marry. They did little or nothing to bring light or hope into dark lives or to care for the suffering.

The monastic orders seemed to have lost their enthusiasm and many monks no longer faithfully followed their Rule. Instead, they were more occupied in managing—and enjoying—the great lands and wealth they had accumulated than in leading strict lives of prayer and obedience. When men saw the riches of monasteries piling up they thought it strange that so little of it was ever used to help the needy, and some demanded that it should be taken away and shared out among other groups of people.

The higher clergy, such as bishops and abbots, who should have set a good example, often did nothing of the kind. They were more like great feudal lords than ministers of God, doing little to rebuke the sinful or keep ill-living clergy in order. They lived in comfort and loved their money. A French bishop in Innocent's reign was described as 'This man who knows no God but money and has a purse instead of a heart', and unhappily there were scores of others like him.

These scandals were at the root of the second great evil, the debased behaviour of people generally. Many were quite indifferent to the Church and its teaching, or openly scornful and contemptuous, even hostile. Though they might still call themselves Christians, they certainly never allowed their religion to inconvenience them in any way, and they lived exactly as they liked, thoughtless, heartless, and gay, or greedy, brutal, and oppressive. The Church had failed men so greatly that they had come to believe that if they went to Mass on certain days, however carelessly and irreverently, their souls were safe, and that a lifetime of black deeds could be wiped out by a hasty death-bed repentance. Many, especially the poor, were unbelievably ignorant and superstitious, and tormented by problems; they often tried to escape from their fear of death and ill-luck by turning to witchcraft and magic, the ancient magic that their pagan forefathers had used, with spells and charms and talismans.

But in spite of indifference and superstitions the great majority of people felt in their hearts a need for religion, and because of this there were many who were ready to follow almost anyone who seemed to offer them some solace in the sorrows of this world and some hope of happiness in the next. In the twelfth century there were plenty who were ready to do this. In many countries of Europe men were to be found preaching and teaching, urging repentance and promising salvation, but they were not the clergy of the Church, and often what they taught and did was quite against its teaching. Yet thousands of disciples believed and followed them, away from the Church, along ways which often led to terrible persecution as heretics. And heretics and heresy were the third of the evils which specially haunted Innocent.

The leaders of these heresies were often mysterious figures, who moved from place to place in great secrecy, and indeed even now only a few of their names are known. Some were very ignorant men, who could not read or write, but who made up for lack of learning by the burning fire of their utterances. Some were good and earnest people, whose devoted and simple lives were in strong contrast to those of the corrupt clergy and who truly longed to show men the way to heaven. Some were sinister, and filled with envy and hatred, some were false rogues. One of these, who said that he was Jesus Christ come again to earth, preached the beauty of poverty and self-denial to his disciples, but himself lived fatly on their subscriptions.

Scandals in the Church, debased lives among lay people, heretics abounding, these were the problems that Innocent wrestled with. He thundered against the deplorable clergy who brought the Church, and so the true teaching of Christ, into contempt, and poured out letters and edicts forbidding them to do this and urging them to do that. They were not to hunt and hawk, or drink in taverns, or wear brightly coloured clothes—red and green he specially mentioned as most unseemly. They were to dress soberly in black, and set themselves earnestly to do their duty. He hounded the bishops to do theirs too, and particularly to watch over and correct their clergy. If they ignored his urgings he sometimes abruptly turned them out of their bishoprics, and this was a sharp punishment, for it cut off their incomes. The Bishop of Sens, who had done little or nothing to follow up one of Innocent's edicts, received a letter which said: 'We nominated you bishop because We thought We were giving God's flock in Sens and indeed in the whole of France a true shepherd. But now your light is out. Now it is nothing more than smoke from a snuffed candle.' Innocent was both angry and hurt by the bishop's indolence, for they were old friends, but he would not allow friendship to stand in the way of reform.

If reform was a slow tough business, even tougher was the rooting out of heresy, especially as there were places where the roots had gone very deep. One of these was the south of France, a rich and prosperous part of the land with thriving towns and brisk trade. It swarmed with feudal lords holding brilliant little courts in their castles, with troubadours entertaining all the world with their songs and stories of love and chivalry, and merchants from every country in Europe coming and going. It also swarmed with heretics, and there were some obvious reasons for this. It was a part of France where people were lively, sharp-witted, and ready to question and criticize anything. They openly criticized the Church, especially as their clergy were some of the worst in France, and the feeling against them was hostile and contemptuous. Many people were anti-Church, anti-pope, anti-priest, and anti-monk; many, especially feudal lords, cast envious eyes on Church wealth. The centre of fashion and brilliance in Languedoc, as this part of France was called, was the court of the counts of Toulouse, and it was also the centre of hostility to the Church. The counts were known to welcome heretics, to listen readily to their preaching, and to allow them to move free and unmolested in their domains. Their example was followed by people of every class, and because of this, 50 years before Innocent became pope, the south of France was known as a dangerous hotbed of heresy. Bernard of Clairvaux himself had gone to Toulouse in 1145 in search of 'a certain Henry, once a monk but now a man of very wicked life who has caught the fickle attention of the people of those parts'. Although at the time Bernard was a sick man, he forced himself to visit 'those places where that singular beast feeds and boldly revels among the flock of Christ, speaking lies'. The word 'boldly' was the right one. Heretics were safe in the land of the counts of Toulouse, even when they were open enemies of the Church, as 'the singular beast' Henry certainly was.

When Innocent became pope he tried endless ways of dislodging heretic preachers and bringing 'the flock of Christ' back to the fold. For ten years he wrote persuading letters and threatening letters; he sent special envoys and special preachers (among them a Spanish monk called Dominic); he urged the nobles, and particularly the reigning Count of Toulouse, Raymond VI, to renounce their own abominable ways and drive out the heretics from their lands. Innocent was not a natural persecutor—he was too intelligent—and he did not want to use force, but in the end he did. In 1208 his special envoy to Toulouse was murdered, and the disgraceful Count Raymond openly rejoiced at the crime. This was too much, and Innocent gave up peaceful persuasion and proclaimed a holy war against heretics all over the south of France. It was a long cruel war which dragged on for years. It destroyed Count Raymond and many others like him, it did terrible damage, it

silenced the voices of the troubadours; but because force is not a good weapon to use against stubborn men who hold passionately to their beliefs, it did not stamp out the heretics but only drove them underground.

This holy war against the heretics in the south of France was not the only one that Innocent proclaimed. He also set going the Fourth Crusade to the Holy Land, because he hoped it might fire in men, especially of the tough fighting class, a new enthusiasm for Christianity if they tried once more to wrest Jerusalem out of the hands of pagans. But the results were not at all what he hoped for. Instead of making straight for the Holy Land, the leaders of the crusading armies decided to interfere in a squabble between two rivals for the throne of the eastern empire; and with this flimsy excuse they proceeded to fling themselves against Constantinople, still, nearly 800 years after Rome itself had fallen, the splendid impregnable capital of the East, a Christian city, beautiful and civilized, but fatally rich. The thought of her fabulous wealth drew the crusaders like a magnet, and far more powerfully than any thought of capturing Jerusalem. They seized the city and for three terrible days raged madly through it, these so-called soldiers of the Cross, slaughtering other Christians, burning churches, looting and destroying. 'They who are supposed to serve Christ rather than their own interests,' wrote Innocent, appalled by the news, 'who should have drawn their swords against pagans alone, are dripping with the blood of Christians.' It was the greatest blow that had ever fallen on Constantinople, and also, perhaps, the greatest shock to Christianity in the Middle Ages. Constantinople never quite recovered; the Crusaders straggled home with their loot, Jerusalem was not rescued, and 'Mercy, Pity, Peace, and Love', those four flowers of the Christian faith, were trampled underfoot, and all that Innocent could do to revive them was not enough. It was a dark moment in history, when some quite different power, some different person, was urgently needed to stir the hearts of men and prick their consciences. Six years later Innocent III and Francis of Assisi met in Rome.

'Why do all men come after thee?' asked Brother Masseo, one of the first companions of St. Francis, looking one day at the thin little man who was his leader, 'And why do men long to see thee and hear thee and obey thee? Thou art not beautiful, thou art not of much wisdom, thou art not of noble birth. Whence comes it then that it is after thee that the whole world doth run?' And indeed, when you look at the rather ordinary face on page 238, you can understand something of Masseo's amazement. The answer that Francis gave Masseo was that God had called him, the meanest of His creatures, to show forth His power to men. It was this that he implicitly believed, and it was because of this that he was able to inspire

St. Francis from the chapel of
St. Gregory, Subiaco, Italy.
Most portraits of St. Francis
were painted long after he died,
but this one is contemporary
and probably the artist had seen
him.

people in their thousands to change their ways, and that he put new life into the Church. But the call of God was not a comfortable thing to receive, and when it came to Francis it drove him to act, at least in the eyes of his family and friends, like a madman and a drop-out.

Until he was 25, Francis was simply one of the liveliest and most extravagant of all the noisy rich young men in Assisi. In fact it was said that 'he strove to surpass all the rest in follies and freaks, idle talk and songs, and soft flowing attire.' He seemed a lucky person, who had been born with a silver spoon in his mouth and certainly had no cares about money, which he spent freely. His father, Pietro Bernadone, was a very prosperous cloth merchant, who, like some of those described in Chapter 13, travelled about Europe serving his customers. Indeed, he was away in France on a business trip when his remarkable son was born, and when he reached home, mellowed by the good profits he had made, he called the boy Francis—in Italian 'Francesco', the 'little Frenchman'. Pietro did not mind his son's extravagance or his wild pranks in the streets of Assisi. He liked him to cut a dash and be popular and successful, and Francis had every intention of being both. He saw himself winning renown as a soldier and a knight errant, seeking adventure, and defending fair damsels in distress.

But he was not merely a spoilt and wild young man. He was invariably gentle and courteous in manner, and absurdly generous, and he hated the sight of suffering in any form (and there was plenty of it to see in medieval Italy), even if he did nothing about it, except to toss coins to beggars and—from a safe distance, for he was mortally afraid of them—to lepers. There were times too, when he behaved rather oddly. Occasionally, streaming home with his friends at night after a late party, waking the sleeping citizens with their laughter and singing, he would suddenly drop out of the group and wander off in a kind of dream which he could not explain even to himself. Then one day in 1205 he left Assisi with a band of friends who had all volunteered to fight for the pope in South Italy. They rode off in the highest spirits to Spoleto, and there spent the first night of their journey. In the morning Francis had mysteriously disappeared. It seems that he was told in a dream or a vision not to go on the expedition, and the power of the dream was so strong upon him that he left his friends and rode home. Everyone in Assisi was astonished when he reappeared, and his father was very annoyed, for he wanted Francis to distinguish himself in the fashionable sport of fighting and he had spent much money on his equipment. Was his son a coward? What was at the bottom of this peculiar behaviour?

After this Francis began to withdraw more and more from his

Assisi, the hill-top town in Italy where St. Francis was born in 1182.

family and friends. He spent much time wandering by himself in the hills and through the olive orchards outside the town walls, moody, puzzled, and uncertain, and you can imagine the gossip and arguments that went on about his strangeness. Then one day he had another strange experience. While out on one of his wanderings he had gone into the half-ruined church of San Damiano on the hillside below Assisi to pray. Over the altar there hung a painted wooden crucifix, and as Francis knelt there alone in the little crumbling church, he thought the figure on the cross spoke to him: 'Francis,' it said, 'repair my church, which, as you see, is falling into ruins.'

Francis got up and hurried home. This at least was something he could do quickly and easily. He took some rolls of good cloth from his father's shop, rode down to the town of Foligno, ten miles

away, sold the cloth and his horse, and walked back to San Damiano. There he thrust the money into the hands of the old priest in charge of the church. It was typical of his quick impatience at that time that when the priest, afraid of offending the wealthy father of this peculiar young man, refused to take it, Francis threw it down in the church and went off, quite pleased with what he had done. But his father was very far from pleased when he heard. He now lost all patience with his son, for he saw him not only as eccentric and unfashionable, but dishonest into the bargain. He turned him out of his house and publicly accused him of theft before the magistrates and the bishop. Then Francis was ordered to appear in public outside the bishop's palace in Assisi and answer the charge, and he electrified everyone by handing over the money and everything of value that he possessed, and then, removing his gay clothes, dropping these too at his father's feet. Standing almost naked before a crowd of onlookers, he said 'Listen, all of you, and understand. Up to now I have called Pietro Bernadone my father, but now, since I am resolved to serve God only, I give him back the money he is so perturbed about, as well as the clothes I wore that belong to him, and from now on I will say "Our Father which art in heaven" instead of "my father Pietro Bernadone".' Then, wrapped in an old cloak which the bishop hastily produced, he walked away through the crowd, some of them silent and amazed, some jeering and scornful, out into the world with nothing.

For the next two years Francis allowed himself to reach the depths of poverty and hardship. He was laughed at by his friends, beaten and thrown in the snow by bandits, driven from the door by monks. He suffered from cold and hunger, he made his home among lepers. He was without money, friends, home, or security. He wandered through villages and towns carrying a broom with which he swept clean the dirty and neglected churches. He also collected and begged stones, and with his own hands repaired San Damiano according to the command he had received. He begged for his food, he slept in the open, he tended the sick and the helpless. Much of this he found almost intolerable, the dirty scraps of cold unwanted food made him sick to look at them, he could hardly bear to touch the lepers, but everywhere he went he thanked God for his goodness; praising him for the sun, the moon, the air, the birds and beasts, for 'Sister Water who is very useful and humble and chaste . . . for Brother Fire . . . beauteous and jocund, robustious and strong'. Everywhere too he preached of the love of God for man and the need for repentance, and his words went to the very hearts of those who heard him, so that scorn and fear turned to reverence and people began to say 'Truly this man is a saint and the friend of God.'

Gradually he was joined by companions, men inspired by his

extraordinary example, who gave up their possessions as Christ had asked his disciples to do. They put on the brown habit and cord, and with him 'suffered many tribulations and hardships from hunger, thirst and cold. Yet all this they bore with fortitude learned from Francis, nor were they perturbed, nor were they saddened, nor did they wish evil to those who treated them evilly.' By 1210 the little group numbered 12, and Francis called them 'fratres minores', the 'brothers of very small account'. At this point he had a strong desire for the pope to recognize them as a religious order, to bless them and approve of their work, and it was to ask for this that the brothers set off for Rome, to seek an audience with Innocent III.

At first he was most unwilling to give them recognition. He did not believe they could possibly go on leading such a harsh life permanently, and if they really wanted to renounce the world, why not enter one of the existing monastic orders in a nice orthodox way and not start a new one? Besides, it might be dangerous to encourage them. Some of the most malignant and persistent heretics had behaved and dressed in much the same way, and how could he be sure that these men would not turn out to be like them, more of a menace to the Church than a help? Innocent hesitated and hedged and sent the brothers away. Then, after a few days of deep and anxious thought, he made up his mind to take the risk, perhaps because he could not resist the appeal of Francis, perhaps because of their obvious loyalty and devotion to the Church, and their promise 'to obey and reverence the Lord Pope Innocent and his successors', or perhaps because he really had the strange impelling dream which is shown in the picture on the page opposite, and really needs no explanation. At any rate, Innocent III approved the Rule of the Order of Fratres Minores, or the 'Friars' as they are now called, and Francis and the brothers left Rome full of joy.

In the next few years astonishing things happened. 'Many among the people, noble and common, clerks and laymen, pierced by God's spirit, began to come to St. Francis, longing evermore to fight under his leadership.' The first 12 friars grew into a multitude and spread far beyond Assisi and Italy. The absolute devotion of the brothers, their poverty—for they would not touch money—, their simplicity and humility, their preaching and their service to the very poor, began to make a deep impression. In 1216 a Frenchman called Jacques de Vitry came across them in Italy and gave them high praise: 'Many people,' he said, 'both rich and poor, leaving all for Christ, have fled from the world and are now called 'fratres minores'. By day they go into the towns and villages to win others by their example. By night they retire to some lonely place and give themselves up to prayer. I believe that, to the disgrace of the bishops who are dumb dogs that will not bark,' (Jacques did not

The dream of Innocent III in which he is said to have seen the Christian church collapsing and the young St. Francis coming to its rescue. From the church of St. Francis in Assisi.

like bishops!) 'the Lord intends before the end of the world to save many souls by these humble men.' He was right, but all the growth and success, and the many souls saved, brought problems, and they were ones that Francis himself found very difficult to tackle. As long as he had only a few ardent disciples whom he knew intimately, he could pass on his ideals to them, teach them, and make sure they were fit for the hard life and the exacting work. But this became impossible when there were hundreds of friars, not only scattered through all Italy but reaching into France, Germany, Spain, England, and the Holy land, and when he himself had gone to Spain or the Holy Land to preach to the pagans there.

In England, for instance, their success was astonishing. Nine friars arrived in 1220 and settled at Oxford, and in six years there were groups working in London, Canterbury, Cambridge, Worcester, Hereford, Bristol, Gloucester, Salisbury, Stamford, Lincoln, Leicester, Northampton, Nottingham, Norwich, and Kings Lynn. The Bishop of Lincoln wrote 'They illuminate our whole country with the light of their preaching and teaching.' But they were far from Assisi and cut off from the personal example of Francis. How were they to manage? The fact was that the Order of Friars was changing, that nothing would stop it, and that because of its size, rules, regulations, officials, and organization were becoming essential. But Francis disliked regulations and organization; he feared that his own ideals of poverty, simplicity, and humility would gradually be lost in a mass of written rules. He still tried to insist that the friars should refuse to touch money or own property, for he wanted them to spend their lives travelling as the spirit moved them, not to be based on a permanent house. He wanted them to live by the few hard rules that Christ once gave to his disciples, and on which he had first founded his order. With great sadness he saw the changes come, the large meetings of friars to discuss the complicated affairs of the whole vast order, the appointment of ministers in charge of distant branches, the regulations about clothes and food, or the hours of fasting and praying. It was all too rigid for Francis, who longed for the brothers to be free. He might still write letters beginning 'I brother Francis, your little servant, beg and beseech you by the love of God that you humbly receive the fragrant words of Christ, and understand and faithfully observe them'; but the truth was that out of the multitude of friars there were bound to be some who if simply left to themselves would not 'understand and faithfully observe', and these needed to be guided, governed, and organized. For a time Francis tried to resist these changes, but it was impossible for him to do so, and in 1220, knowing well that he was not the man to be the head of a great religious organization, he resigned as head of the order, and spent the rest of his life almost as a hermit. He was certainly

unhappy, for he saw his order slipping into the hands of men who, though they loved and reverenced him, yet thought quite differently about it. They longed to use to the utmost the amazing power for good that he had set free. It just happened that they saw him as the famous founder of a great and well-organized army of missionaries, with houses and churches and money; not as the Poverello and his little poor brothers, owning absolutely nothing, as he desired. But some people who knew him best saw Francis as the morning sun, and his life as the dawn of a new day. They said 'At the rising of this sun the earth lay numbed by the frosts of winter, in darkness, and devoid of life. His words and deeds were like a clear light awakening a new and finer day.' He was able to do so much because he touched something that lay deep and strong in medieval men, who, when they thought about God, were impressed not so much by the idea of his power and majesty—they took that for granted—but by the fact that he should make himself weak and lowly. 'The descendants of the Goths and Vandals, who despised weakness, marvelled greatly that the Creator of the world chose to suffer and be poor.' This to them was proof of His love for mankind and Francis had clearly and forcibly shown what it meant. So when men saw the Poverello and his faithful disciples, who had renounced everything the world most values, wealth, power, security, home, and family, and were prepared to risk even life itself in the service of God and his people, the world took fresh hope.

Francis died in 1226; at the end he lay on the bare floor of a little church near Assisi, wrapped only in his habit; two years later he was made a saint. Before that his body was taken up the hill to Assisi quickly and secretly, for fear that it might be stolen, and now it lies buried in an enormous church, built on the edge of the little town by order of the minister general of the Friars, and splendidly decorated inside by two of the greatest of Italian painters, Cimabue and Giotto. All day long crowds of visitors tramp through the great church, listen to the guides, and see the story of the Poverello set forth in the marvellous paintings on the walls. All the same, it seems rather a strange place for the 'little poor servant of God' to be in.

Francis left three orders behind him, which still exist and together have about 50,000 members: the Friars Minor; the Order of Poor Clares, for women; and the Third Order, for people who cannot entirely leave the world, but who want to follow his Rule as nearly as possible. Another order of friars was founded in 1216 by Dominic, the Spanish monk who had wrestled with heresy in the south of France. They were the Friars Preachers, the Dominicians, also pledged to poverty, preaching, and teaching. But from the first they were devoted to learning, too, and Dominic often sent his friars to study at universities, so that many became famous scholars.

St. Dominic. A portrait painted soon after his death. The face is that of a scholar and organiser, very different from that of St. Francis.

Francis, on the other hand, had never wanted his order to be a learned one; he did not even allow the brothers to possess books, which he thought would destroy their humility and distract them from their true work among people. But of course there was deep need of both Franciscans and Dominicans: both, in their different ways, stirred all Christendom to its foundations, and helped to solve the problems that so troubled Innocent III.

Chapter 17
Kings in a new style: Frederick II and St. Louis

This chapter concerns two great thirteenth-century kings. In almost every way they contrast sharply, and yet they have one thing in common: they are both kings in a new style, a more modern style. The thirteenth century has a different air from that of the twelfth. The world of the twelfth century was essentially a feudal world, in which a man like Henry Plantagenet could build up an 'empire' out of a personal collection of fiefs, an empire that would fall to bits again, because there were such frail ties to bind it together. In the thirteenth century we begin to see kingdoms or 'states' that are more firm and compact and more thoroughly under the control of their kings. This is perhaps a rather difficult idea to grasp at first, but it may become clearer as we look at the work of the Emperor Frederick II, especially as ruler of the kingdom of Sicily, and that of King Louis IX in France.

The kingdom of Sicily, as you know from Chapter 11, had been built up by the Normans, and it was quite different from any other kingdom in Western Europe. Here there were impressive ruins which reminded men of the splendour of the Greek and Roman past, marble colonnades, stately arches framing the intense blue Mediterranean sky, and fallen statues of remarkable grace and beauty. There were churches too, from the time of the Emperor Justinian, beautifully decorated with glowing mosaics, and there were fine mosques and minarets which had been built when the island of Sicily was in the hands of the Muslims. Even Jewish synagogues found a small place here.

Palermo, the capital of Sicily, was a city of narrow streets opening out into colourful noisy market places, where Normans and Italians, Jews, Greeks, and Saracens were talking in a babel of languages, bargaining and quarrelling in the warm southern sunshine. There was an amazing variety of race and religion. Towering over the town stood the royal fortress of the Norman rulers of Sicily, and in the early years of the thirteenth century you might have seen a small untidy boy run out from the grim castle into the sunny streets, making his way to a house where he always knew there would be something to eat, for he was hungry. It seemed that no one in the castle bothered much about this sunburnt, fair-haired, sturdy lad, and so he learned to look after himself. He wandered

A thirteenth century statue at Bamberg Cathedral, Germany, which is said to represent Frederick II.

round the stalls in the market place, watching men as they did their business or argued and taking in how people behaved to each other. He had a quick mind, picked up the different languages he heard very easily, and could understand and speak Arabic as well as French and Italian. Most of the merchants and salesmen would give the boy a friendly nod when they met his clear gaze fixed steadily on them, though some would chase him off when they were in a bad temper, believing that small boys are usually up to no good. The young Frederick, for that was his name, would then scamper off to the wonderful gardens which had been laid out by the Norman kings, where he could wander among the fountains and examine closely the exotic flowers and trees and the rare animals to be found there. In later life men were astonished by his detailed knowledge of plants and animals.

Perhaps it sounds a happy childhood, and certainly Frederick enjoyed the freedom and the rich variety of the busy city, but no child likes to feel that there is no one at all to care for him, and even that he has enemies. Frederick's mother and father were both dead. His guardian, Pope Innocent III, did his best to preserve order in Frederick's kingdom while his ward was still a child, but he never troubled to see Frederick or to inquire much into his education. There was a tutor, at least for part of the time, and from him Frederick learned Latin. In the background was the unfriendly figure of Markward of Anweiler, a selfish German servant of Frederick's father, the late Emperor Henry VI. Markward practically ruled the kingdom of the Sicilies for five years, until Frederick was 12 years old, and it was during that time that Frederick led his own free vagabond life among the citizens of Palermo. When Markward of Anweiler's rule came to an end, and the old Sicilian chancellor, Walter de Palear, took charge of Frederick again, he was worried to find that the boy was quite untamed, and remarked that the young king 'would follow only the dictates of his own will'. This was to remain true for the rest of Frederick's life.

Frederick had made it his business to find out something of who he was and what his expectations in life might be. His mother Constance was the heiress of the Norman kings of Sicily, and his father, the German Emperor Henry VI, of the great house of Hohenstaufen, had married Constance in order to add Sicily and southern Italy to his own inheritance of Germany and Lombardy. You will see this more clearly if you look at the map on page 139. Frederick knew that as soon as he was 14 he would be allowed to rule his own kingdom of Sicily. He knew too that he had a claim to his father's title of Holy Roman emperor, but the German princes who elected the emperor had almost forgotten the existence of the boy prince of Sicily, the last of the Hohenstaufen, and had taken

sides either with his uncle, Philip of Swabia, or else with the rival candidate, Otto. In the struggle between these two for the imperial crown success had gone first to Philip and then to Otto.

In the end Otto succeeded too well. He got the upper hand in Germany and Lombardy, and stretched out his hand to grasp central Italy and Sicily itself to add to his possessions. He over-reached himself. The lands of the pope round Rome were in danger, and so was the kingdom of Sicily. The wily Pope Innocent III cleverly intrigued to persuade the German princes to depose Otto and elect Frederick as their emperor instead. It seemed the only possible way to bring Otto to a halt, and it succeeded. To Frederick a miracle seemed to have happened. To be sure he had still many enemies, but the young king was now filled with a sense of his great destiny, and he set off eagerly with a handful of followers to meet the group of German princes who had elected him. His journey through Lombardy was perilous, for many of the great North Italian cities were his enemies. At one point he had to leap on to a horse bare-back and swim across a wide river to escape the wrathful citizens of Milan. On he went through the Engadine pass, and finally arrived before the walls of the city of Constance. The citizens were busily preparing to welcome his rival Otto, who was expected in three hours' time. By now Frederick had gathered 300 followers, and he had with him Berard, Archbishop of Palermo. Berard tackled the Bishop of Constance, and dared him to refuse entry to the rightful emperor, recognized by the pope himself. The harassed bishop finally gave orders for the gates to be opened; Frederick's men entered; the gates thudded back into place and were firmly barred behind them. Otto and his small army arrived, too late.

No man could be fully recognized as Holy Roman emperor until he had been crowned in Rome by the pope, as Charlemagne had himself been crowned on that memorable Christmas Day in the year A.D. 800. But before that, by tradition, must come a solemn coronation and anointing in Charlemagne's own capital at Aachen. It was here that the great Emperor Otto I had been crowned, as you read in Chapter 9, and here too that Frederick's own grand-father, Frederick Barbarossa, that great Hohenstaufen warrior who had died on the Third Crusade, had sat on Charlemagne's throne. As the young King Frederick entered the cool lofty church at Aachen, taking his place in the slow coronation procession, he was deeply moved by a sense of the past. He felt himself to be the true heir not only of the heroic Barbarossa but of that still greater shadowy figure, the Emperor Charlemagne himself. As the cere-mony proceeded and he received from the bishops the orb and the sceptre, he had a sudden overwhelming yearning to place himself within this mighty tradition and to dedicate himself to a great cause.

As soon as the crown had been placed on his head, to the astonishment of those present, he took the Cross and committed himself to lead a crusade to regain Jerusalem.

We cannot hope to understand Frederick unless we see clearly what lay behind that moment of drama. It could mislead us. Frederick in fact had very little interest in the Church. What happened at Aachen was a very personal experience in which he had a sudden exalted sense of his own closeness to the Divine Power. He knew that the rulers of the ancient Roman empire had themselves been worshipped as half divine, and throughout his life Frederick was to think of himself as the successor not only of Charlemagne but of the Caesars. Always he thought of his own power as king and emperor as coming to him directly from God, and not through any bishop or pope. The Church did not come into this at all. One of his bishops once urged him to build 'churches and cloisters rather than to fortify hills and crown the mountain heights with castles'. Frederick ignored the advice. This was not where his interests lay. In later life he was known to mock at religion and to take pleasure in shocking churchmen. His cast of mind was strongly 'secular', which means that he was concerned with the things of this world.

What captured Frederick's imagination at Aachen was not really the idea of regaining Jerusalem but the idea of himself as an heroic emperor. This went very deep. Although he stayed in Germany until 1220 he never rooted himself there. He bought the support of the German princes by giving them many privileges, and then he left Germany in the hands of his young son, and went off to Rome for his official coronation as emperor by the pope. For him this was a great occasion. As the crown was placed on his head he was handed a sword of state, which he brandished three times, while the choir burst into song: 'To Frederick ever glorious, of the Romans unconquered emperor, be Life and Victory.' The words rang in his ears as a challenge, and turning his back on Germany he set out for his native Sicily to put his ideal of imperial power into practice.

Frederick loved power. It was in Sicily that he felt he could grasp it. It was true that in 1220 the strong Norman monarchy had been almost swamped in feudal warfare and Saracen rebellions. Frederick was undaunted. First he made his position clear. He declared that all grants of land to nobles or the Church made in the last 30 years were now cancelled; all these must now be returned to the crown. The feudal lords were outraged and rose in revolt. Frederick was calm and ruthless. He first selected as his victim the most powerful lord, and got the lesser lords to support the king out of jealousy; then he turned on the lesser lords without remorse. In a few years he was master.

Kings in a new style: Frederick II and St. Louis

The revolt of the Saracens could have proved still more dangerous, but Frederick again acted swiftly and astutely. Large numbers of Saracens from the island of Sicily were transported to the town of Lucera on the mainland, which became a flourishing Saracen colony under Frederick's personal protection. Its Christian inhabitants were sent off, its church was converted into a mosque, and Frederick would not allow anyone to try to convert this Saracen community to Christianity. They owed him their safety and their freedom to worship as Muslims. They paid him heavy taxes, and provided him with a troop of devotedly loyal bowmen, whom he could call on at a moment's notice for any campaign and use for just as long as he wanted. Many Christians were scandalized, but Frederick did not care in the least for their opinion.

Order was one essential; wealth was another. Frederick did not rely on feudal dues; his income was much more modern. He charged heavy export duties on the rich Sicilian corn crop, and also on dairy produce and textiles. Foreign ships putting into port at Messina had to pay harbour dues. Some sources of wealth were state-owned: the forests, fisheries, salt, silk-manufacture, iron-mining, and stone-quarrying. All this was still not enough. Frederick also taxed his subjects fiercely, and in the end reduced his kingdom to miserable poverty.

Frederick's methods were ruthless, but his aims were neither simple nor crude. He had a deep respect for the Roman ideal of justice, and he had made a close study of the law code of Justinian, which was described in Chapter 3. In 1231 he issued a law code for his whole kingdom, the *Constitutions of Melfi*. His lawyers examined the Norman, Muslim, and Byzantine laws in use in the kingdom of the Sicilies, and they even took detailed records of unwritten customs that were remembered by old men; but the *Constitutions of Melfi* were far from being a patchy collection of laws from different sources. A full and thorough knowledge of Roman law clearly inspired the *Constitutions*, and the completed work was a systematic law code for the whole kingdom, the first of its kind in the Middle Ages. Throughout this logical, well-constructed code went the theme that the authority of the king was absolute and not to be questioned; it was from him that all justice came.

Frederick valued justice highly. He liked to have men trained in law for all important official posts at court, in local government, or in the towns. They were in short supply at the beginning of his reign, and in 1224 he founded the first 'state' university, at Naples. Other universities had developed from cathedral schools, as at Paris, or from the schools of a great town, like Bologna, but Frederick wanted a university that would serve the needs of the kingdom of Sicily. It must train lawyers for the service of the state.

Two Saracen dancing girls, drawn by Matthew Paris.

252

Other subjects were studied too, and he recalled all scholars of his kingdom who were studying at foreign universities and made them transfer to Naples. He enthusiastically set out all the advantages of his new establishment: delightful and healthy surroundings, cheap lodgings, money advances for poor scholars, an abundance of corn, wine, meat, and fish, and no long journeys to other parts of Europe.

Frederick's own exotic court was a centre for men of learning. The king delighted in witty and brilliant conversation; he could not stand bores. Muslim and Christian scholars were welcomed, and the king's chief minister, Piero della Vigna, was a distinguished writer. His elegant Latin style was later copied all over Europe and he probably had a hand in many of Frederick's speeches and letters. Piero wrote Latin poetry too, and he gathered round him a group of very able pupils, who were carefully trained in his own style of writing. These young men roused the jealousy of some of the other courtiers. There were philosophers, scientists, and medical men too. Frederick had always had a strong curiosity about scientific facts, ever since those lonely days when, as an unkempt boy, he had observed the plants and animals in the palace gardens at Palermo. The emperor himself planned and shared in the writing of a detailed study of birds and bird life called 'The Art of Hunting with Birds'. It was the first thoroughly scientific study of the subject ever made, showing Frederick's close and accurate observations of facts about the natural world.

Frederick's court dazzled and fascinated, by its strangeness as well as by its brilliance. His troupe of Saracen dancing-girls was so vividly described by an English royal visitor that the chronicler of St. Alban's abbey, Matthew Paris, drew two of them in the margin of his book, as he imagined them balancing on spheres. You can see his drawings on this page. The girls were provided with fine linen underclothes, silk capes, and fur mantles. Frederick was married three times, two of his wives dying in childbirth. His third wife was an English princess, but the queen of the moment was kept shut away in her own apartments for most of the time, in the fashion of the East. The dancing-girls saw more of court life.

The male Saracen slaves at court were sometimes taught to read and write in Arabic, and Frederick showed great favour to his faithful servants. Muska and Marzukh, two little black page-boys, often caught the eye of foreign visitors. Most curious of all was Frederick's menagerie. He hardly ever set off on a journey without it, and people would come for miles to get a glimpse of it when he was travelling in the north of Italy. Camels covered with richly embroidered cloths were led by large numbers of slaves, all brightly dressed in gay silk tunics; next came the leopards and lynxes, apes, bears, panthers, and lions, each animal led on its chain by a silk-clad

Saracen slave boy. There was a giraffe, and an elephant with a wooden tower on its back in which trumpeters and bowmen were seated. And apart from all this there were dogs, hawks, owls, eagles, falcons, white and coloured peacocks, and African ostriches. People stood and gaped as the cavalcade went past, and were enormously impressed, as Frederick intended them to be. He knew quite well that all this added to his colourful reputation. He delighted in animals; when he had leisure, hunting and hawking were his pastimes, and he was never happier than when he rode out hawking on his black stallion, called Dragon, with some of his choice falcons and other birds of prey.

Men could jest at Frederick's court about almost anything, even religion, but there was one thing about which no light remark was ever allowed: the power of the king. It was this at bottom which brought Frederick into a terrible struggle with Pope Gregory IX.

Elephant with Wooden tower on its back. This drawing shows the meaning of the inn sign 'Elephant and Castle'.

Gregory followed Innocent III as pope in 1227, when Frederick, after many delays, was on the point of setting out to the Holy Land, to fulfil his crusading vow, taken 12 years before at Aachen. From the first, Gregory distrusted Frederick. Gregory was 86 when he became pope and he lived to be 100. No wonder he complained that Frederick's advisers were far too young. The two men were utterly out of sympathy. Gregory was that same Cardinal Ugolino who had advised St. Francis, and who was ready to fight and die for the well-being of the Church. When Frederick, who was really quite ill, sent a message to the pope that he had been delayed yet again in his journey to Jerusalem because of sickness, the pope did not believe a word of it. He lost all patience and excommunicated the emperor. Frederick was bitterly angry, and as soon as he was well again he set out for Jerusalem without the pope's blessing. He went to claim the crown of the Holy Land in the name of his wife Yolande, who was heiress of the late king of Jerusalem. To the pope's shocked surprise, the emperor was successful, and by diplomacy with the Muslims he regained the Holy City for Christendom. The pope's anger hardened, and Frederick entered the church of the Holy Sepulchre banned and excommunicated. Frederick's belief that he, as emperor, was the chosen of God gave him courage to act in a way that made other men tremble. In rash defiance of the pope's ban, he strode forward and lifted the crown of the kingdom of Jerusalem from the altar of the Sepulchre and placed it on his own head. No bishop would have dared to crown him, but Frederick dared to crown himself.

The later part of Frederick's life was spent in a struggle against the pope so fierce and bitter that it seems to overshadow even the clash between Henry IV and Gregory VII, which had shattered the peace of Europe over 150 years before. Pope Gregory IX suspected that Frederick planned to control the whole of Italy, including Rome itself, and that in his position as king of Sicily and also king of Lombardy he would gradually close in on the lands of the pope in the centre of Italy until the papal power was strangled. With desperate energy, Gregory strained every nerve to stop this. His allies were to be found in Lombardy. The power of the emperor here was very much slighter and looser than it was in Sicily. Indeed there was no comparison. In Lombardy the great town communities were almost independent, and there were sharp rivalries between different towns. This was a situation which the pope could use for his own ends. If certain towns made a stand for Frederick, Gregory could be sure that another group of towns would be ready to fight for the pope. Both Frederick and Gregory threw themselves into the fight with passionate determination to win. Fortune swayed one way and then the other, but as the war dragged on Frederick was pressing his subjects for more taxes than

Castel del Monte. An octagonal fortress built by Frederick II in Apulia.

they could give him. Twice he came very near to success, but each time the pope's party managed to survive. Gregory IX died in 1241, but his successor Innocent IV took up the struggle with fresh zeal. In 1245 Innocent solemnly deposed the emperor. Frederick gathered his army again and marched north, but in 1248 he suffered a crushing defeat in the battle of Vittoria. Frederick's most faithful servants and friends were beginning to desert him. His doctor tried to poison him, and even Piero della Vigna was suspected of treason. Frederick punished every hint of treachery with cruel vindictiveness, and the end of his life was friendless and bitter. He died in 1250 in his native kingdom of Sicily, trusting no one. The English monk Matthew Paris wrote in his chronicle, 'About this time Frederick, the greatest of earthly princes, the wonder of the world . . . departed this life.' Frederick was the last of the great Hohenstaufen emperors.

★　　★　　★

Louis IX, who came to the French throne in 1226 and reigned until 1270, was a saint. Whereas Frederick II mocked the Church, blasphemed against Christ, and made friends with Muslims, Louis was deeply and naturally religious. While Frederick loved extravagant display and flaunted his Saracen dancing-girls and his menagerie before a fascinated public, Louis disliked outward show, dressed simply, and would have preferred the life of a monk to that of a king. It would seem that the two kings had little in common, yet this was not wholly true.

Both Louis IX and Frederick II valued justice above most other things, and they believed that justice must come from the king. We can see this in a very down-to-earth way in the case of King Louis, because there happened to be a young man at his court who watched what the king did very closely, and then wrote it all down, simply because he admired the king and wanted people to know about him. Happily for us, the Lord Joinville had a very vivid way of describing things; one sees the scenes that he describes so clearly that one never forgets them. For this reason we shall look at St. Louis mostly through the eyes of Joinville. This is what he tells us about Louis's administration of justice:

> I have sometimes seen him in summer go to administer justice to his people in the public gardens in Paris, dressed in a plain woollen tunic, a sleeveless surcoat of wool, and a black taffeta cape round his shoulders, with his hair neatly combed, but no cap to cover it, and only a hat of white peacock's feathers on his head. He would have a carpet laid down so that we might sit round him, while all those who had any case to bring before him stood round about. Then he would pass judgement on each case.

257

Louis was generous in his justice too. One day a young man called Renaud de Trit brought the king a charter stating that Louis had granted a certain piece of land to Renaud's family. The test of a genuine charter was the seal, and when Louis looked at this one he saw at once that it was so broken that all that was left of the picture was the legs of the king with his feet resting on a footstool! Louis handed the charter, with the fragment of seal dangling pathetically from it, to some of his councillors and asked them for their opinion. They all said that the king had no need at all to take notice of this charter when the seal was in such a state. The king listened to their advice, and then sent one of them off to bring a charter from the royal chest which he knew had a seal similar to the one that was broken. Then he addressed his councillors: 'My lords, here is the seal I used before I went overseas, and you can clearly tell from looking at it that the impression on the broken seal corresponds exactly with that of the one that is whole. Therefore I could not with a clear conscience keep back this land.' Louis asked for advice and listened to it, but in the end he relied on his own judgement.

In 1259 his council were furious with him for making too generous a treaty with Henry III of England. They felt sure that Louis could have insisted on keeping Aquitaine in his hands, as well as the other Plantagenet lands in France. Louis thought he could too, and he knew perfectly well that his councillors felt that he was being too soft; but he deliberately let Henry keep Aquitaine, because he considered it better to have Henry as a grateful and contented vassal than as a disgruntled enemy.

In handling people Louis had complete sureness of touch. This rare quality comes out in one of Joinville's most delightful stories; it is worth retelling here in full. There is nothing that can bring us closer than this to Louis as a person.

The incident occurred on Louis's first crusading journey. Things were going very badly, and the king asked his advisers if they thought he should return home. They all said that he should, except for the young Lord Joinville, who felt bitterly disappointed and ashamed at such a course. He advised the king to go on. The other lords were very angry with Joinville and sneered at him as they all went in to dinner. Joinville suspected that the king too was angry with him, and he felt thoroughly miserable. What happened next is best told in Joinville's own words:

> While the king was hearing grace I went over to a barred window in an alcove. I passed my arms through the bars of the window and stood there thinking that if the King went back to France I would go to the Prince of Antioch, who was a relative of mine, and had already asked me to come and join him.
>
> While I was standing there the King came up to me, and leaning on my shoulders put both his hands on my head. I thought it was Philippe de

Seal of St. Louis. The importance of the seal is brought out in the story of Renaud de Trit. This photograph shows clearly the way in which the seal was attached to a document.

Nemours, who had already plagued me too much that day, because of the advice I had given. So I exclaimed: 'Stop bothering me, my good Philippe.' By chance, as I was turning my head, the King's hand slid down over my face, and I recognized who it was by the emerald ring on his finger. 'Keep quite quiet,' he said, 'for I want to ask how a young man like yourself could be so bold as to advise me to stay here, against the advice of all the great and wise men of France who have advised me to return.'

'Your Majesty,' said I, 'even if such a bad idea had ever entered my mind, I would never have advised you to go back.' 'Do you mean to say', he asked, 'that I should be doing wrong if I went back?' 'Yes, sir, so God help me' said I. Then he said: 'If I stay here will you stay too?' 'Certainly,'

Statue of St. Louis at Mainneville, made less than forty years after his death. He is shown very simply dressed, wearing a plain crown.

I answered. 'I am very well pleased with the advice you have given me,' he said. 'But don't speak of this to any one until the week is up.'

Poor Philippe de Nemours, who is mentioned in this story, was evidently far less tactful than the king. On another occasion he was boasting to the king that the French had cheated the Saracens of some £10,000 in a treaty arrangement. Joinville tells us how he had to tread heavily on Philippe's foot to make him stop talking, because Joinville realized that the king was far from pleased at any dishonest dealing, even with enemies.

Both Louis's Crusades ended in failure. On the first, Robert of Artois foolishly advised that the army should attack Cairo. They ended up floundering in the maze of streams which form the Nile delta. The second of his Crusades was diverted to Tunis in the hope of converting the Muslim ruler of that city; it accomplished nothing, and on this Crusade the king died. It seems strange that Frederick II, who entirely lacked the true crusading spirit, should have had so much more success.

Louis was sensitive and deeply religious, but he was also full of sturdy common sense. He would speak his mind plainly too. The French bishops wanted him to promise that he would confiscate the goods of any man whom the Church had excommunicated. He told them straight that he would do no such thing, since he knew that the Church sometimes excommunicated a man who was later proved innocent. Even the pope did not escape Louis's reproofs. He told Innocent IV that he was demanding far too much money from the French clergy, and wanting too many posts in the French Church for his own chaplains and clerks. This was bold talk to the head of the Church, but Louis was very much aware of his rights and responsibilities as king.

'Right from his childhood,' writes Joinville, 'King Louis had compassion on the poor and suffering.' Many of us are tempted to push the horrors of disease and war and the misery of old age and poverty out of our minds, because we find it too painful to think of them. Louis was one of those rare men who force themselves to face up to these things. He kept on thinking of ways in which he could do something about it. He founded hospitals for the sick; he gave money to widows who had been left desperately poor, and to 'poor craftsmen who through age or sickness could no longer ply their trade'. Every day at his court he had a number of old and crippled men to sit near his own table at dinner or supper, and he saw to it that they were served with the same food as he had. He was tireless too in trying to spare his subjects unnecessary taxes and in checking high-handed or corrupt officials, for Louis was no fool, and he realized that many of the royal officials needed a firm hand.

With heretics Louis was pitilessly stern. Scores of Frenchmen accused of heresy were burned to death in his reign. Was there any difference between this and the cruelty of Frederick II, who would have men hideously tortured to death when they had betrayed him? Frederick's cruelty was personal; Louis's was not, for he believed that he was defending the Christian faith.

The complete trust felt for St. Louis, even beyond his own kingdom, was so great that men came to him of their own accord to ask him to settle their quarrels. From Germany, Spain, and Flanders came appeals for his judgement. The most famous case was when he was called upon to judge between the English king, Henry III, and his rebellious barons. He judged in favour of the king. It could not be otherwise, for Louis believed as firmly as Frederick II that the authority of a king came from God, to whom alone he was responsible.

Indeed Frederick II and Louis IX had many things in common. Both of them were intensely active kings; both were exceptionally able; both were confident and strong. Both revered justice, and believed that to give justice to their subjects was the supreme task of kingship. But there the likeness stops. It is for you to decide which is the greater man, and you will not all think alike.

Chapter 18
Men of Art and Men of Learning

I and Pangur Ban my cat
'T is a like task we are at.
Hunting mice is his delight
Hunting words I sit all night.
'Gainst the wall he sets his eye
Full and fierce and sharp and sly.
'Gainst the wall of knowledge I
All my little wisdom try.

Irish poem of the eighth century

Pangur Ban had a lot in common with modern cats, but he spent most of his time trotting in and out of a cold monastic cell. He appeared to be interested only in the mice, but probably he relented from time to time, wove his way in and out of his master's legs, and occasionally curled up on a corner of his cloak, which trailed conveniently onto the floor as the monk sat at work with his books. Pangur Ban lived in the eighth century, and his master was a Celtic monk who spent much of his time in study. You can tell from the poem that he did not find this at all easy. Knowledge presented itself as a high, thick, stone wall, and the monk was acutely aware of the littleness of his own wisdom as he tried to penetrate this wall. Even when he felt that he had grasped an idea, he was often at a loss for words to express his thoughts, and he 'hunted' them far into the night, pausing just occasionally from the effort, to sit back and watch Pangur Ban at his mousing.

In the Dark Ages, which followed the barbarian invasions and the collapse of the Roman world, much of the learning which had been a commonplace among Greek and Roman scholars was lost. The loss was not complete and it was not final, thanks to the Benedictine monasteries. Between the barbarian settlement and the year A.D. 1000 there were always some monks in the West, scattered in their isolated monasteries, who took the business of learning seriously, like Pangur Ban's friend. Manuscripts were laboriously copied out and handed down to the next generation, sometimes copied carefully and accurately, sometimes hurriedly with many mistakes. Some of these manuscripts were the works of Christian writers, like Pope Gregory the Great, some were works of famous Roman writers and poets, such as Cicero, Livy, Virgil, and Ovid, and there were some copies made of the writings of the ancient

Greek philosophers Plato and Aristotle, although only a very few of Aristotle's works were still known in the West at this time.

In the chaos and hardship of repeated raiding by Goths, Vandals, Franks, and Huns, and then later, in the ninth century, by Vikings, Magyars, and Muslims, it was very hard indeed to give one's mind to anything except mere survival. The sufferings of the monks of Noirmoutier, described in Chapter 7, bring this point home. In constant fear of attack, frequently on the move to find a safer refuge, struggling to survive the disastrous effects of famine and devastated lands, the monks must often have felt that the life and interests of the scholar were meant for safer and more leisured times than theirs. Yet man's urge to learn is surprisingly strong, and throughout the very worst of the Dark Ages the Benedictine monasteries managed to pass on a thin thread of knowledge from the past.

Copying is one thing, but understanding what you copy is often more difficult. Some monks copied the works of ancient writers almost blindly, and when they came to be read a few generations later by some eager young monk, he would find himself baffled and discouraged by simply not being able to understand what the original writer had meant. Like Pangur Ban's master, he found that knowledge was a thick wall and it needed tremendous effort to make any dents in it.

In this dark picture there were a few shafts of light. First, at the very entry into the Dark Ages stands the splendid figure of Boethius. He was a scholar in the full broad tradition of Roman learning, and he was a respected man in the court of Theodoric, king of the Ostrogoths, in about the year 500. Boethius planned to hand on to the future the works of the Greek philosopher Aristotle, as well as those of Roman writers, but his fine plan was cut short when he was put to death by his barbarian king, though not before he had translated into Latin one of Aristotle's most important books, on *Logic*, the art of reasoning. This was to have great influence in Western Europe 500 years later.

In the following centuries, as we have seen, most of the learning of the ancient world was almost lost to sight; scholarship was only to be found in the monasteries, and when men sought for knowledge it was never *new* learning that they wanted, but simply the recovery of parts of the *old* learning of Greece and Rome. The whole aim of scholars was to master what had once been known and was now lost. One big step forward was taken by the Emperor Charlemagne, about 800. At his court school at Aachen the study of the Latin language and literature was vigorously encouraged, for the emperor, like all the scholars of this period, believed that this knowledge would help in a fuller understanding of the Bible and of Christian

The crown was the supreme symbol of royal power. This splendid example, the imperial crown of the Holy Roman Empire, was made in the late tenth or early eleventh century. It is now on view in the Kunsthistorisches Museum, Vienna.

Sardonyx chalice encrusted with jewels from the abbey of St. Denis in Paris. This is a fine symbol of the wealth lavished on the church.

generatio

teaching. Charlemagne's revival of learning was planned for him by the Englishman Alcuin, from York, as you discovered in Chapter 6, and it was Alcuin, you will remember, who was so deeply distressed by the news of the Viking attacks on Lindisfarne, which threatened cultural life in England.

It is from Alcuin too that the type in which this book is printed and the style of your own handwriting have come. The ordinary writing of the period before Charlemagne was so spiky and untidy that it was often almost impossible to read. If you look at the illustrations on this page, you will see the contrast between such scrawl and the Carolingian script which Alcuin made standard. This clear neat hand meant that manuscripts were much easier to read and much more likely to be accurately copied in future.

The handwriting used in Gaul before the time of Charlemagne was closely related to this late Roman script. The words are 'L Caecilio Lucando sesterftuis mille sescentos'.

A page from the Bible, written in clear 'Carolingian script'.

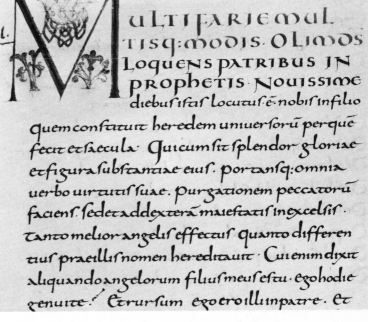

As Boethius stands at the entry to the Dark Ages, another great scholar stands at their close: Gerbert, a French abbot, who became pope as Sylvester II in the year 999. Gerbert is a lonely figure. His learning ranged much further than that of the scholars of Charlemagne's court, and he had mastered a good deal of the scientific knowledge of the ancient world as well as its literature, and, thanks to Boethius, the *Logic* of Aristotle. He looked to the world of Greece and Rome as the source of all light and learning, and the present seemed very dark to him by contrast. His brilliant mind only seems to emphasize the ignorance and lack of understanding in the men around him. He had few pupils and few people to talk to or discuss things with, and for this reason his influence could only be limited.

The next century brought the stirrings of change. Apart from the learning which went on in the monasteries, most cathedrals too had their own schools, often not very good ones. A few were good. In the year 1006 Fulbert, who had been in charge of the cathedral school at Chartres, became bishop there, and Fulbert was not only a scholar; like Alcuin, he was a born teacher. He could interest anybody in anything, and the range of his own interests was very wide indeed. Science, mathematics, music, literature, logic; all of them fascinated him, and the solving of one problem simply led him on to the next. He loved discussing learned matters with his friends and with pupils, and one of his pupils looked back long after he had left Chartres to the conversations they had had with Fulbert in the calm summer evenings in the little garden by the city chapel. Fulbert had a large, serene mind, eager and inquiring, but never restless, and always tolerant and generous towards other people's ideas. One historian recently found a delightful correspondence between two of Fulbert's former pupils after they had left Chartres and had been appointed to important positions in the cathedrals of Liège and Cologne. Ralph from Liège writes to his friend Reginbald about a statement by Boethius that the inside angles of a triangle add up to 180°. If you look at Figure (i) you will see that Boethius meant the angles ABC, BCA, and BAC.

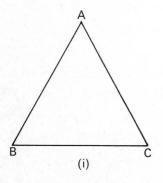

(i)

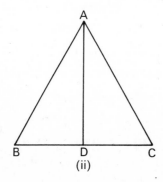

(ii)

Ralph, however, does not seem to have thought of this, and he had the bright idea that Boethius might have meant that you should drop a perpendicular from A to BC as in Figure (ii). He then pointed out happily that angles ADB and ADC added up to 180°, and that probably those were the 'inside' angles of the triangle. It is easy enough for us to smile at Ralph busily going off on the wrong track, but how was he to know? When he was passing through Chartres he had called on Fulbert and discussed the problem with his old master, and he tells his friend that in the end he convinced Fulbert! We do not know what Reginbald's view was; perhaps he was just completely puzzled.

The story is worth repeating because it shows that even shortly after the year 1000 men were still trying their 'little wisdom' against a formidable and baffling wall of ancient knowledge, which had to be re-learnt, and they were still very far from mastering even simple problems. But with the rise of the cathedral schools in the eleventh century there came to be many more scholars, many more people with whom to discuss your problems, and much more chance of puzzling your way through eventually to the right answers. It was the start of a new age of expansion and advance that belongs particularly to the twelfth and thirteenth centuries, but which was certainly beginning in the eleventh. We shall come to these developments later.

Just as men have an urge to learn and stretch out towards new knowledge, and never more so than in our own generation, so too they have an urge to create things of beauty. In this respect the period before A.D. 1000 is full of interest. As you look back in history to any particular period and examine the buildings, the painting, the sculpture that it produced you will find that these can only be understood if you go deeper still, to find out how men thought at the time. The men of the Dark Ages looked back again and again to the lost world of the Roman empire. They attempted to recover its learning bit by bit, as we have seen, and it was natural that in art too they should turn to the Roman past for models.

Sometimes they attempted direct copies. If you look at the picture of Charlemagne's palace chapel at Aachen on page 268, you will see that there is something clearly Roman in its style; and in fact it is as near to an exact copy of the church of San Vitale, built in Ravenna for the Emperor Justinian, as Charlemagne's builders could manage. What was Roman was good, as far as Charlemagne and his court were concerned, and so the builders at Aachen struggled painfully to re-learn forgotten methods of Roman vaulting and to build in the classical manner. Yet the result is not purely classical, even though Charlemagne actually took some of the

Right *Abbey gatehouse at Lorsch, Germany : ninth century.*

Charlemagne's palace chapel at Aachen, modelled on the church of San Vitale in Ravenna.

capitals of pillars and other stones from Ravenna and had them put up again in the Aachen chapel. The builders were Franks, they were 'barbarians', and the chapel at Aachen looks like what it was— a Frankish imitation of a Roman building.

The chapel at Aachen was impressive, but elsewhere the urge to imitate Roman styles sometimes resulted in pretty poor work. This was not always so. Sometimes a builder would mingle Roman with barbarian art in a very pleasing combination. If you look at the picture on this page of the abbey gatehouse at Lorsch in Germany, built in the ninth century, you will see that much of the design is Roman. The three round archways are like those of a Roman triumphal arch, and you will recognize the lower and upper rows of pillars as being the kind that one sees on Greek and Roman buildings. But there is nothing Roman about that row of little pointed gables across the top of the upper pillars, nor in the intriguing speckled pattern which covers the surface of the whole gatehouse and quite changes its appearance: these are purely Frankish touches. The man who designed this gatehouse was clearly a true artist, able to use different traditions in his own way, and to bring them together in a pleasing whole.

Symbol of St. Matthew from the Book of Durrow.

Some of the most lovely works of art in the whole of this period are the illuminated Gospel books, written and painted in Ireland and Northumbria in the seventh and eighth centuries. Here we have an art which is essentially 'barbarian', in this case Celtic and Anglo-Saxon, and is only gently touched by Roman influence. The Greeks and Romans liked to represent the human figure in painting and in sculpture. The Greeks had first brought this to a high stage of perfection, as you can see by looking at Greek statues, and the Romans closely followed their example. The barbarians, on the other hand, were much more at home with patterns than with people, and their genius in designing beautiful patterns has rarely been equalled. On their bleak headlands, and beside groups of roughly-built beehive cells, Irish craftsmen set up stone crosses of firm shapely lines, engraved with intricate interlaced bands and circles. You can see a photograph of one of these on page 273. Anglo-Saxon metal-workers bent over delicate designs of blue and red glass set in a fine gold framework like a tiny honey-comb, and produced brooches and clasps of the rare beauty of the finds at Sutton Hoo in Suffolk, now to be seen in the British Museum. In the seventh century these skills were to be carried over to the art of painting on parchment.

One of the earliest illuminated Gospel books from this period is the Book of Durrow; there is a photograph of one of the paintings from this book on the page opposite. It may have come from Ireland or from the Anglo-Saxon kingdom of Northumbria; scholars are not sure which. Although the page is slightly spoilt by damp, and has to be shown here in black and white, the original, which is kept in Trinity College, Dublin, is painted in soft glowing reds, yellows, and greens that bring out the rich pattern of broad interlacing bands which frames the page, and the minute delicate work on the mantle of the figure which represents St. Matthew. But the figure itself, as you see, is a little odd! The face is quite satisfactory, and may have been copied from a manuscript that had come from the Mediterranean world, where Roman influence was still strong, but arms were obviously left out as being much too difficult, and notice what has happened when the artist came to the feet! There can be no doubt at all that the style of this page is barbarian. The artist has a confident mastery of pattern, but is a little desperate when it comes to the human figure.

In the seventh century the Anglo-Saxon kingdom of Northumbria welcomed a flood of influence from the Roman world, which came through the Church. We know, for instance, that Benedict Biscop, the founder of the monasteries of Wearmouth and Jarrow, darted off to Rome year after year, untroubled by the strenuous journey, and he always came back laden with books and pictures from

monasteries in Gaul and in Italy. His biographer says that on one occasion

> he made his fourth journey to Rome and came back loaded with more abundant spiritual merchandise than before . . . . He brought back large quantities of books . . . and pictures of sacred representations to adorn the church of St. Peter which he had built; namely a likeness of the Virgin Mary and of the twelve Apostles with which he intended to adorn the central nave, on boarding placed from one wall to the other, also some figures from Church history for the south wall, and others from the Revelation of St. John for the north wall.

All these, you notice, were paintings of *people*. Such paintings would now be seen by Anglo-Saxon artists who were already practised in the skills of pattern-drawing, partly from their own native metal-work and partly through the influence of Irish missionaries. From these Roman books and pictures the monks of Northumbria began also to learn how to draw the human figure in the Roman way.

On pages 274 and 275 you will see two pages from the richly illuminated Gospel book which was made by the monks on the island of Lindisfarne, off the Northumbrian coast, at the end of the seventh century. It was decorated inside and out by Anglo-Saxon monastic craftsmen, as we know from a statement at the end of the book: 'Eadfrith, Bishop of Lindisfarne, wrote this book to the glory of God, of St. Cuthbert, and of all the brotherhood of saints upon this island; and Ethelwald, Bishop of Lindisfarne, made the outside binding, and decorated it with his utmost skill; and Billfrith the hermit forged the outer metal-work and set the gold and gems within it; and Aldred, a humble priest, wrote the glosses in English.'

On one of the pages shown, the new delicate 'string' interlace has replaced the heavier broad-banded interlace of the Book of Durrow, and if you look closely you will see woven into the maze of patterns some of the gulls, cormorants, and other sea-birds which flew over the Farne islands and perched on the rocks, as they do today. The monk who designed this page knew them well, and, like many another craftsman of his race, he twisted and twirled them into his designs. In this he was thoroughly 'barbarian'. But the designer of the Lindisfarne Gospels had come under the spell of Rome too. Look at the portrait of St. Matthew on page 275, and compare it with the figure of St. Matthew in the Book of Durrow. You will be able to work out for yourself how much the Lindisfarne artist had learned from the books and paintings that men like Benedict Biscop had brought to the north from those Mediterranean countries where the Roman skill in figure-drawing had not been lost.

*Celtic Cross at Ahenny,
Ireland. Irish craftsmen were
skilled in making beautiful
patterns of interlacing bands.*

Before we leave this group of Gospel books we must look at one more, perhaps the finest of them all, the Book of Kells. It was probably designed in the monastery on the Island of Iona, off the Scottish coast, and later taken to Kells in Ireland. The intricate patterns of the Lindisfarne artist are always very restrained, but the artist of the Book of Kells who drew the decorated initial facing page 265, is so carried away by sheer joy in his work that in and around his wonderfully delicate sweeping curves and spirals, trumpets, circles, and diamonds there hide delightful little angels—and even cats and mice playing together near the bottom of the page. There is a note of exhuberant delight in this book that is very rare in the Dark Ages as a whole.

Carpet page from the Lindisfarne Gospels.

Figure of St. Matthew from the Lindisfarne Gospels.

Men of Art and Men of Learning

Joy was far from being the dominant note in the art of Western Europe during this period. The prevailing atmosphere was stern and harsh, for the times were harsh and disturbed, and men were far more aware of the power of evil than of the forces of light and hope. If we look at the picture of Durham cathedral on the page opposite, which was built in a span of 40 years, covering the year 1100, we can learn much about the mood which gripped the West until about the middle of the twelfth century. Men were still copying the Roman style of building ('Romanesque' it is sometimes called), but Durham cathedral echoes the mood of its own age. Here was a church that was half fortress, built on solid rock above the river Wear, a stronghold from which the Norman bishops of Durham could resist the forces of the Scots or of the Anglo-Saxon rebels. Resistance seems to be the keynote of the whole structure. It is as though it was planted there not only to resist worldly enemies, but, through the holiness of its monks, to resist all the mysterious powers of evil in a world that was difficult to understand but likely to be hostile. Its massive round pillars and superb semi-circular arches have a solid strength which seems to defy attack, and in the dimly-lit nave the bold zigzag patterns, carved deeply into the stone pillars, even now create a sense of stern barbaric splendour. Durham cathedral was built to overawe. If you came in friendship you could find safety there, but if you were an enemy you would be fought off with all the ferocity of the savage beast which held the door knocker in its jaws, and which you can see on page 278.

The men who built Durham cathedral, and many other Romanesque buildings throughout Western Europe, did not think of God as mild or benevolent. One of their favourite subjects was the Last Judgement; and the sculptured figure of Christ in Majesty, rewarding the righteous with the joys of heaven and sending the wicked to the most grisly fate of horrible torment, dominates many a Romanesque doorway. The one at Conques, photographed on page 279, is remarkably well preserved, so that you can see on the right-hand side all the gruesome details of the horned devils, grinning horribly at the sufferings of their victims, and the jaws of Hell, opened greedily to swallow the damned souls. On page 286 the figure of Christ, this time from the church at Barnack in Northamptonshire, looks out with a severe, unyielding face, determined on stern justice rather than mercy.

The century from 1100 to 1200 is one of the most restless and exciting and creative times that Western Europe has ever known. You have already learnt that it was a time of expansion, of busier trade, and the rise of thriving merchant life in the towns. Men moved about more. They went on pilgrimages, often far afield, to Rome or to Compostella in Spain, and they went off to the East on

276

Above *Tympanum at Conques Cathedral. The sharp details have hardly been blurred by 800 years of wind, sun and rain. In the centre Christ sits in judgement. To the left the blessed enter paradise and to the right the damned are hurried into the horrors of hell.*

Left *Door knocker of Durham Cathedral. The eyes of this splendid beast once flashed in coloured enamel.*

Crusades. Kings were wresting power from the hands of unruly feudal nobles and establishing their will more firmly, enforcing law and experimenting in new methods of government. In the Church St. Bernard broke away from the stiff traditions of Benedictine monasticism of the old Cluniac kind, and set up monasteries in a new style, bound together into the firmly-governed Cistercian Order, which had houses scattered throughout Western Europe. Such vigorous new life could not leave either art or learning untouched.

Fulbert, the good Bishop of Chartres, had been a pioneer in the building up of a cathedral school whose fame drew men to Chartres from Italy, England, and Germany, as well as from all parts of France. By the early twelfth century there were many schools of this kind, busy with teachers and crowds of young students who knew that time spent in the schools was now one of the quickest ways to promotion in the Church and even in royal government. Many were eager to learn, and they would move on from one school to another in search of the best teachers and fresh subjects

of study. The basic skills were to be had anywhere; for further studies you had to travel.

To study law a man would go to Bologna in Italy if he could. Here there was a group of keen scholars studying the code of Roman law drawn up by Justinian in the sixth century. They lectured on it, wrote about it, and argued tricky points of meaning. Irnerius was the greatest teacher here, and the students who went to his lectures became so steeped in the ideas of the ancient Romans on law and government that they began to think differently about the laws in force in their own countries. The new study of Roman law certainly influenced the thinking at Henry Plantagenet's court, where, as you know, there was a strong practical interest in law and a readiness to work out new methods. Indeed Henry's court was a centre of culture, for his interest in new ideas attracted writers and poets to his household as well as lawyers.

At Bologna, too, and also in Rome, a newer system of law was being studied; this was the law of the Church, 'canon' law. Pope Gregory VII had stirred up energetic searches into the documents lying half forgotten in the dusty store-rooms of some of the Roman churches, so that he could bring to light statements made by earlier popes backing the authority and power of the Head of the Church in Rome. In the twelfth century the man who brought these studies into a neat orderly book was a Bolognese scholar called Gratian, and his work on canon law remained an authority. Italy was the place for the study of medicine too, and the school at Salerno was rapidly regaining the medical knowledge of the ancient world and adding to it.

Italy offered so much; but if you were interested in logic or in theology, then you would do best to turn your back on the Alps and make for the cities of France: Chartres or Laon, Rheims or, above all, Paris. Paris was the place for logic, and Paris too was where you would find, in the early twelfth century, that incomparable teacher Peter Abelard. It is difficult to explain the fascination of logic for the men of the twelfth century. It was essentially the art of reasoned argument, developing a line of thought from one point to another— and of course we still talk about a 'logical' argument. It made men better able to understand the working of their own minds, and better able also to understand the world about them, to classify objects and actions and ideas into groups and give them names, so that they became manageable and understandable. This brought quite a new sense of mastery over themselves and over the world around them. They no longer felt helpless before the wall of knowledge.

The most colourful figure in this new excitement over learning was undoubtedly Peter Abelard. He had first gone to Paris as a

young student, gifted with a brilliantly quick mind, full of self-confidence, and full of contempt for men who were slower than himself. At Paris, and then at Laon, where he went to study theology, Abelard disagreed sharply with his masters. He seemed to spin a web of quick, clever argument all round them until they were caught struggling. One of them withdrew for a time into a monastery, and the other became a bitter enemy. In a short sketch of his life Abelard tells us of his own high ability, for he was not modest, and describes one of his masters, Anselm of Laon, as an old man whose words were like 'smoke without light'. Abelard soon set up as a lecturer himself, first in Laon and then in Paris. His lectures were clear and lively, and soon attracted very large audiences. He had many enemies among those who were jealous of his ability or who disliked his confidence, but his dynamic personality and sparkling wit and sarcasm drew devoted crowds of young students. His lectures were far more entertaining and much easier to remember than those of most other masters.

It was also in keeping with Abelard's stormy temperament that he should have a passionate love affair with the niece of one of the canons of the cathedral in Paris. Heloïse was taught as a private pupil by Abelard, and was herself very clever and gifted. She did not want Abelard to marry her because she said that this would stand in the way of his career. She asked him how a man of learning could possibly put up with the screams of babies or the stupid chatter of nurse-maids trying to soothe them. In the end they parted and Heloïse went into a convent, but she continued to exchange letters with Abelard till his death, and she never ceased to be in love with him. Their letters have survived, and there is a fourteenth-century carving of the lovers on the capital of a pillar, which you can see above.

In many ways Abelard's views seem very modern. One of his books is called *Scito te ipsum*, 'Get to know yourself', and it shows very clearly the interest of twelfth-century scholars in understanding their own minds and their own behaviour. Abelard believed that you should not condemn a man for a crime that he commits, if the man himself believes that he is doing right. He pointed out, for instance, that the men who put Christ to death believed that they were doing their duty as Roman soldiers. This approach angered some people very much, and Abelard was thought to be a dangerous teacher. In another book he set side by side the sayings of various Christian writers, showing that these great men often contradicted each other. St. Bernard was horrified by such lack of reverence, although Abelard genuinely believed that he was helping scholars to arrive at the truth, for he was a sincere Christian. He once wrote to Heloïse that he would not wish to be a man as great as Aristotle, if that would mean that he would

Abelard and Heloise, on a fourteenth century carved capital in the Conciergerie, Paris.

be separated from the love of Christ, for this, he said, was the rock on which he had built his life. St. Bernard eventually persuaded a council of churchmen to condemn Abelard's writings, and Abelard, deeply hurt and discouraged, set off to Rome to appeal to the pope. He was ill and weak by now, and the kind Abbot Peter the Venerable of Cluny went out to meet him on the way, and persuaded him to come to Cluny and spend the rest of his days quietly there. He died in 1142, and Abbot Peter wrote to Heloïse a letter full of admiration for Abelard's good qualities; he comforts her, and reminds her that for both herself and Abelard 'beyond the tomb there is peace'.

The love story of Abelard and Heloïse was real enough, but we should have been unlikely to hear of it if it had happened a century earlier. As well as new learning and new art, the twelfth century produced the first popular romances. The hero of the greatest of these was King Arthur, accompanied by the Knights of the Round Table. The interest of these stories is often the devotion of a knight to his lady and the knight's own quest for adventure. Earlier tales, like the great Song of Roland, dwelt on a man's loyalty to his lord and heroic acceptance of a cruel fate. This was in keeping with the grim mood of the period before the twelfth century, but the romances woven around the story of King Arthur give room for greater tenderness, more colourful variety of adventure. The audience which enjoyed such tales would also keep alive the true love story of Abelard and Heloïse.

The schools of Paris were to develop in the next generation into one of the early universities of the West, for a university, as we know it, is a creation of the Middle Ages. Many new problems and anxieties lay ahead, for new learning brought new dangers from the point of view of the Church. In Chapter 16 you learnt that this was a time when heresy was spreading, and this turning away from the teaching of the Church was sometimes to be found among scholars too, who were almost intoxicated with new ideas. In the thirteenth century some of the works of Aristotle, so far unknown in the West, filtered in from Spain in translations which came from Muslim sources. Aristotle of course was a pagan philosopher, and by the time that his works had been translated and commented upon by Muslims they led men's thoughts very far away from the Christian view of the meaning of life, and the nature of God and the universe. At one point the pope forbade masters at Paris to lecture on these newly known works of Aristotle, but in the middle of the century St. Thomas Aquinas came to grips with the problem in a very clear-headed way. He wove into Christian teaching much of Aristotle's learning, but he also stated quite clearly which of Aristotle's ideas he thought a Christian must turn down. Some scholars might disagree with him, but Aquinas's work was so brilliant and so sound that students were once more allowed to hear about the new works, since they now had Aquinas's writings to guide them.

A few other famous schools developed into universities at this time. Oxford did; so also did Bologna, the great law centre. Bologna was a university under the firm control of its students. It was the students who made the rules, and if a professor was a minute late in starting a lecture or went on a minute too long he was fined! He was fined too if he did not bother to explain difficult passages, or if he did not get through the syllabus. The students at Paris and Oxford did not have so much of an upper hand, but they were often rowdy and unpopular with the townsfolk, and, like modern students, they were often short of money and always writing home for more. Parents often had a word to say before sending the required amount. One father writes to his son, 'I have recently discovered that you prefer play to work, and strumming on the guitar while others are at their studies, whence it appears that you have read but one volume of law, while your more industrious companions have read several.' This student is told that he must 'repent utterly of his careless ways'. One suspects that he will have difficulty in getting his next allowance out of his father unless the reports improve.

We must turn now to the new styles in art, and Abelard's approach to learning may help us to understand some of the changes

that are taking place here. Abelard was deeply interested in people, and one of the features of the twelfth and thirteenth centuries was 'humanism'. This word is used to cover many ideas, but we can use it quite simply to mean an interest in people, in their feelings, their relations with one another, and the everyday occupations of their lives. The artist of the Christ in Majesty at Barnack, on page 286, was not a humanist; he was making Christ a symbol of justice, and not a person with human feelings. This is also true of the figure of the Virgin and Child shown here. This was carved for a German

The Golden Virgin of Essen. This tenth century carving is beautiful but very formal and awe-inspiring.

Virgin and Child, Chichester: a thirteenth century wall painting which is full of human warmth and tenderness.

abbey in the tenth century. The Child sits enthroned on his mother's knee, holding a book in his left hand and raising his right hand in solemn blessing; there is nothing really childlike in the figure at all. But now let us look at the same subject from the later period, when artists have been touched by the new humanism. The Virgin and Child in the thirteenth century wall-painting in Chichester, which you can see on this page, are quite different. The Virgin is no longer just a throne for her Child; she is a real mother, full of charm and tenderness and delight in her baby, and

285

the Christ Child is shown here as a real baby, with his arms round his mother's neck, smiling up into her face. This artist has captured a truly human relationship.

It is the same with other representations of Christ. There is a more sensitive emphasis now on the human sufferings of Christ on the Cross than on his mere power as a judge. You will see this if you look at the detail of the Danish crucifix on this page, and contrast it with the Barnack picture of Christ in Majesty.

Left *A figure of Christ sculptured in stone in the church at Barnack, Northamptonshire. The date is about 1050.*

Right *Detail from a Danish crucifix carved about 1150, now at Tirstrup.*

Sculptured figure from Chartres Cathedral: a woman washing wool.

Before the twelfth century it would be rare for an artist to portray any subject that was not directly religious, but if you look at the lovely series of carvings on Chartres cathedral you will see that a sculptor will now take everyday life as his subject, and find beauty in homely occupations. Shepherds guard their grazing sheep, and farmers tend their vines across the west front of this magnificent church, and on this page you may see the graceful figure of a young housewife washing wool.

287

It is easy to find many examples of the humanism of the scholars reflected in various forms of art, but does it seem likely that one will be able to find any sign of their love of argument, of, for example, Abelard's passion for logic? The photograph on the page opposite of the Angel Choir in Lincoln cathedral, built after 1250, may help us to find an answer to this. This choir is built in the new 'Gothic' style of architecture. It is wholly different from that of Durham cathedral. Instead of heavy solid pillars and rounded arches, there are clusters of pillars, delicately fluted, supporting pointed arches. The whole design is more intricate and elaborate, and one has the impression of innumerable slender pillars and delicate lined ribs of stone, beautifully controlled to produce an elegant and satisfying whole. Surely the brilliant lecture, in which many small threads of evidence are gradually brought together into one powerful and convincing conclusion, has its parallel here. But the design of the east window is most revealing of all. Here a large circle rests on two lesser circles, each of which rests on two lesser circles still. This was just like the division of a book into chapters, chapters into sections, sections into subsections, that delighted the heart of the medieval scholar. It was part of the new-found delight in order that showed itself in both building and learning.

Perhaps you have already noticed that the Gothic style marks a step away from Rome. The rounded arches of Durham may still have something in common with the Colosseum, but Lincoln has nothing. This marks a new confidence felt by the craftsmen of this period, a confidence in their own ideas. This was also true of one of the greatest of medieval arts, which also develops in the twelfth century and owes nothing to Rome, the making of stained glass. No photograph can give a true impression of the quality of the light which filters into the nave of a medieval cathedral through the deep blues and reds, clear greens and glowing gold, of the stained-glass windows. Chartres is perhaps the most beautiful of all, and much of the glass here is of the twelfth century. It is only possible to reproduce one photograph, to give some idea of the design and of the colour; the bringing of the good news to the shepherds, on the facing page. The shepherds stand against an intense blue background, within a circle of deep red. Their tunics and cloaks are of gold or a dusky mauve, and their stockings gold, red, or green. The balance of colour is masterly, but its true radiance depends on the light which streams through it from the sunshine outside. In England, too, there are some rich collections of stained glass. Perhaps the finest is in the windows of York Minster, where it ranges from the delicate misty 'grisaille', in shaded patterns of grey, to the glowing colours of some of the later windows, one set of which was given by the merchant gilds of York.

Early in the twelfth century a German monk wrote a book on

Stained glass in Chartres Cathedral showing angels announcing to the shepherds the good news of the birth of Christ. The deep blue, red, and gold glow intensely as the light shines through the glass, and there is a sense of excitement and expectancy in the figures of the shepherds.

The Cathedral at Siena, the earliest of the great Gothic cathedrals in Italy, begun in 1196 and finished in 1215.

Angel Choir in Lincoln cathedral, thirteenth century.

various crafts, among them the making of stained-glass windows. He is intensely practical. 'If you want to construct glass windows, first make yourself a smooth wooden board, of such a width and length that you can work two sections of each window on it.' He goes into details of mixing colour and 'how to make shadows and highlights in draperies', but the chief impression is of extremely hard manual work. It is taken for granted that the reader will have to make his own kiln, to make iron trays for use in firing the glass, and will have to know how to cast lead to bind the pieces of glass together; it is even assumed that he will have to make his own bellows—from rams' skins. Theophilus had no desire for fame; he only tells us his name, no more. For most of the men who built the soaring Gothic cathedrals, carved crucifixes, illuminated manu-scripts, or designed stained glass we have not even a name. The medieval artist did not advertise himself. In a sense Theophilus spoke for them all when he wrote in his book, 'God is mindful of the humble quiet man, the man working in silence, in the name of the Lord.'

A pupil of Bishop Fulbert of Chartres said that the men of his day were like dwarfs on the shoulders of giants. For him the giants were the scholars of Greece and Rome, whose learning seemed so magnificent to the men of eleventh-century Europe as they looked back in admiration to the ancient world. But a dwarf on the shoulders of a giant can see a little further than the giant himself, and in the two centuries after Fulbert's death the life of Western Europe took a leap forward which was to help to shape the future history of the world. It was the vigour and creative power of this civilization, first seen in the period we have just been studying, that was eventually to burst out in invention and exploration, in art and in literature, with a force that sometimes swept up other civilizations in its own. This lay far in the future, but the seeds of the success of the West had already been sown.

Chapter 19
Epilogue

This book has spanned a thousand years of European history and in that great stretch of time millions of men and women lived and died and tremendous changes came about. These changes did not of course occur suddenly and obviously—this very seldom happens—they arrived so slowly and so gradually that most people living between 300 and 1300 would hardly be aware from day to day and year to year that their lives, home, work, food, their ideas and outlook, were steadily altering bit by bit. But for us, looking back from the twentieth century into that far past, it is possible to recognize and pick out some of the main differences between a portrait of Europe in 300 and one in 1300.

If, for instance, you compare the maps on page 10 and page 292 you can see at once how differently Europe was divided up. The vast sprawl of the Roman empire which dominates the first map has disappeared from the second. In the west, as you know, its great mass had crumbled before the movements of barbarian invaders and then, as these settled themselves inside its boundaries, the land was gradually pieced together into much smaller units. Some of these, shown on page 292, are not unlike the states you see on a map of Europe today in size and shape but there are others which no longer exist at all. One of these is the Holy Roman Empire, Charlemagne's empire restored by Otto the Great, always entirely different from the empire of the Caesars in spite of its name, its emperor a German and chosen by Germans.

The eastern (Byzantine) part of the empire managed somehow to survive all through the thousand years. In 1300 it still had another 153 years of life before it too disappeared from the map, but it had shrunk a great deal since Constantine built its new capital city in 330, and filled it with matchless treasures from Greece and Rome. And though its emperor still lived in the palace looking out over the Bosphorus to Asia Minor his power was much diminished and he was continually harassed by rivals and enemies. Amongst these enemies were the Muslims, newcomers to the map of Europe and nowhere to be found on it in 300. By 1300 they were firmly established from the Persian Gulf to Spain, a permanent fact of history, and a very important one, since there are now nearly 500,000,000 of them in the world and you cannot open a newspaper without reading something about them.

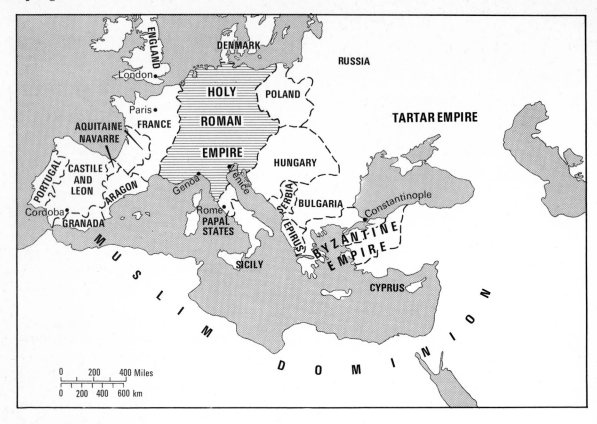

Europe in 1300.

With the break-up of the Roman power in the west many things were lost and not only physical things like roads, walls, aqueducts and legions but also the feeling of unity which men in every part of Europe had once had, the feeling that they were all citizens of one great empire, unified, as it were, under the emperor and the imperial eagles. By 1300, having quite lost this unity, they thought of themselves as separated into groups, Englishmen or Italians or Burgundians or Greeks or Frenchmen; as men of their feudal lords or subjects of their kings. They had, however, gained a unity of another kind which came from religion, for except for Muslim territories and tiny settlements of Jews, all Europe was now Christendom and all men were supposed to belong to the Christian Church where they worshipped in the same service—the Mass— and in the same language—Latin—no matter where they lived. It was a Church which in a thousand years had changed almost beyond recognition. In 300 Diocletian outlawed and persecuted Christians and they could only meet to worship in small groups and secret places, always in peril of their lives. But in 1300 Christianity was the accepted and official religion of Europe and the Church had reached a position of immense power and influence, its great

wealth shown openly in splendid buildings—cathedrals, churches, and monasteries—and in stately ceremonies. And though some of its clergy might be ignorant and unworthy men they were certainly not fugitives. Bishops were princes of the Church, equals of any great feudal lord; kings and rulers used the clergy as councillors and high officers of state; the Pope was ready to challenge any earthly monarch. But the great strength of the Church came from other things besides wide lands and wealth and astute officials. All through the centuries in spite of its faults it had managed to show people by teaching and example that mercy and peace were better than cruelty and bloodshed. The simple goodness of men like Aidan of Northumbria and Alcuin, of Boniface the missionary to the Germans, and the 'little poor man' of Assisi, as well as the steely persistent courage they could show, influenced thousands while they lived and countless more after they were dead.

The Church had also always managed to keep alive the idea of education and learning as things good in themselves. In so doing it had preserved in its libraries some of the priceless treasures of the past which might have been lost for ever, the writings of Greek and Roman scholars without which the world would be a much poorer place. There had gone out, too, from the schools attached to cathedrals and monasteries a steady stream of educated men who, often in a very dark world, passed on continually their love of learning as a counterpoise to love of war. And we must never forget that the Church gave encouragement and opportunities to artists and craftsmen of many kinds so that they were able to express their ideas of form and beauty and to develop new and startling power and originality in the building and decorating of cathedrals and churches, in soaring arches, traceried windows, in marvellous carving and glowing colour. Without the Church learning, education, and peaceful arts would have been extinguished for a very long time, and there would have been no preaching of a gospel of love and hope. What the effects of that would have been on us today we can only guess.

When the movements and attacks of barbarian peoples had slowed down and ended, the fabric of life in Europe was slowly repaired. One result of this was greater security and rather more food since it was safe to go into the field and work, so that by 1300 the population of Europe had grown greatly, though not far ahead lay disasters of famine and plague which in a short time were to cut the numbers by, in some places, a half or a third. Another result was that over the years the towns grew and changed, developing perhaps from the old ghost of a Roman city, half empty and ruinous, first to become a small fortified place with a stronghold and a church built out of the ancient stones, and later a thriving bustling place of several thousands, a centre of buying and selling

so full of people that the houses spilled out beyond the encircling walls, but still small by our standards.

Whenever this happened the men of the countryside round strove to make a little extra money by supplying food to the people living and working in the town. They did not know how to increase their crops rapidly by better ways of farming as modern farmers often do, so they had to use more land. Forests were cleared, marshes drained, brambles and thorns grubbed up, and the ploughs bit into fresh soil. In fact the descendants of people like Actard and Erlindis were no longer content to grow just enough to feed and clothe themselves and the family, and to satisfy the demands of the lord. They aimed at a surplus knowing well that they could sell it in the nearest town. And of course as these country people chaffered and bargained in the market place over eggs and cheese and spare sheepskins, they noted the greater freedom of the townsmen and envied it. They heard of the bargains struck between lords and burgesses to exchange money for service and their own desire to escape from the bonds of service sharpened.

As the towns grew and the roads became safer—though many were still what Chaucer called 'broken and noyous'—so trade and travel increased everywhere. The Mediterranean sea and the cities on its shores or within easy reach were still thought of as the centre of the world's trade. Venice and Genoa, Pisa and Florence were some of the largest, richest and busiest cities in Europe. Even now it is surprising to read the list of goods which could be bought and sold in Venice in 1300—furs, leather, grain, salt, oil, copper and iron, tin and mercury, timber, fruit and soap, animals and slaves, textiles and scent; and the precious spices which helped to smother the worst smells and tastes of medieval cooking when food was mouldy or going bad (there was little or no fresh meat from Michaelmas to Easter)—pepper, ginger, cinnamon, cloves, capers and caraway seeds. You can probably pick out from this list the goods which came from northern Europe, for merchants there were very active and prosperous too, in England and Flanders, Northern France and the Baltic towns. Many of them were ready to push out from well-known tracks and familiar markets in new directions, as the Polo family pushed out to the Far East; and though in 1300 most merchandise was still drawn towards the Mediterranean the time was not far off when the pull of its markets would lose some of its power before the magnet of the Atlantic and the New World.

The history of mankind is never frozen or without movement. The craftsmen of the Middle Ages ventured into new and marvellous skills, the sailors and merchants into unknown lands and seas, the scholars continually sought fresh knowledge and ideas. All were in movement of one kind or another, either of mind or body.

And though in 1300 a high proportion of Europeans were still submerged, unfree and very near the starvation line, even these were generally rather better off and nearer to personal freedom than in 300. For almost everywhere the pattern of society was slowly changing. There was no longer the same urgent need for protection which had driven men like Bruno to become the vassals of a powerful lord, and so the bonds between lord and man weakened and so did the haughty power of the feudal nobles. The neat threefold division of 'God's house' into those who prayed and those who fought and those who worked was changing too, for it was less easy to distinguish the third group which in the days of Alfred of England had been only the poor, the landless, and the unfree. The edges of this third group were becoming very blurred for now it had to include many who were far from poor or servile—burgesses, merchants, lawyers and prosperous craftsmen. Already in England in 1295 some of the townsmen were important enough for Edward I to summon them to his Great Council. As for the humble villein on the manor the conviction that he was bound before anything else to provide food, clothes and money for those above him was by no means as firm as it had been. Lords had begun to see the profit in commuting service for rent, in paying wages to workers on the demesne instead of forcing sullen villeins to do week-work and boon-work. And whereas at one time the useful little saying

> 'For the lord and eke the clerk
> Live by him that does the work'

seemed perfectly natural and proper, some men were beginning to have very different ideas. An English poet of the fourteenth century, William Langland, was to warn lords not to oppress their poor labourers for in Heaven their positions might change and

> 'Though he be thine underling now, well may hap in Heaven
> That he be worthier set and with more bliss than thou'

and for many of the 'underlings' the thing uppermost in their minds was not only where their next meal was coming from but the question

> 'When Adam delved and Eve span
> Who was then the gentleman?'

Clearly there were many changes ahead as the fourteenth century dawned over Europe.

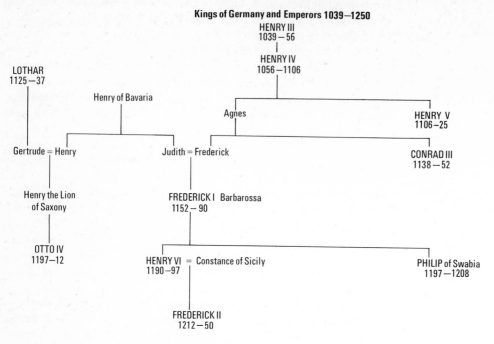

Kings of Germany and Emperors 1039–1250

HENRY III
1039 — 56

HENRY IV
1056 —1106

LOTHAR
1125 —37

Henry of Bavaria

Agnes

HENRY V
1106 —25

Gertrude = Henry

Judith = Frederick

CONRAD III
1138 —52

Henry the Lion
of Saxony

FREDERICK I Barbarossa
1152 — 90

OTTO IV
1197—12

HENRY VI = Constance of Sicily
1190 —97

PHILIP of Swabia
1197 —1208

FREDERICK II
1212 —50

Note : Otto IV and Philip of Swabia were rival kings between 1197 and 1208

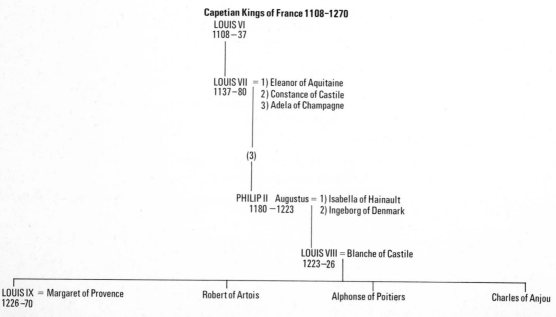

Capetian Kings of France 1108-1270

LOUIS VI
1108 — 37

LOUIS VII   = 1) Eleanor of Aquitaine
1137—80   2) Constance of Castile
                 3) Adela of Champagne

(3)

PHILIP II   Augustus = 1) Isabella of Hainault
1180 —1223   2) Ingeborg of Denmark

LOUIS VIII = Blanche of Castile
1223 —26

LOUIS IX = Margaret of Provence
1226 –70

Robert of Artois

Alphonse of Poitiers

Charles of Anjou

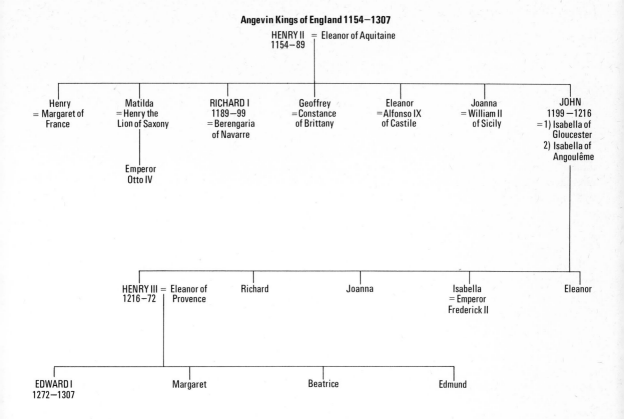

Angevin Kings of England 1154–1307

HENRY II = Eleanor of Aquitaine
1154–89

Henry
= Margaret of
France

Matilda
= Henry the
Lion of Saxony

Emperor
Otto IV

RICHARD I
1189–99
= Berengaria
of Navarre

Geoffrey
=Constance
of Brittany

Eleanor
=Alfonso IX
of Castile

Joanna
= William II
of Sicily

JOHN
1199 –1216
=1) Isabella of
Gloucester
2) Isabella of
Angoulême

HENRY III = Eleanor of
1216–72   Provence

Richard

Joanna

Isabella
= Emperor
Frederick II

Eleanor

EDWARD I
1272–1307

Margaret

Beatrice

Edmund

Bibliography

I. GENERAL

There are as yet only a few books for young readers on purely Continental topics, but for this period many of those on English history have a wider relevance and can be good starting points for further work. For instance, the first two volumes in the 'Portrait of Britain' series, *Portrait of Britain before 1066* and *Portrait of the Middle Ages* provide useful general reading.

For the adult reader, using this book for teaching, some of the most useful among recent books are:

H. St. Le B. Moss, *The Birth of the Middle Ages* (O.U.P.).

R. W. Southern, *The Making of the Middle Ages* (Hutchinson).

R. H. C. Davis, *History of Medieval Europe* (Longmans).

C. N. L. Brooke, *Europe in the Central Middle Ages* (Longmans).

There are two volumes in the series 'The Making of European Civilization' that not only contain useful monographs by specialists written for the general reader, but also a wealth of magnificent illustrations, which are invaluable material for children working on their own. They are:

The Dark Ages, ed. D. Talbot Rice (Thames & Hudson).

The Flowering of the Middle Ages, ed. Joan Evans (Thames & Hudson).

The short classified bibliography which follows has been divided in each section into two categories; (a) junior and (b) adult:

(a) Books suitable for the age range 12–13, for which our book is intended.

(b) A list of some recent publications, which, while obviously not exhaustive, may be of particularly interest to adults using the book.

II. RULERS AND PEOPLE

(a) *Junior Section*

'People of the Past' series (O.U.P.):

A Saxon Settler (R. Sutcliff).

A Viking Raider (A. Boucher).

An Eleventh-Century Mason (J. Paget).

A Thirteenth-Century Villein (P. Andrewes).

'Then and There' series (Longmans):

The Vikings (G. L. Proctor).

Alfred and the Danes (M. Reeves).

The Norman Conquest (M. Reeves).

'Clarendon Biographies' (O.U.P.):

Alfred the Great (H. R. Loyn).

William the Conqueror (D. Walker).

Frederick II of Hohenstaufen (P. Andrewes).

T. Talbot Rice, *Everyday Life in Byzantium* (Batsford).

P. Muntz, *Everyday Life in the Age of Charlemange* (Batsford).

A. Fox & A. Sorrell, *Roman Britain* (Lutterworth Press).

(b) *Adult Section*

For chapters 1, 2, and 3 see Moss, *Birth of the Middle Ages* (O.U.P.).

Procopius, *The Secret History* (Penguin) is a lively source for Justinian.

Gregory of Tours, *The History of the Franks*. A source for the history of barbarian rulers and people.

For Chapter 5 see Moss, who devotes 3 chapters to Islam, and Bernard Lewis, whose study, *The Arabs in History* (Hutchinson) sets the rise of Islam in the wider context of the modern world.

Chapter 6: Donald Bullough, *The Age of Charlemagne* (Elk) is beautifully illustrated; and see Einhard's *Life of Charlemagne* (Univ. of Michigan Press, and paperback).

Chapter 7: Gwyn Jones, *History of the Vikings* (O.U.P.).

Chapter 11: C. H. Haskins's classic *The Normans in European History* (Ungar, New York, and paperback).

The best edition of *The Bayeux Tapestry* is the one edited by Sir Frank Stenton (Phaidon Press, 1965).

Chapter 15: R. W. Barber's *Henry Plantagenet* (Barrie & Rockliff); G. O. Sayles, *The Medieval Foundations of England* (Methuen), provides a clear account of Henry II's government.

Chapter 18: See M. Wade Labarge's biography of *St. Louis* (Eyre & Spottiswoode), but there is really no substitute for the contemporary biography of the king by Joinville, in Joinville and Villehardouin, *Chronicle of the Crusades* (Penguin, 1963); E. Kantorowicz's *Frederick II* (Ungar, New York), is fascinating if partisan.

III. THE CHURCH

(a) *Junior Section*

'People of the Past' series (O.U.P.):

   A Northumbrian Missionary (F. Grice).

   A Twelfth-Century Benedictine Nun (C. Northcote).

'Then and There' series (Longmans):

   The Golden Age of Northumbria (H. E. Davidson).

   Medieval Pilgrimages (G. Scott Thomson).

   The Medieval Monastry (M. Reeves).

Mary R. Price, *Bede and Dunstan* (O.U.P.).

A. Duggan, *Growing up with the Norman Conquest* (Faber).

J. Williams, *Knights of the Crusades* (a Cassell 'Caravel' book).

E. K. Milliken, *English Monasticism, Yesterday and Today* (Harrap).

A. Duggan, *The Story of the Crusades* (Faber).

R. R. Sellman, *The Crusades* (Methuen).

(b) *Adult Section*

The Rule of St. Benedict, ed. J. McCann (Burns, Oates) is a key document for an understanding of the period and much of the material can be understood by children; D. Knowles, *Saints and Scholars* (C.U.P.) has an illuminating chapter on the significance of the Rule.

* Asterisk indicates books containing source material.

Chapter 10: For the conflict between Empire and Papacy see especially C. N. L. Brooke, *Europe in the Central Middle Ages* (Longmans), and relevant documents in *Sources for the History of Medieval Europe*, ed. B. Pullan (Blackwell).

Chapter 12: Many of the books on Cluny are out of print, but for details of the daily round there see especially R. Graham, *English Ecclesiastical Studies* (S.P.C.K.), where there is much to interest children, and J. Evans, *Monastic Life at Cluny* (Archon Books). N. Hunt, *Cluny under St. Hugh* (E. Arnold) is a scholarly monograph which has a more general interest. For St. Bernard, G. G. Coulton's sketch in *Five Centuries of Religion*, Vol. I (C.U.P.) is a useful starting point and there is an excellent English edition of *The Letters of St. Bernard of Clairvaux*, ed. B. Scott-James (Burns, Oates). For a good general account of monasticism in England see J. C. Dickinson, *Monastic Life in Medieval England* (Black). The standard work, of course, is D. Knowles, *The Monastic Order in England*, 2nd edn. (C.U.P.).

Chapter 14: S. Runciman, *A History of the Crusades* (C.U.P.); also R. Pernoud, *The Crusaders* (Oliver & Boyd), which is imaginative and stimulating. The 'little book' is *Gesta Francorum*, ed. and trans. Rosalind Hill (O.U.P.); in the same series, relating to the Third Crusade, is *The Chronicle of Richard of Devizes*, ed. John Appleby. The English translation of the *Itinerarium* is out of print.

Chapter 16: *St. Francis of Assisi, the Legends and Lauds*, ed. Otto Karrer (Sheed & Ward), gives plenty of source material suitable for children. The edition of *The Little Flowers of St. Francis*, ed. Dom Roger Huddlestone (Burns, Oates), may be recommended, and *St. Francis of Assisi* by Omer Englebert, trans. E. V. Cooper (Herder), is very readable. John Moorman, *A History of the Franciscan Order* (Clarendon Press), is a full and scholarly work, and D. Knowles, *The Religious Orders in England* (C.U.P.), Book II, Chs. ix–xx, is excellent.

IV. TOWNS, CASTLES, AND THE COUNTRYSIDE

(a) *Junior Section*

'People of the Past' series (O.U.P.):
  A Thirteenth-Century Villein (P. Andrewes).
'Then and There' series (Longmans):
  The Medieval Village (M. Reeves).
  The Medieval Town (M. Reeves).
  The Medieval Feast (R. J. Mitchell).
  The Medieval Castle (M. Reeves).
  The Medieval Tournament (R. S. Mitchell).
A. Duggan, *Growing up with the Norman Conquest*, and *Growing up in the Thirteenth Century* (Faber).
E. Oakeshott, *A Knight and his Castle* (Lutterworth Press).
W. O. Hassall, *How they Lived, 55 B.C.–A.D. 1485* (Blackwell).
Christine Price, *Made in the Middle Ages* (Bodley Head).

(b) *Adult Section*

Chapters 8 and 13: *The Cambridge Economic History* (C.U.P.) is authoritative, but very specialized. F. Heer, *The Medieval World* (Mentor, New York), is a readable introduction by a Continental scholar. There are books with

useful material for children in a recent Batsford series: see especially J. J. Bagley, *Life in Medieval England;* E. R. Chamberlin, *Life in Medieval France;* and M. Rowling, *Everyday Life in Medieval Times*. H. S. Bennett, *Life on the English Manor* (C.U.P.), is humane and informative, and so is Eileen Power's *Medieval People* (Methuen).

For a detailed but readable study of feudalism see Marc Bloch's *Feudal Society* (Routledge, and paperback). G. Duby, *Rural Economy and Country Life in the Medieval West*, trans. C. Postan (E. Arnold), is first-rate. So, too, is *Medieval Trade in the Mediterranean World* by R. S. Lopez & I. W. Raymond (Columbia Univ. Press). Richard Barber, *The Knight and Chivalry* (Longmans), is useful and lively.

V. ART AND LEARNING

(a) *Junior Section*
'People of the Past' series (O.U.P.):
An Eleventh-Century Mason (J. Paget).
'Then and There' series (Longmans):
The Golden Age of Northumbria (H. E. Davidson).

Since much of the material for this aspect of the period is visual, children can use adult books. In addition to the two books in the 'Making of European Civilization' series already mentioned in the General section—which are outstanding—there are also J. Beckwith, *Early Medieval Art* (Thames & Hudson), and A. Martindale, *Gothic Art* (Thames & Hudson), both more modestly produced and much less expensive, but with good illustrations. There are excellent reproductions in the Fontana Unesco Art Book, by J. Sweeney *Irish Illuminated Manuscripts* (Milan).

(b) *Adult Section*
R. W. Southern, *The Making of the Middle Ages* (Hutchinson) is indispensable, and there is a lively and readable account of universities in C. H. Haskins, *The Rise of the Universities* (Cornell Univ. Press, and paperback). A useful selection of source material may be found in *Medieval Culture and Society* (Harper & Row, New York), and a systematic treatment of the history of thought in D. Knowles, *The Evolution of Medieval Thought* (Longmans). There is a good survey of the twelfth-century renaissance in C. N. L. Brooke, *Europe in the Central Middle Ages* (Longmans). *Theophilus: De Diversis Artilus*, ed. C. R. Dodwell (Nelson), is a delightful account of the techniques of various crafts by a medieval craftsman.

Index

Aachen (Aix-la-Chapelle), palace at, 79, 82, 86, 89, 131; palace chapel at, *98*, 250, 251, 267–9, *268*; palace school at, 93–5, 264

Abbasid dynasty, 78, 79, 80; *see* Mansur, Harun al Raschid, al Mamun

Abelard, Peter, 179, 280–2, *282*

Abu Bakr, kinsman of Muhammad, 66; Caliph, 69, 70, 79

Acre, port of, besieged and captured in Third Crusade, 211–12, 213

Actard, villein on the estates of Saint German des Prés, 118, 120, 121, 122, 123, 124, 125, 126, 185

Adhemar of le Puy, 200, 201

Afghanistan, 49

Africa, North, corn supplies from, 18, 31, 37; invaded by Vandals, 28, 42; reconquered by Justinian, 43; conquered by Muslims, 64, 72–3, 196

Ahenny, cross at, *273*

Aigues Mortes, 188

Alaric, the Visigoth, 24, 25–6, 28, 29, 30, 33

Alcuin, friend of Charlemagne and scholar, 82, 91, 92, 93–5, 99, 100, 102, 265, 266

Aleppo, 219

Alexandria, 11, 182; captured by Arabs, 72

Alexius Comnenus, Emperor (Byzantine), 198–202

Alfred, the Great, 101, 110, 111, 147, 148, 187, 295

Ali, cousin of Muhammad, 66

Alice, sister of Philip Augustus, 209

Allah, Muslim name for God, 67, 68, 75

Alps, 30, 60, 101, 138, 141, 144, 174, 199, 280

America, 226; discovered by Vikings, 106

Amr ibn al-As, 70, 71

Angers, castle of, *228*

Angevin Empire, Chapter 15, 247

Anglo Saxon, Anglo Saxons, attacks on Britain, 27; conversion to Christianity, 61–2; attacked by Vikings, 101; traditions in government, 224–5; art, 271–2

Anglo-Saxon Chronicle, 147, 151, 160

Anjou, county of, 208, 215, 220, 227; counts of, *see* Geoffrey Plantagenet, Henry Plantagenet

Anna Comnena, 162, 200, 201–2

Anselm, St., Archbishop of Canterbury, 172

Antioch, 11, 35, 182, 219, 220; captured by Bohemond, 202–4

Apulia, 162

Aquitaine, 220; invaded by Muslims, 74; acquired by Louis VII, 218; as part of Angevin Empire, 208, 221, 224, 227, 258; Dukes of, 215, *and see* William I, William IX, William X

Arabia, 35; description of, 64–5; life of Muhammad in, 66–8; after death of Muhammad, 69–71

Arabs, 64, 65, 66; conquests by, 69–78

Aristotle, 76, 264, 266, 282

Armies of Roman Empire, 13, *16*, 22, *23*; of Justinian, 42–3; of Charlemagne, 91–2; of Frederick II, 252; of King Henry II, 227–8; of Crusaders, 200, 201, 208; of the Arabs, 71–8

Armour, *see* Clothing

Arsuf, battle of, 205

Art, of the Byzantine Empire, *38*, *40*, *41*; of the Muslims, 75, 76, 79, *81*; of the Court School of Charlemagne, 87, *94*, 95

Styles in, Anglo Saxon, 271–2; Celtic, 271, 273, *275*; Greco-Roman, 269–72; influenced by humanism, 284–7

Illuminated Gospel Books, *270*, 271–3, *274–5*; stained glass, 288–90; *see also*, Buildings, Painting, Sculpture

Assisi, 232, *240*, 241, 242, 244, 245

Assize, of Arms, 227; of Clarendon, 226

Ataulf, the Visigoth, 24, 25, 27

Augustine, St., Archbishop of Canterbury, 61–2

Avars, 91

Baghdad, description of, 78; life in, 79–80

Baldwin I (of Lorraine), King of Jerusalem, 200, 202, 204

Baldwin IV, King of Jerusalem, 207

Barbarians, peaceful penetration of Roman Empire by, 22; invasions of Roman Empire, 12, 21–34, 101, 182; their kingdoms, 24; settlement within Empire, 26–30. *See also* Dacians, Franks, Germans, Goths, Visigoths, Ostrogoths, Huns, Lombards, Saxons, Vandals

Barnack, Christ in Majesty at, 284, *286*

Bayeux, city of, 149; Tapestry, 149, *150*

Beaumont du Périgord, market at, 190

Bede, 61, 82

Bedouins, their way of life, 64–5

Belfort, 180

Belisarius, general of Justinian, 43

Benedict Biscop, 271–2

Benedict of Nursia, St., 167; his life, 50–2; his Rule, 52–8, 171, 174, 175, 176

Benevento, 58, 60

Berard, Archbishop of Palermo, 250

Berbers, 72, 73, 74

Berengaria of Navarre, wife of Richard I, 209, 211

Bernard of Clairvaux, St., his Cistercian ideals, 172, 175–81, 279; personality and letters, 179–80; approves Second Crusade, 206; against Eleanor of Aquitaine, 219–20; against Abelard, 179, 180, 281; against heresy, 236

Black Death, 129

Blois, county of, 215; Countess of, 227

Boethius, 264, 266, 267

Bohemond, son of Robert Guiscard, 197, 200–4

Bologna, university of, 252, 280, 283–4

Boniface, St., 85, 86

Boothby Pagnall manor house, *119*

Bordeaux, 217, 218, 222

Boulogne, 164

Britain, in Roman times, 11; invaded and subdued by Anglo-Saxons, 27, 61

Brittany, Bretons, 227; fief of French crown, 215; claimed by Henry II, 228

Bruges, 187

Brunhild, Queen of the Franks, 60

Bruno, 112, 113, 295

Buildings, of Emperor Diocletian, 15; in Roman towns, 182; of Theodoric, *32*; in Constantinople, 35–7; of Justinian, 43–6, *44*; of Charlemagne, 86, 98, 99, *268*; of Arabs, 73–6, *73, 75, 77*; of Henry II, 228, *228*; of Frederick II, 251, *256*; Roman influence on, 269, 276; Gothic style in, 288, 290.

Churches and Cathedrals, Byzantine, 45–7 (Sancta Sophia, *47*); Ostrogothic (Theodoric's Mausoleum, *32*); Carolingian, 86 (Palace Chapel at Aachen, *98, 268*); Ottonian (St. Cyriakus, Gernrode, *134*); Saxon in England, 159 (Earl's Barton, *158*); Norman in England, 156–9, 276 (Melbourne, *159*, Ely, *157*, Durham, *277*); Norman in Sicily (Church at Palermo, *156*); Gothic in England, 288 (Lincoln, *289*). *Monasteries*, Benedictine, 53 (St. Ambrogio, Milan, *53*, Lorsch gatehouse, *269*); Cluniac, 164–9, *165, 166, 168*; Cistercian, 175, 176, *176, 177, 178*; *see also* walls, castles, houses

Burgundy, 33, 164, 175; Dukes of, 215; Duchess of, 173

Burhs, 111, 187

Bury St. Edmunds, 187–8, 198, 231

Byzantine Empire, Byzantines, Greeks, Chapter 3, 78, 247, 291; oppressive government in, 70; loses provinces of Syria, Egypt, North Africa to Arabs, 71–3, 196; loses Asia Minor to Turks, 198; rulers of, *see* Justinian, Heraclius, Alexius Comnenus

Byzantium, *see* Constantinople

Caen, 222

Cairo, 261

Calabria, 162

Caliph, *see* Abu Bakr, Omar, Omayyad dynasty, Abbasid dynasty

Camaldoli, 174

Canossa, 145, 174

Canterbury, 62, 229; Archbishops of, 152; *and see* Lanfranc, Anselm, Thomas Becket

Canute, King of Denmark and of England, 147

Carausius, 14

Carolingian Empire, *see* Charlemagne

Carthage, 28

Cassiodorus, 30–1

Castles, in England, 154 (Thetford *155*, Rochester, *155*); in Sicily,

247, 251 (Castel del Monte, *256*); in France, 216, 220, 228 (Angers, *228*); in Syria, 205–6 (Krak des Chevaliers, *205*); attraction for merchants, 187

Cathay, *see* China

Cathedrals, *see* Buildings and Art

Ceylon, 195

Champagne, county of, 215, 220

Charlemagne, King of the Franks, 64, 74, 79, 82; court life, 89, 266; appearance, *88*; campaigns, 91–2; coronation in Rome, 96, 250; as Emperor, 134, 135–7, 138, 185, 186, 250–1, 264, 265, 267; bust of, *88*; empire of, 130, 131, 291, its government, 96–9, its break up, 100–15, 147, 215

Charles Martel, 74

Charles (the Simple), King of the Franks, 147

Chartres, 266, 267, 279, 287, 288, plate facing, *288*

Chichester, 187; painting of Virgin and Child at, *285*

Chilperi, King of the Franks, 84, 87

China, 49, 78, 195

Chi-Rho monogram, 38, 273; *see also Labarum*

Christianity, 64; persecuted in Roman Empire, 17; Constantine's conversion to, 18; Clovis's conversion to, 34; Ethelbert of Kent's conversion to, 34; conversion of English to, 61–2; Muhammad's break with, 67; tolerated by Muslims, 76; Charlemagne forcibly converts Saxons to, 92; part played by, in life of a villein, 128; power of, by 1300, 292–3

Churches, *see* Buildings

Cimabue, 245

Cipangu, *see* Japan

Citeaux, abbey of, 175, 181

Cities, *see* Towns

Clairvaux, abbey of, 175, 178, 179

Clarendon, 221; Assize of, 226

Classes of society, 111, 116–18, *117*, 295; *see also* Lordship, Knights, Villeins, Merchants, Monasticism

Index

Clermont, Council of, 146, 199

Clothing, of Roman soldiers, 21, 22, *23*; of Franks, 33; of Justinian's guards, 37; of Viking warriors, *105, 106*; of crusading knights, *203, 206*; laid down in Assize of Arms, 227; of Franciscans, 232; of Saracen servants, 253; of Justinian, 38–9; of Charlemagne, 87, of St. Louis, 257

Clotilde, wife of Clovis, 33–4

Clovis, King of the Franks, 31–4, 83, 84

Cluny, abbey of, life in, 164–73, 197, 283; abbots of, *see* Hugh, Peter the Venerable

Coins, the *aureus*, 15; of Diocletian, *13*; of Constantine, *13*; of Theodoric, *29*; Arabic, minted by Normans, 76; silver penny of Charlemagne, 96, *96*; silver penny in England, 224

Cologne, 266; Reginbald of, 266–7

Columbus, Christopher, 195

Communes, 193

Compostella, Church of St. James at, 198, 279

Conques, cathedral at, 276, *279*

Conrad of Montferrat, 207

Constance, wife of Henry VI, 249

Constance, city of, 250

Constantine the Great, Emperor, *13*, 37; reorganisation of Roman Empire, 15; defence of Empire, 15–17; dealings with Christians, 17; conversion to Christianity, 18; founding of Constantinople, 20, 35, 291

Constantinople, city of, founded as new capital by Constantine, 20, 21, 35, 291; description of, 35–7; walls of, *36*; Nika riots in, 39–40; rebuilt by Justinian, 45–6; reached by Vikings, 108; looted in First Crusade, 201; looted in Fourth Crusade, 195, 237; fell to Turks, 45; Emperor at, 29, 30, 59, 75, 196, 200; *and see* Byzantine Emperors; Patriarch of, 62

Cordova, 75–6; mosque at, *77*

Coronation, of Kings, of Pepin as King of the Franks, 86; of Otto I as King of Germany, 130–1; of Frederick II as King of Germany, 250; of Frederick II as King of Jerusalem, 255; of William I as King of England, 151. of Emperors, of Charlemagne, 96; of Otto I, 135; of Frederick II, 251

Court life, of Justinian, 37–9; of Caliphs of Baghdad, 78–80; of Charlemagne, 85–90, 93–5; of Henry II of England, 221; of Eleanor of Aquitaine, 227; of Frederick II, 253–4; of feudal lords of southern France, 236

Crown, imperial, plate facing *264*

Crusades, 81, 276; ideas behind them, 197–8, 251; First Crusade, 198–205, 206, 219; (People's Crusade, 200–1); Second Crusade, 180, 206, 219–20; Third Crusade, 208–13; Fourth Crusade, 237; Crusade of Frederick II, 255; Crusades of St. Louis, 258, 261

Ctesiphon, 71

Cuthbert, St., 82, 272

Cyprus, 210–11; ruler of, *see* Isaac

Dacians, 22

Damascus, surrendered to Arabs, 71; Great Mosque at, *73, 74, 75,* 78

Danes, *see* Northmen

Danube, river, 20, 21, 25, 101

Datini, family of, 191–2, 194

Denmark, 102

Desert, way of life in, 64–5

Dijon, 175, 180, 184

Diocletian, Emperor, 13–15, 292

Djem, 183

Domesday survey, 154, 188; description of, 160; extract from, *161*

Dominic, St., 236, 245, *246*

Dues, of a villein to his Lord, 126; harbour, 252

Durham cathedral, 156, 276, 288; nave of, *277*; door knocker of, *278*

Durrow, Book of, *270, 271, 272*

Eadfrith, Bishop of Lindisfarne, 272

Earls Barton church, *158*

Edessa, crusading state of, 202, 204, 206

Edmund, St., King of East Anglia, 187, 198

Education, Muslim, 68; at palace school at Aachen, 93–5; of Frederick II, 249; in cathedral schools, 266–7, 280–1; in the universities, 283–4. *See also* Learning

Edward, the Confessor, King of England, 148, 149

Edward I, King of England, 295

Edwenna, 185

Egypt, as province of Roman Empire, 12, 70; conquered by Arabs, 71–2; as part of Muslim Empire, 78, 80

Einhard, biographer of Charlemagne, 87–9, 90, 92, 94, 96

Ekkehard, 196

Eleanor of Aquitaine, wife of Louis VII of France and later of Henry II of England, her upbringing, 217; marriage to future Louis VII, 218; life in Paris, 218; on crusade, 218–20; divorced by Louis VII, 220; married Henry Plantagenet, 220–1; relations with him, 227, 229, 231; court at Poitiers, 227; tomb of, *230*

Eleanor, Queen of Castile, daughter of Eleanor of Aquitaine, 227, 229

Elephants, 79–80, 90, *254*

Ely, 151, *157*

Emperors, Roman, *see* Constantine and Diocletian; worship of, 14, 15, 251

Engadine Pass, 250

England, conversion of, 61, 62; Alcuin's ties with, 82; attacked by Vikings, 102, 110; invaded and conquered by Normans, 147–60; acquired by Henry II, 221; government of, 223–6, 227; rural life in, 121, 123; merchants from,

186; towns in, 187, 192, 193; students from, 218, 229; Cluniacs in, 170; Cistercians in, 176, 179; Franciscans in, 244. *See also* Buildings, Castles

Kings of, *see* Ethelred the Redeless, Canute, Edward the Confessor, William I, William II, Henry I, Stephen, Henry II, Richard I, John, Henry III, Edward I

Erlindis, wife of Actard, a villein, 118, 120, 123, 126

Essen, Golden Virgin of, *284*

Ethelbert of Kent, 34, 61, 62

Ethelred the Redeless, King of England, 110, 147

Ethelwald, Bishop of Lindisfarne, 272

Eusebius, biographer of Constantine, 18

Exchequer, of Normandy, 222; of England, 222, 224

Exeter, 151

Fairs, 185, 192

Farming, in Roman Empire, 11–12; on the estates of Charlemagne, 90; among Saxons, 92; among Northmen, 103; in Medieval Europe, 116, 120–6; on Cistercian lands, 176, 178; near towns, 189; general improvement of, 294

Fastrada, wife of Charlemagne, 92

Fealty, oath of, 112–13, 160, 202, 210

Feudalism, 115; in Norman England, 160; in France, 215, 221; challenged by growth of national feeling, 231, 251. *See also* Vassals, Lordship, Kingship, Knights

Flanders, 187

Florence, 174, 191

Foederati, 25, 29

Foligno, 240

Fonte Avellana, 174

Fontévrault, abbey of, Plantagenet tombs in, *230*

Fountains abbey, 176

France, origin of name, 34; emergence as a country, 109–10; invaded by Muslims, 74; by Hungarians, 101; by Vikings, 102–3, 108, 147, 148; clergy of, 141; monasteries in, 164, 170, 175; Franciscans in, 244; schools in, 281; heresy in, 236–7, 262; and crusades, 197, 199, 200, 208; rural life in, 118–27, 129; merchants in, 186, 191–2, 239; communes in, 193; feudal disorder in, 214–16; increase of royal power in, 216, 218, 229–31, 257–8, 262; Kings of, *see* Louis VI, Louis VII, Philip II (Augustus), Louis IX

Francis of Assisi, St., *238*; meeting with Innocent III, 232, 237; early life, 239; conversion to a new life, 240–1; followers, 242; problems he faced, 244–5; Innocent III's dream of, *243*

Franks, 28, 43; their way of life, 25; settlement in Gaul, 31–4; and the Church, 60; defeated Muslims, 74; under Merovingians, 83–5; part of Carolingian Empire, 100

Frederick I (Barbarossa), King of Germany and Emperor, 208, 250

Frederick II, King of Germany, King of Sicily and Emperor, 262; his childhood in Sicily, 247–50; his bid for crown of Germany, 250–1; his state in Sicily, 251–4; relations with Pope, 254–7

Friars, Dominican, 245–6

Friars, Franciscan, 242–6

Fulbert, Bishop of Chartres, 266, 267, 279, 290

Gaiseric, leader of Vandals, 27–8, 42

Galla Placidia, 24

Gaul, 42, 43; province of Roman Empire, 12, 97; invaded by barbarians, 27; controlled by Franks, 33

Genoa, 197, 294; part played in First Crusade, 204

Geoffrey Plantagenet, Count of

Anjou, father of Henry II, 220

Geoffrey de Vinsauf, 208, 210

Gerbert, *see* Sylvester II

Germanus, general of Justinian, 43

Germany, 138; emergence of, 109; and Otto I, 130–7; and Henry IV, 144; and Frederick II, 249–51; investiture of bishops in, 141–2; princes of, 144–5; and the crusades, 208; Cluniacs in, 170; Cistercians in, 175; Franciscans in, 244; rural life in, 124–5

Gibraltar, 73

Gilbert de Heugleville, 152

Giotto, 245

Glastonbury, 152; Thurston, abbot of, 156

Godfrey, Duke of Lorraine, 200, 201, 202

Godric, son of Edwenna, 185

Gokstad, ship, 106

Golden Horn, 37

Gospel Books, *270, 271–3, 274, 275*; *see also* Book of Durrow, Lindisfarne Gospels, Book of Kells

Gothic, *see* Buildings

Goths, 20, 22, 35, 245; division of, 25, 28; *see also* Visigoths and Ostrogoths

Government, of late Roman Empire, 14–15; of Byzantine Empire by Justinian, 39–45; of Empire of Charlemagne, 96–9; of Muslim Empire by Caliphs, 76, 79; of Italy by Theodoric, 30–1; of Gaul by Clovis, 34; by his successors, 83–4; of dominions of Henry Plantagenet, 221–7; of Kingdom of Sicily by Frederick II, 251–2; of France by St. Louis, 257–62; new methods of, 280

Gratian, 280

Great Khan, the, 195

Greece, ancient, culture of, 20, 263, 264, 266, 269, 283, 290, 293; preserved in Arab world, 76, 80, 81

Greenland, 106

Gregory, Bishop of Tours, writer, 34, 84, 87

Gregory I, the Great, Pope, 58–63, *59*, 64, 263
Gregory, monk of Cluny, 172–3
Gregory VII, Pope, 142–6, 164, 173, 255, 280
Gregory IX, Pope (Cardinal Ugolino), 232, 254–7
Gundrada, wife of William of Warenne, 164–5, 170, 173

Hadrian's Wall, 11
Harold, Earl of Wessex and King of England, 102, 149, 151; in Bayeux Tapestry, *150*
Harold, Hardrada, King of Norway, 149
Harun al Raschid, Caliph, 79, 90
Hastings, battle of, 151, 162
Hattin, battle of, 207
Hauteville, Tancred of, *see* Tancred
Headingham Hall, *114*
Heloïse, 281–2
Hejira, 67, 76
Henry III, King of Germany and Emperor, relations with the Pope, 138, 141, 142, 145
Henry VI, King of Germany and Emperor, 249
Henry the Fowler, Duke of Saxony and King of Germany, 111–15, 130
Henry I, King of England, 172, 221
Henry II (Plantagenet), King of England, 220; married Eleanor of Aquitaine, 220; government of his dominions, 221–7, 247, 280; his buildings, 228; expansion of his territories, 228–9; his quarrels, 229; his tomb at Fontevrault, *230*
Henry III, King of England, 258, 262
Henry, son of King Henry II, 229
Henry IV, King of Germany and Emperor, conflict with Pope Gregory VII, 142–6, 164, 173
Henry, monk of Dijon, 180
Heraclius, Emperor (Byzantine), 70, 71
Heresy, 235, 236, 242, 262
Hohenstauffen rulers, *see* Frederick

I, Henry VI, Frederick II, Philip of Swabia
Holy Land, in Muslim hands, 146; pilgrimages to, 148, 197–8; crusades to, Chapter 14, 219, 237, 255; Franciscans in, 244
Holy Roman Empire, in time of Charlemagne, 96; in time of Otto I, 135; in time of Henry IV, 139; in time of Henry VI and Frederick II, 249
Rulers of, *see* Charlemagne, Louis the Pious, Otto I, Otto III, Henry III, Henry IV, Frederick I, Henry VI, Otto IV, Frederick II
Homage, act of, 112–13, 141, 146, 147, 160, 217, 218; by crusader knight, *203*
Homs, 205, 206
Hospitallers, Military Order of, 206
Houses, of lords, in the early Middle Ages, 112, *113*, *114*; manor houses, 118, *119*; of villeins, 119–20; of towns people, 189
Hugh, Abbot of Cluny, 145, 165, 171, 172; description of, 173–4
Hugh de Payns, 180
Hugh of le Puiset, 216
Humanism, 285–7
Hungarians, 101, 130, 264
Huns, 25, 29, 184, 264

Iceland, 106
Île de France, 215, 216, 217
India, 49, 71, 78, 80, 195
Innocent III, Pope, 232–7, 242, 249, 250, 255
Innocent IV, Pope, 257, 261
Investiture, of bishops, 141–2, 146
Iona, 273
Iraq, 71
Ireland, 228; its monks, 50–1; attached by Vikings, 103, 106; its art, 271–3, *273*
Irnerius, 280
Isaac, ruler of Cyprus, 210
Islam, religion of, 64–9, 72, 78, 252; conversion of Turks to, 198; conquests of, 69–78

Istanbul, 35; *see* Constantinople
Italy, 170, 175, 218, 272, 280; invaded by Visigoths, 26, 27, 33; by Ostrogoths, 30–1; plundered by Vandals, 28; reconquered by Justinian, 43; invaded by Lombards, 58–9; raided by Hungarians, 101; south subdued by Normans, 162; Gregory I and, 59–60; Charlemagne and, 96; Otto I and, 134–7; Henry III and, 138; Henry IV and, 141–6; St. Francis and, 237–46; Frederick II and, 251–7; Benedictine monasticism in, 50, 53; merchants in, 191, 192, 193, 194–5, 197; communes in, 193; learning in, 280

Jacques de Vitry, 242
Jaffa, port of, captured by Richard I, 212
Japan, 195
Jarrow, monastery of, 82, 271
Jerome, St., 26
Jerusalem, 26, 201; place of pilgrimage, 198; in Muslim hands, 80, 196, *75*; captured in First Crusade, 204; recaptured by Muslims, 207; objective of later crusades, 212, 219, 237, 251; kingdom of, 206; coronation of Frederick II in, 255
Kings of, *see* Baldwin I, Baldwin IV, Frederick II
Jews, 47, 64; and Islam, 66, 67, 70, 80; settlements of in Western Europe, 247, 292; massacre of, 180
Joanna, Queen of Sicily, daughter of Eleanor of Aquitaine, 227, 229
John, Count of Mortain and King of England, 229, 231, 233
John Gualbert, 174
John Russell, of London, 193–4
Joinville, biographer of St. Louis, 257, 258–61
Juries, 226
Justice, in dominions of Henry II, 225–7; in kingdom of Frederick II, 252, 257; in France under

St. Louis, 257–8; *see also* Law
Justinian, Emperor (Byzantine), 50, 70, 96, 247, 252, 267, 280; his life and reign, 35–49; portrait of, in mosaic, *38, 40*

Kadesiya, battle of, 71
Kells, Book of, 273, plate facing *265*
Ketton, Robert of, 81
Khadijah, wife of Muhammad, 66
Khalid ibn al-Walid, 70, 71
Kingship, symbols of, 130, *136, 137,* 140, 250, plate facing *264*; of Theoderic in Italy, 29–31; of the Merovingians, 83–5; of the Carolingians, 85–99; of the Saxon house in Germany, 130–4; feudal kingship of William I in England, 160; of Henry II, 221–7; of Louis VI in France, 214–16; the 'new style' of kingship of Frederick II, 250–7; of Louis IX, 257–62
Kingston Bagpuize, 152
Knights, 116, 146, 180, 223, 239; crusading, 201–13, *203, 213,* 227 (*see also* Templars, Hospitallers); of the Round Table, 227, 283. *See also* Feudalism
Koran, 68; translation from Arabic into Latin for Peter the Venerable, 81
Krak des Chevaliers, *205,* 205–6

Labarum, 18, *19*
Land, as source of wealth, 110, 112, 116, 128–9, 160, 167, 169
Lanfranc, Abbot of Caen and Archbishop of Canterbury, 154
Languedoc, 236
Laon, 281
Law, in dominions of Charlemagne, 97, 101; in dominions of Henry II, 225–7; in Sicily under Frederick II, 252; Roman, 47–8, 252, studied in Bologna, 280, its influence, 252, 280; Canon, 280; Salic, 34
Learning, in monasteries, 56, 74, 95, 263–6, 293; in cathedral schools, 266–7, 280, 281, 283, 293; in

universities, 283; at the court of Charlemagne, 92–5, 264–5; at the court of Henry II, 280; at the court of Frederick II, 253; in the Arab world, 76, 80; encouraged by St. Dominic, 245; rejected by St. Francis, 246
Leicester, Earl of, 193
Leo III, Pope, crowns Charlemagne, 96, 138
Leo IX, Pope, 138–141
Leopold, Duke of Austria, 212–13
Lewes, priory of, 170
Liege, Ralph of the church of, 266–7
Lincoln, 288, *289*
Lindisfarne, monastery of, raided by Vikings, 82, 102, 265; Gospels, 272, 273, *274, 275*
Loire, river, 108, 220, 228
Lombards, 54, 58, 59, 93, 96, 100; states of, *see* Lombardy, Benevento, Spoleto
Lombardy, 145, 186, 250, 255
London, 62, 151, 182, 185, 187, 190, 193, 222, 224
Lordship, over vassals, 112–15, 133; over villeins, 116–18, 121, 124–7, 129, 192–3, 295
Lorsch, gatehouse at, 269, *269*
Louis VI, King of France, 214–18
Louis VII, King of France, 179, 217; on crusade, 218–20; divorced Queen Eleanor, 220
Louis IX, St., King of France, 247, 257–62, *260*
Louis the Pious, King of the Franks, and Emperor, 100, 101, 108–9, 184
Lucera, 252
Luitgard, wife of Charlemagne, 93, 99

Magyars, *see* Hungarians
Maine, province of, 208
Malaya, 69
Mamun, Caliph, 80
Manor, the, 118, 120–9, 176, 185
Mansur, Caliph, 78–9
Marco Polo, 195
Marie de Champagne, daughter of

Eleanor of Aquitaine, 227
Markets, 185, 187, 189–90, *190,* 249
Markward of Anweiler, 249
Marseilles, 197
Martino da Canale, citizen of Venice, 194
Marzukh, 253
Masseo, Brother, 237
Matilda, wife of Henry I, King of England, 172
Matilda, wife of William I, King of England, 149
Matthew, St., *270, 271, 272, 275*
Matthew Paris, 253, 257
Maxentius, 18
Mecca, 64, 67, 68, 71; pilgrimage to, 65–6, 69
Medina, 64, 67, 71, 73
Mediterranean Sea, 28, 43, 101, 106, 184, 196, 197, 294; countries bordering, 70, 72, 195, 271, 272
Melbourne church, *159*
Melfi, Constitutions of, 252
Merchants, way of life of, 189–95; part played in crusades by, 204; their settlements in Syria, 206; of Pisa and Genoa, 197; of Florence, 191, 194; of Venice, 195; of York, 288; in Paris, 218. *See also* Datini family, Polo family, Pietro Bernadone
Merovingian Kings, 83–5, 86
Messina, 208–9, 252
Michelangelo, 45
Milan, 193, 250; archbishopric of, 142
Mills, *125,* 129, 176
Missi dominici, 97–9
Monasticism, Egyptian, 52, 55, 56, 173; Celtic, 50–2, 55, 263; Benedictine, its origins, 50–2, its character, 52–8; Cluniac, 164–73, 279; Cistercian, 174–9, 280
Mongols, 80
Monks, *see* Monasticism
Monte Cassino, monastery of, 52–8, 172
Mosaics, of Ravenna, 44, *38, 40, 41*; of Damascus, 74

Index

Muhammad, 64, 65, 70, 81; life of, 66–7; teaching of, 68
Musa, Arab governor of North Africa, 73, 74
Muska, 253
Muslims, 64, 257, 291; beliefs of, 68–9; conquests of, 69–78, 184, 195, 196, 292; way of life, 75–81, 163; raids on Europe by, 101–2, 128, 130; in Sicily, 163, 247, 252, 253; attitude of Christians towards, 197–8; attacked by Christians, 106, 202–13; negotiations with Frederick II, 255; leaders of, see Muhammad, Caliphs, Amr, Khalid, Nureddin, Saladin

Napoleon, 130
Narses, general of Justinian, 43
Nika riots, 39–41, 45
Nile, river, 11, 261
Noirmoutier, monastery of, 108–9, 264
Normandy, 149, 162, 208, 217, 227; origins of, 110, 147–8; govern-ment of, 222–3, 224; Dukes of, see Robert I, Robert II, and the Kings of England: William I, Henry I, Henry II, Richard I, John
Normans, in Sicily and Southern Italy, 76, 145, 162, 247–9, 252; their conquest of England, 147, 149–60; their attacks on Byzantine Empire, 199; their part in the Crusades, 200–4; see also Normandy
North Sea, 17, 21, 33
Northmen, their way of life, 103; ships of, 106, 106, 107; explorations of, 106–8; raids by, 82, 91, 101, 102, 108–11, 112, 115, 130, 147, 148, 187, 196, 215, 264, 265; treasure of, 104; weapons of, 105
Northumbria, kingdom of, 82, 93, 95, 271–3
Norway, 102, 106, 149
Nureddin, 205–6

Odovacar, 30
Offa, King of Mercia, 186
Omar, Caliph, 69, 70, 72, 79
Omayyad dynasty, 73, 75, 78
Orb, imperial, 137
Orleans, 215; Bishop of, see Theodulf
Osbern Gifard, 152
Ostrogoths, 25, 28, 29–31, 34
Otto I, King of Germany and Emperor, 130–7, 250, 291
Otto III, King of Germany and Emperor, 136
Otto IV, King of Germany and Emperor, 250
Oxford, 81, 154, 187, 283, 284

Painting, 271–3, 285; see also 117 (the three estates); 122 (woman by her fire); 123 (milking); 125 (windmill); 128–9 (dancers); 129 (pig killing, bees entering hive, flailing); 136 (Otto III); 153 (Norman soldiers); 203 (Crusader doing homage); 233 (Innocent III); 238 (St. Francis); 243 (dream of Innocent III); 246 (St. Dominic); 253 (dancing girls); 254 (elephant); 270 (St. Matthew, Book of Durrow); 274 (carpet page, Lindisfarne Gospels); 275 (St. Matthew, Lindisfarne Gospels); 285 (Virgin and Child, Chichester); Book of Kells, plate facing 265
Pakistan, 69
Palermo, 76, 247–9, 253; church of San Cataldo at, 156
Palestine, 196, 206, 211; Festus, governor of, 47
Pangur Ban, 263, 264
Papacy, see Pope
Paris, 34, 81, 214, 215, 218, 229, 257, 280, 283, 284
Paul, St., 47, 59, 62
Pepin the Short, King of the Franks, 85
Persia, Empire of, 69, 70; Justinian's wars against, 39, 49; its army defeated by Arabs, 71;

nature of its conquest by Arabs, 75, 78–80
Persian Gulf, 78, 291
Perugia, 192
Peter Abelard, 179, 218, 281–3, 284, 285, 288
Peter, St., 59, 272
Peter the Hermit, 200–1
Peter the Venerable, Abbot of Cluny, 80–1, 172, 282–3
Pevensey, 151
Pharos lighthouse, 72
Philip II (Augustus), King of France, 209; on crusade, 208–12; in France, 229–31
Philip, Duke of Swabia, 250
Philippe de Nemours, 258–9, 261
Picts, 15
Piero della Vigna, 253, 257
Pietro Bernadone, father of St. Francis, 239, 241
Pilgrimages, 185; popularity of, 197–8; to the Holy Land, 197–8, 212; to Rome, 164, 180, 185, 276–80; to Compostella, 198, 276–80; to Bury St. Edmunds, 187, 198; of Muslims to Mecca, 66, 69
Pisa, 191, 197, 294
Poitiers, 74, 220, 222, 227, 229
Polo, family of, 195, 294
Pont du Gard, 183
Pope, 135, 137, 149, 174, 179; election of, 142; authority of, 59–60, 62, 85–6, 142–6, 213, 233, 250, 280; see Gregory I, Leo III, Sylvester II, Leo IX, Gregory VII, Urban II, Innocent III, Gregory IX, Innocent IV
Prester John, 195
Prüm, abbey of, 124
Pyrenees, 27, 74

Quraish tribe, 66, 73

Ravenna, 26, 43–4, 99; exarch of, 58, 86; church of San Vitale in, 267–9; and its mosaics, 38, 40, 41; Theodoric's tomb at, 32
Raymond IV, Count of Toulouse, 200, 201, 202, 204

Raymond VI, Count of Toulouse, 236

Raymond, Prince of Antioch, uncle of Eleanor of Aquitaine, 219

Reeves, 118, 125

Rievaulx abbey, *176*, 177

Reform, of the Church, 138–42, 173; need for, 234–5

Relief, 115

Remigius, St., 141

Renaud de Trit, 258

Rheims, 108, 184, 281; council at, 141

Rhine, river, 20, 21, 27, 92

Rhone, river, 102

Richard I, King of England, 229, 231; on crusade, 208–13; in Aquitaine, 227; his tomb in Fontevrault, *230*

Richard Anstey, 224

Richard Fitz Nigel, Treasurer, 223–4

Robert of Artois, 261

Robert, Count of Flanders, 200

Robert I, Duke of Normandy (the Devil), 148

Robert II, Duke of Normandy, 200

Robert Guiscard, 162–3, 197, 199

Robert of Molesme, 175

Robert, monk of Cluny, 170, 174

Rochester, keep, *155*

Roger I, Count of Sicily, 162–3, 197

Rognvald, Viking warrior, 108

Roland, song of, 282

Rollo, Viking leader, 110, 147, 148

Roman Empire, 10, 50, 96, 100, 130, 131, 251, 291; decline of, Chapter 1, 52, 58; attacked by barbarians, Chapter 2, 58; towns in, 17, 182; rulers of, *see* Diocletian and Constantine

Romanesque, *see* Art and Buildings

Romauld of Ravenna, St., 174

Rome, ancient civilisation of, 20, 47, 58, 96, 263, 266, 267, 269, 272, 280, 288, 290, 293; admired by barbarians, 24, 30; copied by Arabs, 75; admired by Charlemagne, 267; admired by Frederick II, 251, 252

Rome, Church of, 59, 62, 146; *and see* Pope

Rome, city of, 15, 18, 20, 21, 28, 31, 61, 93, 182, 237, 250, 271, 279, 282; sacked by Visigoths, 24, 26; plundered by Hungarians and Saracens, 101–2; St. Peter's Church in, 45, 96, 135, 171; rival factions in, 138; church councils in, 140, 142; pilgrimage to, 164, 185; Gregory I and, 58, 59; Leo IX and, 141; Gregory VII and, 145; Otto I and, 134–5; Henry IV and, 142; Frederick II and, 251, 255

Rosamund Clifford, 229

Rothenburg, 188

Rouen, 222

Russia, 25, 35, 78, 106

Saint Denis, abbey of, 85

St. Gall, abbey of, 74

Saint Germain des Prés, abbey of, 118, 121, 126

Saladin, Muslim leader, 207, 208, 212, 213

Salerno, 145, 280

Salisbury, 156

San Damiano, church of, 240–1

San Miniato, 174

Sancta Sophia, church of, 20, 37, 47, 48, 75, 108; description of, 45–6

Saracens, *see* Muslims

Saxon Shore, 15, 17, 27

Saxony, Saxons, 25, 100; Charlemagne's treatment of, 91, 92; Duke of, *see* Henry the Fowler

Scandinavia, 78, 102, 148

Scotland, 106, 175, 228

Sculpture and carving, 271, 276, 285, 287; *see also 16* (Trajan's column); *19* (Labarum); *23* (Roman soldiers and standards); *63* (Vicar of Rome); *83* (Charlemagne on horseback); *88* (Bust of Charlemagne); *94* (Ivory book cover); *133* (book cover); *209* (Bust of Philip Augustus); *214* (Crusader tomb); *230* (Fontevrault tombs); *248* (Bust of Frederick II); *260* (Statue of St. Louis); *273* (Ahenny cross); 278 (Durham door knocker); *279* (Last Judgement, Conques); *282* (Abelard and Heloïse); *284* (Virgin of Essen); *286* (Danish crucifix); *287* (woman washing wool, Chartres)

Seals, of William the Conqueror, 148, 149; of Henry Plantagenet, 221; of St. Louis, 259

Seine, river, 147, 218

Sens, Bishop of, 235

Services, of a vassal to his lord, 112–15, 160; of a villein to his lord, 124–7

Ship burial, 106 (Gokstad); 186 (Sutton Hoo)

Sicily, 26, 59, 149; plundered by Vandals, 28; conquered by Muslims, 76, 81, 102, 196; reconquered by Roger de Hauteville, 162–3, 197; in Third Crusade, 208–10; Frederick II and, 247–9, 251–5

Sidonius Apollinaris, 33

Slaves, 74, 78, 191–2, 253–4

Slavs, 91

Spain, 28, 60, 78, 91, 149, 170, 175, 198, 217, 291; invaded by Vandals, 27; under Visigoths, 42; seaboard recovered by Justinian, 43; conquered by Muslims, 73, 74, 75–6, 81, 196; Christian reconquests in, 197; monks in, 170, 175, 176; friars in, 244

Spoleto, 58, 60, 239

Sport, of Charlemagne, 89; of Henry II, 222; of Frederick II, 254

Stanton Harcourt, 152

Stephen (of Blois), King of England, 223

Stephen Harding, 175, 176, 181

Stoke Gifford, 152

Subiaco, 50

Suger, Abbot of Saint Denis, 217; Chalice of, plate facing *264*

Sutton Hoo, 186, 271

Sweden, 102, 106–8

Sylvester II, Pope, 266

Syria, 67, 70; fall of province to the Arabs, 71, 72, 196; under Arab rule, 75, 78, 80; in crusading period, 202, 206

Tancred of Hauteville, 162; family of, 162, 197
Tariq, Berber soldier, 73, 74
Taxes, in Roman Empire, 15, 97; in Byzantine Empire, 44–5, 70; in Italy, collected by Gregory I, 59; in medieval towns, 194; in Kingdom of Sicily, 252
Tedald, appointed by Henry IV as Archbishop of Milan, 142
Templars, Military Order of, 180, 206
Temple Church, London, 180
Tenedos, island of, 43
Thames, river, 187, 223
Theodora, wife of Justinian, 38, 40–1, 44; portrait of in mosaic, *41*
Theodoric the Ostrogoth, 29–31, 35, 42, 86, 87, 264; his tomb in Ravenna, *32*
Theodulf, Bishop of Orleans, 99, 101
Theophilus, 290
Thetford, 154, *155*
Thomas Becket, Archbishop of Canterbury, 223, 229
Thomas de Marle, 215–16
Thorstein, Viking leader, 108
Tirstrup, crucifix at, *286*
Tostig, 149, 151
Toulouse, county of, 215; counts of, *see* Raymond IV, Raymond VI
Tours, city of, 34, 220, 228; victory of Charles Martel at, 74; Bishop of, *see* Gregory
Towns, town life, in Roman Empire, 182; in Constantinople, 35–7; in Cordova, 76; in Baghdad, 78–80; in medieval Europe, 128, 276, 293; in Lombardy, 255; growth of, Chapter 13
Trade, in Roman Empire, 11; in Byzantine Empire, 35, 49; of Arabs, 67, 78–9; in medieval Europe, 128, 184–7, 197, 294;

through Syrian ports, 204
Travel, in Roman Empire, 11; of Vikings, 106–8; of royal courts, 86, 221–2; of pilgrims, 198, 276; of friars, 242–4; of students, 218, 280; across the Alps, 144–5, 271; to the East, 195; difficulties of, 97, 184–6; increase of, 186–7
Treasure, of Visigoths in Spain, 74; of Caliphs in Baghdad, 79; of Charlemagne, 87; Viking hoard of, *104*
Troubadours, 217, 219, 227, 236
Troyes, 192
Tunis, 261
Turks, 50, 198–9, 201, 202, 204; fall of Constantinople to, 45
Tyre, city of, 207

Ugolino, Cardinal, *see* Gregory IX
Universities, 245; of Bologna, 252, 280, 283–4; of Naples, 252–3; of Oxford, 283–4; of Paris, 218, 252, 284
Urban II, Pope, 146; his preaching of the First Crusade, 199–200
Urse d'Abbetot, 154

Vallombrosa, 174
Vandals, 25, 31, 34, 245; in Gaul, 27; in Spain, 27; in North Africa, 28, 42
Vassals, their relations with their lords, 112–15, 133, 295; of French King, 215–16, 221, 258; of Henry Plantagenet, 221, 223, 227; in Aquitaine, 218; bishops as, 141
Vence, street in, *191*
Venice, 194, 195, 294
Vézelay, 188, 189
Vikings, *see* Northmen
Villeins, their way of life, Chapter 8, 184, 295; accepted as lay brothers into Cistercian Order, 178; in crusades, 201
Visigoths, 24, 25, 29, 31, 34, 99; in Italy, 26–7; in France and Spain, 27, 73, 74, 76

Vittoria, battle of, 257
Volga, river, 78

Wales, 228
Walls, of Rome, 17; gateway in, *16*; of Constantinople, 35, *36*; of Rheims, 108, 184; of Dijon, 184
Walter Map, 223
Walter de Palear, 249
Waltham, 156
Wardship, feudal right of, 115
Weapons, of Roman army, 22; of Justinian's army, 42; of Franks, 33, *86*, 87; of Vikings, *105*, 106, 110; required in Assize of Arms, 227
Wear, river, 276
Wearmouth abbey, 271
Wessex, 148
Westminster, 149, 151, 156
William the Conqueror, Duke of Normandy, King of England, 110, 221; his upbringing, 148; his invasion and conquest of England, 149–60; 162, 164; in Bayeux Tapestry, *150*
William I, Duke of Aquitaine, 197
William IX, Duke of Aquitaine, 217
William X, Duke of Aquitaine, 217
William de Harecourt, 152
William Langland, 295
William of Malmesbury, 152
William II (Rufus), King of England, 172
William, Earl of Warenne, 198; his visit to Cluny, 164–73; his foundation of Lewes Priory, 170
Windsor, 224
Woodstock, 224
Worcester, 154
Wren, Christopher, 45

Yarmuk, battle of, 71
Yerebatan, cistern at, *44*
Yolande, wife of Frederick II, 255
York, 11, 62, 82, 151, 265, 288–90
Yugoslavia, 13

Zahra, al, 76

55658